P9-DTR-716

THE COMPLETE
Job-Finding
GUIDE

for
Secretaries
and
Administrative
Support Staff

PAUL FALCONE

American Management Association

New York • Atlanta • Boston • Chicago • Kansas City • San Francisco • Washington, D.C.
Brussels • Mexico City • Tokyo • Toronto

This publication is designed to provide accurate and authoritative information in regard to the subject matter covered. It is sold with the
understanding that the publisher is not engaged in rendering legal,
accounting, or other professional service. If legal advice or other expert
assistance is required, the services of a competent professional person
should be sought.

Library of Congress Cataloging-in-Publication Data

Falcone, Paul.
    The complete job-finding guide for secretaries and administrative
support staff / Paul Falcone.
        p.   cm.
    Includes bibliographical references and index.
    ISBN 0-8144-7885-9
    1. Secretaries--Vocational guidance. 2. Job hunting.   I. Title.
HF5547.5.F35 1995
651.3'023'73--dc20   95-7338
                                                                   CIP

© 1995 Paul Falcone.
All rights reserved.
Printed in the United States of America.

Printing number
10 9 8 7 6 5 4 3 2 1

Contents

To my lovely wife, **Janet**, our darling daughter, **Nina Rose**, and our newest addition, our son **Sammy**: Thank you for giving me more love, support, and encouragement than any papa deserves.

And to my mom and dad, **Dorothy** and **Carmine**: Thank you for teaching me that I could do anything and be anything I wanted. You've given me the tools necessary to make this first book a reality.

Acknowledgments

This book could never have come about without the support and guidance of friends and teachers who have taken me under their wing. Gail Angel and Ileene Bernard of the London Agency, my two mentors in the world of business, took a chance on a neophyte and constantly challenged me to reach new heights. Dick Kaumeyer, managing partner of Right Associates and UCLA instructor, guided me through the publishing process and created a role model for me to follow. Kathy Shepherd of the Focus Agency and president of the Los Angeles chapter of the California Association of Personnel Consultants took it upon herself to champion my career and get me out in front of audiences. I am grateful to Delonna Kaiser, an "HR professional's HR professional," Dick Fearn of The Human Element in Los Angeles and UCLA instructor, Lucille Pearson of Global Resources LTD in Rancho Palos Verdes, Peter Shapiro, vice-president of human resources with ElectroRent Corporation in Van Nuys, and Larry Comp and Terri Lauter of Humanomics in Granada Hills, California—all close friends who have been instrumental in editing and critiquing my manuscript as it made its way through the proofing process. My thanks also go to Peter Leffkowitz of the Morgen Consulting Group in Kansas City, Missouri, search industry trainer par excellence and the man who influenced my business style and public speaking skills more than he'll ever know. My newfound friends at AMACOM, Tony Vlamis, senior acquisitions and planning editor, and his outstanding assistant Theresa Plunkett guided me every step of the way. Editors Barbara Horowitz, also of AMACOM, in conjunction with Janet Frick, significantly enhanced the quality of my manuscript. And last, but certainly by no means least, thank you to two executive secretaries extraordinaire, Sandy Fogel and Ann Sanborn. Your candid insights provided untold value in the development of this book.

Introduction

Promise yourself to become an insider in the employment field. Pick up your highlighter and a pencil and share the secrets that have worked for some of the most rewarded executive assistants and administrative support staff in corporate America. Allow an employment trainer to walk you step by step through the intricacies of getting hired in today's tough market.

Why Is This Book Needed?

How-to-interview books and resumé guides abound. The demand for information in our society has led to a proliferation of books for specific employee groups: recent MBAs and college grads, senior-level executives in career transition, and professionals looking to break away from corporate bureaucracies and turn entrepreneurs. All these groups have their needs met on the shelves of your local bookstore.

What's conspicuously lacking, however, is a book devoted specifically to your needs as secretarial and office support staff. Unfortunately, not enough authors are aware of the intricacies and pitfalls of the secretary's unique employment process. But the pressures common to executive secretaries and office personnel will only get more intense as technology changes, international competition heightens, and the demand for skilled candidates increases.

U.S. companies are recognizing that key secretarial and administrative employees play ever-increasing roles in their companies' profitability. Computers have become critical tools that save time and decrease expenses. Few members of an organization are so closely tied to the PC and have the opportunity to exploit its applications as you, the corporate administrative secretary. Your role in the business world has consequently taken on new significance in the last decade and will continue to expand dynamically into the next decade. This book is meant to empower you with the strategies and tactics necessary to maximize your career options by taking control of the hiring process as much as possible.

If you've made a commitment to keeping abreast of stronger job opportunities in superior companies, then *The Complete Job-Finding Guide for Secretaries and Administrative Support Staff* will serve as a unique guide that contains the sophisticated tools and approaches you'll need to gain control over your career. It will introduce you to the most current strategies of effective interview preparation and resumé writing. It will bring you inside the hiring process by articulating the concerns, emotional hot buttons, and the mind-sets of human resources professionals and contingency recruiters. And it will introduce you to methods of researching employers and provide a step-by-step guide for following up with a company after an interview. Finally, it will address the changes in employer values caused by the 1990s recession, and it will provide suggestions on how to position yourself to satisfy corporate America's new needs.

Your Expanding Role Is Crucial to Your Company

Executive secretaries and administrative assistants make $30,000 to $60,000 a year and above—more than many supervisors and middle managers. Prime administrative jobs are offering more variety, reward, and independent decision making than ever. The secretarial function has the potential to save companies significant amounts of money in terms of decreasing costs and saving time. (For example, desktop publishing and graphics softwares produce camera-ready artwork with the touch of a button, bringing in house what formerly had to be expensed to outside vendors.) As a result, companies are putting more and more emphasis on the selection process because nothing less than their bottom line is at stake.

Our global economy has ensured that executive travel will remain a mainstay of daily business life. Consequently, you're expected to guard the fort and ensure a smooth work flow in your boss's absence. You're increasingly gaining recognition as your boss's representative and back-up, along with the authority to make decisions just like every other member of the management team. You're expected as well to possess the communication skills and understanding necessary to deal effectively with multiple cultures, and the technical skills to produce correspondence with pinpoint grammatical and contextual accuracy. With these increased responsibilities come increased opportunities for self-expression, creativity, and independence of judgment. In short, your administrative secretarial function has evolved from a job to a career alternative.

This trend is still in its infant stage. The personal computer (PC) of the 1980s altered corporate America forever. It allowed information to be transferred from the highest to lowest members of an organization with lightning speed, replacing the role of the middle manager as purveyor of information. The corporate pyramid got smashed from that point on by having its midsection drastically reduced. The early 1990s are conse-

Figure F-1. The transition from the traditional U.S. corporate pyramid into flatter, more flexible business structures.

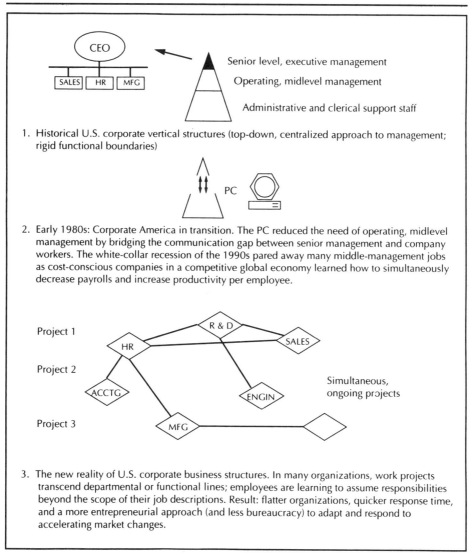

1. Historical U.S. corporate vertical structures (top-down, centralized approach to management; rigid functional boundaries)

2. Early 1980s: Corporate America in transition. The PC reduced the need of operating, midlevel management by bridging the communication gap between senior management and company workers. The white-collar recession of the 1990s pared away many middle-management jobs as cost-conscious companies in a competitive global economy learned how to simultaneously decrease payrolls and increase productivity per employee.

3. The new reality of U.S. corporate business structures. In many organizations, work projects transcend departmental or functional lines; employees are learning to assume responsibilities beyond the scope of their job descriptions. Result: flatter organizations, quicker response time, and a more entrepreneurial approach (and less bureaucracy) to adapt and respond to accelerating market changes.

quently giving way to flatter organizations with horizontal lattice network matrixes rather than the traditional, vertical, pyramid-like structures. (See Figure F-1.)

If the tops and bottoms of the traditional corporate structure are predominantly what's left after middle management's downsizing, then we can expect all remaining functions to increase in efficiency and productivity in order to compensate. The secretarial-executive relationship will become the key power-partner alliance at the top level.

Prime administrative positions are becoming highly sought after and more competitive as companies increase their demands and lengthen the hiring process. The approval for a key executive's assistant will come from multiple interviewers: corporate recruiters, higher-level human resources professionals, department members (potential co-workers), and finally, from the executives themselves. All this in an effort to identify the most outstanding candidates.

It's a very exciting time in the professional career development of office administration workers. The talent emerging from their ranks today is nothing less than astounding. To meet your needs as an executive assistant in the 1990s—as ghostwriter for your boss, negotiator, team builder, and discretionary confidant—this book walks you through every one of those skills needed by one of the most exciting and fastest-developing professions in corporate America: the executive secretary and administrative support employee.

For Whom Is This Book Written?

If you guessed secretaries, administrative assistants, and other administrative support staff, you've got almost the whole answer. With 20 million of you out there in corporate America and employers' expectations rising in ever-tightening labor markets, the need for this book has never been greater. These administrative support workers I'm alluding to include:

- Office managers
- Legal assistants
- Customer service representatives
- Receptionists
- General office clerks
- Sales assistants

But you're not the only readers who will potentially benefit from this hands-on, how-to employment guide. Human resources professionals and office supervisors responsible for nonexempt staffing within their companies will gain a lot of insightful information regarding:

- Traditional interview queries and their interpretations
- How to use what I call "silent interviewing" to account for the links in progression in a candidate's career development
- Questions to expect from candidates during an interview
- Common compensation practices for nonexempt personnel
- Holistic interview questions that measure the whole person
- Why I don't recommend hypothetical questioning techniques
- Behavioral interview questions that ensure spontaneity and base a candidate's answers on concrete, verifiable past actions
- Illegal interview questions that must be avoided at all costs

☛ Advanced reference-checking questions, offer letters, and more

Yet a third potential audience for this book includes all contingency (agency) recruiters in the field of administrative support staffing. For those sales professionals in the search and placement industry, this work would serve as an introduction to the processes and pressures involved in the clerical and administrative support hiring processes. There's no such thing as enough training in the recruitment business, and I see this as the only book of its kind that uniquely synthesizes the dual aspects of the employment process: the how-to-strategize side that recruiters teach candidates, plus the human resource professional's insights into candidate selection and rejection. It's critical that contingency recruiters understand the mind-sets of their clients—the human resource practitioners—and this book lays out the game plan for screening interviews, company research methodologies, cost-per-hire determinations, and line management questioning techniques.

Allow Me to Introduce Myself

Before we go any further, allow me to introduce myself and make a case for my qualifications in the field. I'll start by saying that I've created a unique niche for myself in the employment world in that I'm equally involved in training human resource professionals and contingency recruiters. After spending six years as director of training and as a contingency recruiter with The London Agency, one of the largest administrative support placement firms in Los Angeles, I was recruited myself to join a client company, Aames Financial Corporation, as its human resources manager. So I have actively worked as a contingency recruiter and handled the full responsibilities of a corporate staffing manager. I have a master's degree from UCLA along with three certifications in human resources management, and I sit on two boards of directors: (1) PIHRA, The Professionals in Human Resources Association, and (2) the California Association of Personnel Consultants (CAPC), a nonprofit trade organization governing the search and placement industry. I've published multiple articles regarding corporate recruitment and selection in human resources journals. And I'm an ongoing guest lecturer in UCLA's human resources management program and a motivational speaker at the state and national levels.

The credentials are important so that you understand my own orientation and training in the employment field. (You want to keep my opinions in perspective, after all!) My love lies on the training side of the employment business: Training my own candidates to maximize employment opportunities is where I began; training recruiters to make a living in the world of contingency search is how I advanced; and training human resource professionals in some of the most sophisticated interviewing techniques is where I ended up. Hence, a book that brings together all three groups as players on one playing field: the world of employment.

How Is This Book Structured?

This book was written to be accessible and easy to use. You would probably get the most out of it by starting with Chapter 1 and reading through the material sequentially. It is, after all, written to walk you through the employment process step by step.

On the other hand, each chapter represents an individual, functional unit that covers the selected topic as thoroughly as possible. So if you have a first round of interviews tomorrow morning with the human resources department, then Chapter 6 would immediately provide you with questions to expect from the corporate interviewer, questions to ask the employer during your meeting, and information regarding initial salary discussions.

Similarly, if you purchased this book two hours before your interview with the department or line manager who will have final say over the decision to bring you aboard, then jump right into Chapter 7's discussion of what to do when you meet with line management decision makers.

If you need to research a company and have anywhere between ten minutes and two weeks to gather information, then Chapter 1 will walk you through the library and pick the books off the shelf for you.

Chapter 2 is a step-by-step guide for building your own business network from scratch and tapping into the hidden job market as effectively as the most skillful recruiter. Initially approaching companies and presenting yourself on a problem-to-solution level takes guts and a thorough self-understanding of where you'll help each company most. Chapter 2 provides you with the tools required to conduct successful introductions and exploratory interviews.

Chapter 3 is the ultimate resumé and cover letter organizer to begin your job search campaign. It focuses on customizing your resumé to respond to a particular company's needs, and it lays out the format and content that make administrative resumés stand out from the pack.

Chapter 4 develops strategies for maximizing your chances of landing multiple interviews by writing top-notch cover letters in response to classified ads. (By the way, did you know that it's possible to find out who the company is behind the post office box listed in a blind newspaper ad?)

Chapter 5 gives you a chance to do some personal position-building vis-à-vis the two most influential powers in the employment chain: agencies and human resources. Walk a mile in their shoes to understand their fears, motivations, and goals. Only with that knowledge can you enhance your chances of (1) setting up multiple interviews, and (2) securing multiple job offers. Knowledge is power, and this chapter lets you study their handbook!

Chapter 8 suggests complimentary approaches to following up with a company after an interview to keep your candidacy alive. Calling the employer and asking, "Did you make a decision yet?" doesn't quite achieve your goal. We'll develop strategies for adding value to your candidacy with each contact you make!

Turn to Chapter 9 first if you're already at the salary negotiation stage of the game by the time you get hold of this book. Learn to evaluate the noncash components of the company's offer. Insist on written offer letters confirming starting date and salary to protect yourself from negligent verbal promises or other misunderstandings. Chapter 9 also discusses how to decide whether you're really ready to leave your current job, and why you must know *before* an offer is made.

Chapter 10 answers some of the most often asked questions about resumé writing and interviewing responses. It provides the fascinating details that you need to stay on top of the power curve. I highly recommend that you read this chapter before going on any interviews.

The Appendixes are full of career-enhancing tools that will allow you to maximize your own career development. Look there for the finishing touches to a job-search strategy that will make your job-finding campaign fun, rewarding, and effective. If you're wondering whether your interview outfit is too hip, go straight to Appendix B for wardrobe tips. Need information regarding professional certifications in your field? How about networking organizations and journals dedicated to administrative support staff, human resources professionals, and contingency recruiters? Refer to Appendix C. If you've ever wondered what employers are asking about you on a reference check, Appendix A has it!

So sit back, relax, and enjoy our behind-the-scenes look at the administrative support employment process, while gaining invaluable knowledge to enhance all aspects of your personal career development.

Part I

Honing Your Career Tools: Gearing Up for Empowerment

Chapter 1

Targeting Companies in Your Marketplace: The Laser in Your Library

Welcome to the world of sales. You may never have thought of yourself as a salesperson, but you're about to create a customized program for marketing the most unique product in the world: you. And no matter how long you've been in the business world, what makes this doubly challenging is that you're both salesperson and product! You constantly sell yourself and your qualifications, your skills and your knowledge. So self-marketing is all about understanding your product's features and benefits, figuring out where that product could add the most value, and determining who would want that product most.

In this chapter we'll take a brief stroll down Library Lane to give you a glimpse of all the companies out there that you might want to pursue. You've heard of that mysterious and elusive term the **hidden job market?** Well, it's hidden on the bookshelf right behind the reference librarian's chair! And this chapter will put your fingertips on the pulse of your local job market: who's hiring, whose sizes and earnings are doubling, whose benefits packages top the charts, who has the most interest in your anthropology degree, and whose corporate cultures are most favorable in terms of promotion through the ranks.

I know what you're thinking. "Wait, I thought this book looked promising. It's supposed to tell me things I really need to know, like how to answer 'Where do you see yourself in five years?' I also want to learn how to decode a company's post office box in the Sunday classifieds, and how I can figure out the real salary range for a given position. So why does this exciting book begin with the dullest topic on earth? I want to know how to get a job, not become a librarian."

Well, bear with me for a moment. I'm about to ask you for your first and only leap of faith. This whole book is based on one concept: **empowerment.** It will give you all the tools you need to successfully conduct a fun and rewarding job search campaign. But, as with anything else, success depends on planning, and the library is your first step in the planning process.

Know Your Market

One of the primary rules in sales is to identify and segment your market. The definition of successful marketing is "to identify a need and fill it." Similarly, the job search process rests on a foundation of information that will empower you to maximize the results of your efforts by efficiently identifying your market and understanding the needs that have to be met. (After all, no matter how good your interviewing and networking skills, if you're targeting companies that are downsizing, you'll end up with zero interviews and job offers.) Besides, there's absolutely no better way to stand out from your competition and walk away from this experience feeling that you've learned something than by doing your homework on the front end.

Now, there are two reasons why understanding the needs of the companies that you're targeting is so crucial: First, as we'll see in Chapter 5 while exploring the mind-set of human resources practitioners, companies want to keep their costs-per-hire down. (The **cost-per-hire** is simply a company's total annual recruitment costs divided by the number of newly hired people.) So if you introduce yourself to a company that you've identified at the library and that company indeed grants you an interview, then your potential cost-per-hire will be exactly zero. No employment agency fees, no classified ad expenses, no internal referral bonuses, zero! That's great for you because you're considered a **windfall** or **bonus hire:** The company did nothing and ended up getting a great employee. Naturally, the company is delighted to be so lucky!

The second reason why proactively researching the dominant and growth-oriented companies in your marketplace makes sense for your job search campaign centers around something I call **informed candidacy.** It's a simple concept: Companies simply can't afford mistakes in the Nasty Nineties. It's too expensive, and there's too much liability in making even one mis-hire. Have you noticed that companies are taking a lot longer to hire people? Multiple rounds of interviews, skills analysis, reference checking, credit histories, drug tests, handwriting profiles . . . If corporate America seems paranoid about hiring people, it's because the costs associated with turnover can be deadly.

The solution? Candidates who have taken the time to research a company and know its key players, short-term marketing strategies, and long-term corporate missions have a greater chance of succeeding as part of the company because they're better prepared to meet the challenges faced by that organization. Why? Simply because those individuals identified and recognized those corporate challenges before beginning work there. The chances of a corporate culture mismatch or of a miscommunication in the interviewing process would consequently be greatly diminished. So more realistic expectations translate into fewer surprises and less turnover.

Here's another case in point: Have you ever interviewed with an employer, and it turned out that she went to high school with your cousin and dated your brother's college roommate? Do you recall that feeling of comfort and confidence you got when you could name-drop and share experiences? Well, those personal interviewing connections are very rare. But why shouldn't every interview include name-dropping and shared knowledge? Let's look at it another way: How much do you think you'll stand out from your competitors if you know the CEO's name, her alma mater, and the fact that she's doubled corporate revenues in the past four years?

The Library: A Job Hunter's Treasure Trove

Think about it: The library is a vast, free source of untapped information that puts at your fingertips all the facts and ideas you'll need to stand out clearly as a rarity among your peers. The day an interviewer tells you, "My gosh, you know more about our company than most of our employees do!" is the day you'll gain a lot more salary negotiation leverage when it comes time to accept that offer! And it makes the whole process of job search more fun and rewarding, which is what this book is all about.

Personally, I would recommend that you target companies for at least two to three weeks in the library if you're currently in career transition. It will take that long to really cover your marketplace if you live in a metropolitan area. If you're in a rural area, the time commitment to market research may be significantly lower. Still, you'll be amazed at all the target companies you'll develop in the nearest city.

Not to get too far ahead of myself, but take a guess what the most creative and appreciated follow-up agenda is for staying in touch with a company where you've already interviewed: A piece of library research either about the company or its industry with a handwritten note attached saying "I found this information in the library today and thought you might want to add it to your PR files. I'm doing everything I can to research your company and understand what makes it unique." See Chapter 8 for more about this impressive follow-up strategy to clinch an offer.

*   *   *

Well, did I get your attention? I hope so! There's only one obstacle left: Most people don't know how to use the library. I admit that the library can be intimidating, but too many people let that intimidation stand in their way. The folks that do venture into the hallowed halls of the public library get hit pretty quickly with information overload because they're not sure what they're looking for, never mind how to find it! So it's only been the chosen few who could maximize its use. Until now, that is.

Let me make this as fun and interesting as I can. Let's take a walk together through those long and endless library aisles right now, from the comfort of your living room chair. We'll pick out exactly what books you want, and tomorrow when you go to the library, you can just go pick up exactly what you need and then leave.

We're seeing niche job markets today where certain skills and experience have greater significance for certain companies. Qualified administrative support staff will be in greatest demand in those organizations that are staffing up with talented and creative teams of individuals who can bring new products swiftly to market. The key to beginning the job search process, therefore, lies in knowing how to cherry-pick the winning companies that are increasing revenues and adding to staff. They're out there. You've just got to be willing to spend an hour or so a week in the library to find them.

Remember that the 1990s is a variable economy, which means that you'll need a **bottom-up approach** to targeting the companies you'll want to pursue. As opposed to the top-down approach where you pursue hot *industries* and then select particular firms within those industries, bottom-up planning assumes that particular *companies* are doing well regardless of the industries they're in. In other words, although high-tech entertainment, cable telecommunications, and international trade may be hot industries in this decade, many businesses in those fields may be contracting or folding.

On the other hand, even though aerospace as a whole is dwindling away, certain companies in the field are making very successful transitions out of military and into commercial applications. These are obviously extreme examples, and, of course, you need to know which industries will produce the greatest likelihood of sustaining job growth. But what's important to you is the organization right down the street. *The bottom line remains that you've got to look to particular companies nowadays more than overall industries for finding your next home.* (New industries grow around the success of booming companies, and isolating those organizations with the greatest growth potential needs to be the critical foundation for your job search campaign. Again, that's got to be the new game plan for career development 2000.)

*   *   *

People are usually attracted to companies for various reasons:

- The perception of the way the company treats its people
- The organization's financial stability
- Its revenue and staffing growth
- Its line of business/industry
- Its perception as a hot company making the news
- An emotional link or bond that ties a person to a particular company

Let's begin with the last one, and then work our way backward. First, a personal note to prove a point: I have a bachelor's and master's degree in German. (Don't ask: I'm a nice Italian kid from Brooklyn. My parents still haven't figured it out!) So when I began a career as a recruiter, my first client targets were German, Swiss, and Austrian companies in the Greater Los Angeles area. There was a natural connection: I could speak German with the clients who were from overseas, or, if the company didn't have any German-speaking employees in Los Angeles, I could offer to help out if they ran into any language snags or if something needed translation. It worked like a charm. They were the easiest new business development calls I ever made, and they served as a beautiful beginning into a new industry and career path for me. More important, they were lots of fun.

Now, with the exception of such personal or emotional links that attract people to companies or industries, all the other reasons can be found in the library. Companies making the news, revenue and staffing growth, and financial stability are clear indicators of the companies you should be pursuing. So let's put together a program for systematically identifying the superstar organizations in your area.

Typical Research Situations

Here are the two major ways to use your research.

1. *You'll want to know how to research a particular company where you have an interview already scheduled.* After all, nothing is more impressive than showing an interviewer that you value his time and your career so much that you spent time in the library before the meeting researching that company to understand its history and to identify its needs.
2. *You'll want to know how to locate or cherry-pick the dominant local companies that you'll target in your new job search campaign.*

There are two research modes available: passive and active. Both are critical, and they complement each other well. **Passive research** means you're locating company information in large volumes of directories with somewhat outdated information. The *Dun & Bradstreet* and *Standard & Poor's* tomes are wonderful sources of extremely valuable information, but they're usually published only once a year. Hence, they tend to be a little outdated. I've heard library scientists estimate that 30 percent of the information is already outdated by the time the new volume hits the shelf. I doubt that's an exaggeration considering the speed of change in corporate America due to employee turnover, corporate acquisitions and divestitures, and relocations. Still, even though nuances of data become outdated, the vast majority of the information provided remains relevant, so we definitely want to pursue these sources.

Active research, on the other hand, bases itself on who's been making the news lately. Magazine and newspaper write-ups can give you much more up-to-date information than the annual volumes of *Standard & Poor's*, for example, but write-ups tend to focus on only one particular hot issue or perspective. Hence, they lack the overall scope that you'll find in a *Standard & Poor's* type of manual. So let's learn to use both active and passive research to maximize the information-gathering process.

The most useful library resources depend on the *time frame* available to you to invest in your research, as the next three hypothetical situations show.

Situation 1: You Have Only Ten Minutes to Gather Basic Information About a Company Where You'll Be Interviewing Later Today

There's nothing tricky about this one, I promise. Here's what you want to find out:

- The company's core business, that is, its primary product line or service
- Its size in terms of number of employees and/or sales revenue
- Its headquarters (HQ) location and the year it was founded
- The names and titles of its key players
- Its competitors

There are two works available that will serve you best for your limited research mission:

☐ *Standard & Poor's Index: Register of Corporations, Directors and Executives* (New York: Standard & Poor's)

☐ *Dun & Bradstreet's Million Dollar Directory: America's Leading Public and Private Companies* (Bethlehem, Pa.: Dun & Bradstreet)

(Note: The check boxes in front of the books' names are for your convenience. Simply check off the books or periodicals in this chapter that you'll want to pick up as soon as you arrive at the library.)

Let's briefly cover how to use these two works. First, look up alphabetically the company where you'll be interviewing. Make a photocopy of the page with the company's entry, and you're off and running. Ten minutes of your time, and—*zap*—you've got a listing of boards of directors, exchanges where the organization's stock is traded, primary and secondary business lines, and so on. Even the fact that the company's banking, certified public accountant, and law firms get listed can be significant: Wouldn't it be wonderful if the law firm where you used to work currently provides counsel to the company where you're now interviewing? It's exactly those types of connections that put you in the know and create a situation for shared knowledge during an interview.

You'll also see the company's SIC code in these listings. SIC stands for Standard Industrial Classification. These four-digit codes basically help government and private industry identify large business groupings of companies by the activities that those companies engage in. For example, you'd find the American Management Association under the activity subheadings shown in Figure 1-1. That's because the AMA is involved in newspaper, magazine, and book publishing. The four-digit classification, however, is the main one you need. (The two- and three-digit subclassifications shown here represent how you locate that four-digit code.) Note that one company may have multiple codes depending on its lines of business.

Why is this significant to you? Because the SIC code reveals the organizations that compete with a firm in its local market. I call the exercise of identifying company competitors "clustering within an industry." If one investment banking firm is interested in pursuing you, for example, then others will probably be interested in you as well. You should consequently target the other investment banking outfits by letting them know that you're currently interviewing with a competitor of theirs. (Feel free to identify the name of the investment firm that you're alluding to, if you like. A little name-dropping goes a long way in enhancing your candidacy, and that's a very effective way of developing more interviews for yourself.) In showing that you know the key companies in the industry and are

Figure 1-1. SIC code determination.

Manufacturing

27 Printing, Publishing, and Allied Industries (two-digit subheading)

  271 Newspapers (three-digit subheading)
  272 Periodicals
  273 Books
  2731 American Management Association (four-digit classification
      code)

being considered for a position at a competitor, you'll identify yourself as an insider and, you hope, create enough curiosity that the competitor firm will agree to meet with you on an exploratory basis. We'll develop this idea a lot more in Chapter 2.

One final word about SIC codes. They're great for facilitating computer database searches of groupings of companies according to area, size, and other criteria. They're of course handy resources for targeting any company's competitors. But they're limited by their inability to keep pace with the progress that allows corporate America to reinvent itself constantly. For example, some of the hottest pockets of job growth will be in the areas of high-tech interactive media, clean-fuel transportation, and advanced telecommunications. Yet no SIC codes exist as of this writing to measure growth in those areas.

There is one other resource that will fit perfectly into your ten-minute time schedule. Many libraries subscribe to the

☐ *Value Line Investment Survey* (New York: Value Line Publishing)

a monthly updated collection of stock performance forecasts for publicly traded corporations. *Value Line* services investors who are considering purchasing a particular firm's stock, so it grades the organization's historical stock performance as well as its potential earnings predictability. (Note that *Value Line* doesn't list companies alphabetically; instead, it presents companies in industrial clusters; one booklet may cover the automotive industry, another may cover banking and finance, and a third booklet may examine the performance of companies in the tool manufacturing and warehousing sectors.)

The detailed company information is wonderfully unique for you because it's so neatly packaged onto one page and because it's one of the few resources that targets a company's short-term challenges and weaknesses. *Value Line* typically forecasts a corporation's stock performance in the next six- to twelve-month period (along with a three- to five-year outlook). Consequently, it focuses on the company's current challenges: slack product demand, industry weaknesses, employee turnover and layoffs, heightened competition, and stock price volatility (i.e., how often the price of the stock fluctuates).

Obviously, such information provides invaluable insights into what's happening behind the scenes. You'll become an informed candidate with realistic expectations of the challenges you could face as part of the larger corporate family. More important, you'll be able to present yourself to the company on a problem-to-solution level—that is, as someone who offers a practical solution to at least one of the company's concrete problems. Here are some examples:

> Ms. Employer, I've learned in my research that the demand for magnetic tape drives has been flat for the past four years. That obviously means that you're looking for fresh ideas to jump-start the entire marketplace. I feel I could add a lot to a company striving to give 110 percent to creative new marketing ideas. There's nothing more exciting than working together to build the momentum for greater success, and I hope that I'm given the opportunity to contribute to your organization's efforts.

> I did some research in *Value Line* on your organization's stock performance, and what stood out most to me was your stock's volatility. I'm sure that being in a cyclical industry has its own unique pressures. I'd just like to share with you that I'm prepared in advance for the ups and downs that come with swiftly changing markets. I believe I could add a sense of stability and balance to my own particular work area, and that could be helpful to you in a constantly changing business environment.

> I've taken the liberty of doing some homework before our meeting, primarily because I value your time, but also because I'd like to get the most possible out of our interview. An issue that surfaced several times was the heightened competition in the airlines industry. Apparently, the fare wars are bleeding everyone's profit margins despite the increased volume of airline travelers. I'm bringing this up only because I'd like you to know that I understand there will always be pressures when revenues are being squeezed. Typically when revenues are down, motivation falls down with it. Well, I believe that every person's atti-

tude really affects the overall work environment. I've always been kind of a cheerleader to rally the troops, and that might be something this department would appreciate until things eventually settle down.

Talk about turning negatives into positives! The point of this exercise is to show you how you can key into the happenings of a company in as little as ten minutes. When you develop positive information on a company, share it as well:

> The fact that your revenues have almost doubled in the past four years combined with the fact that you're planning on increasing from a 150-person company to a 300- to 500-employee organization in the next two or three years shows me that you're a dynamic organization in a hypergrowth mode. I have a track record of juggling multiple tasks and moving at a lightning pace, and I've worked in a company before that's undergone that type of rapid change. Knowing the pressures associated with hypergrowth would allow me to make a unique contribution to your organization, Mr. Employer.

In developing challenging information about the organization, you might want to talk about your role as part of the solution to the company's problem. No one employee can turn the tide of an industry gone flat or stabilize the vagaries of cyclical markets. However, by taking a micro approach to a macro problem, you'll reveal yourself as a big-picture person who can come up with realistic and practical solutions to any problem, no matter how big or small. Just look what you've accomplished with only ten minutes of library research!

Situation 2: You Have at Least an Hour to Thoroughly Research a Company Where You're Awaiting an Interview

Allow me to preface this section with a caveat: My research selections are by no means exhaustive. There are plenty of research books available in the business section of your local library. However, I've suggested those that I find easiest to track down and use. They also readily provide the most lucid information without a lot of financial ratios and other esoteric details.

Keep in mind as well that you must copy your research and *show it to the interviewer during the meeting!* It's not sufficient to passively mention that you've gone to the library. You get no credit for that! The way to stand out from your competition is to keep your notes *visible* in your lap. And by all means, one of the questions you should raise during the interview should come from one of your photocopied research pages. Literally hold up the article for the interviewer and ask for an explanation of some technical fact or other. That's how you cement the picture of "I've done my homework" firmly in the employer's mind. Nothing is more impressive and complimentary to an interviewer than a candidate who's done the research beforehand. Nothing!

Now, if you're interviewing with a *larger* (greater than 2,000 employees), relatively well-known company, the first place to look would be in the

> ☐ *International Directory of Company Histories* (Editor Adele Hast, St. James Press, Chicago, 1991)

These multiple-volume hardcover books will typically be found in the business reference section of the library near *Standard & Poor's* and *Dun & Bradstreet*. The directory's volumes are broken down into the following categories:

Volume I:	Advertising–Drugs
Volume II:	Electrical & Electronics–Food Services & Retailers
Volume III:	Health and Personal Care Products–Materials
Volume IV:	Mining and Metals–Real Estate
Volume V:	Retail–Waste

If your company falls into any of the broad categories listed, this is your number one bet for detailed (two to six pages) chronologies of company histories and corporate culture issues.

For a real hands-on feel for what's happening in a company now or what's being written about a company in the press, try the

> ☐ *Reader's Guide to Periodical Literature*

That's right, the one you learned to use in high school. *The Reader's Guide* compiles recent magazine articles, so if you're interested in seeing what *Forbes* or *Fortune* Magazine has to say about a particular company, check out the *Reader's Guide* first.

Here's how it works: Simply look up the name of the company in the most recent paperback edition. Then work backward through previous paperback editions, which appear monthly, until you get to last year's hardcover edition. (Each year the paperbound updates get compiled into an annual hardcover edition.) Anything older than a year is probably out-dated for your research purposes. Discussing old news with an inter-viewer gets you some points for your effort, but it won't enhance your candidacy much because you're not currently in the know. But landing one juicy magazine article which was indexed in the *Reader's Guide* will do wonderful things for your confidence and your chances of landing that job.

If the *Guide* shows that an article appeared in *Business Week* two months ago, ask the librarian to help you locate the hard copy of the mag-azine issue. If the library doesn't carry the particular magazine where the article appeared, it will probably carry the magazine on microfiche (film). The librarian can help you locate the microfiche and set the film up in the machine. The whole process should take less than ten minutes, and you can make a paper photocopy of the article straight from the microfiche machine. (In many ways, it's actually more convenient and quicker to lo-cate and copy articles from microfiche than from hard copy!)

One book I've found particularly useful is

> ☐ *Hoover's Handbook of American Business: Profiles of Over 500 Major Corporations* (Gary Hoover; Austin, Tex.: Ref-erence Press, 1994)

Available both in the library and in your local bookstore, it packs onto one easy-to-copy page all the essentials necessary to make you a savvy insider: key executives, company history, core and ancillary lines of business, stock analysis, and industry competitors. It's written in alphabetical format, so its ease of use can't be beat. And you'll really get a grip on where the company's been and where it's going.

Also available both in libraries and bookstores is

> ☐ *Everybody's Business: A Field Guide to the Leading 400 Com-panies in America* (edited by Milton Moskowitz, Robert Levering, and Michael Katz; New York, Doubleday Cur-rency, 1990)

This work is probably the best of its kind in terms of identifying what makes a company tick emotionally, primarily through its detailed descrip-tion of **corporate culture** (i.e., a company's values, ideals, mission, pace, and management style). Moskowitz and his co-authors do a good job of humanizing an organization, giving you a feel for what it would be like to work there.

Finally, if you happen to be interviewing with an organization which has a fairly high-profile CEO (or other corporate officer), take a peek at

> ☐ *Who's Who in Finance and Industry* (Wilmette, Ill.: Marquis Who's Who)

The biographical listings sketch the education, civic activities, and political affiliations of many of America's most prominent business leaders. There is no greater compliment you can pay a company than by taking the time to profile its commander-in-chief. That kind of research can make you stand head and shoulders above your peers.

One final excellent resource for large company research before we move on is

> ☐ *Dun's Employment Opportunities Directory (The Career Guide)* (Bethlehem, Pa.: Dun & Bradstreet)

Dun's provides thorough facts regarding company hiring profiles. It specifically addresses:

- ☛ Benefits programs
- ☛ Career development opportunities
- ☛ *Educational specialties* the company typically hires
- ☛ The employment officer to contact for employment opportunities

This refreshingly unique look at the employment marketplace is particularly helpful in applying your college degree or field of study to the workplace.

*   *   *

I know what you're thinking. These are great research materials if the company you're interviewing with happens to be one of the *Fortune* 500. But what if you're meeting with a *small company* (with fewer than 500 employees)? Where do you dig up these pearls of knowledge that will impress an interviewer so much that she'll find it hard not to hire you?

Well, it's true that the smaller the company, the less it will have documented research. So for small to medium-sized (500 to 2,000 employees) companies on the move, the best strategy is to get into the active research mode and scour magazines and journals: The passive research tomes we've been inspecting up to now just won't work. Therefore, if the first thing that comes to mind is the *Reader's Guide to Periodical Literature,* good for you: You're getting the hang of this research stuff!

The journal calendar in Figure 1-2 yields a double purpose. It's an excellent source for researching smaller companies where you've got an interview pending; it's also going to lead into the next section of this chapter. I'm listing it now, though, because this active journal calendar will thoroughly document many smaller companies that are making the local news. Bear in mind that the 1990s will witness tremendous growth in America's small to medium-sized firms. There will actually be a decline in job growth at *Fortune* 500 companies:

- In 1980, *Fortune* 500 companies employed 16 million workers.
- In 1990, *Fortune* 500 companies employed 12 million workers.
- By the year 2000, *Fortune* 500 organizations will employ fewer than 8 million.

Therefore, combine the annual publications listed in Figure 1-2 with intermittent specialty issues like *Business Week*'s "Hot Growth Companies" (May issues) and "Global 1000" (July issues) and you'll have a sophisticated database that any recruitment firm would envy!

Note: These publications' editorial calendars may change slightly from year to year, so be sure to check with your local librarian if you're having difficulty locating a particular issue.

Another good source of information is

☐ *Ward's Business Directory* (Washington, D.C.: Gale Research, 1994)

Ward's is divided into two volumes:

Volume I: *Large U.S. Companies*
Volume II: *Smaller U.S. Companies*

Ward's also serves your purpose of locating smaller firms within a format you're used to: namely, by listing companies alphabetically, geographically (by zip code), and by SIC code. You'll like *Ward's* because of its ease of use, clear format, and attention to usable detail. However, you'll get

Figure 1-2. Annual business research calendar.

January

Fortune: annual "Survey of Corporate Reputations"
Forbes: "Annual Report on American Industry"
Business Week: "Business Week 1000: America's Most Valuable
Companies"*

February

Fortune: "America's Most Admired Corporations"

March

Business Week: "Corporate Scoreboard"

April

Fortune: "The Fortune 500: The Largest U.S. Industrial Corporations"
Forbes: "Annual Directory Issue" and "The Forbes 500"

May

Inc.: "Inc. 100: The Fastest Growing Publicly-Held Companies in the
Country"*
Fortune: "The Fortune Service 500"
Business Week: "Hot Growth Companies"

July

Fortune: "The Fortune Global 500"
Forbes: "The Forbes International 500 Survey"

August

Fortune: "The Fortune Global Service 500"

October

Inc.: "Inc. 500: The Fastest Growing Privately-Held Companies in the
Country"*

November

Forbes: "The 200 Best Small Companies in America"*

December

Forbes: "The 400 Largest Private Companies in America"

*Indicates that many smaller companies are profiled in these issues.

only statistical information with *Ward's* as compared with some of the previous works we've showcased.

For International Jet-Setters Only. By the way, if international companies are the way you want to go, then locate the

> ☐ *International Directory of Corporate Affiliations* (Wilmette, Ill.: National Register Publishing Company)

It will provide you with a large selection of foreign multinational companies with operations here in the United States, as well as U.S. companies with presence overseas.

Furthermore, the *Directory of American Firms Operating in Foreign Countries* (New York: Uniworld Business Publications, 1994) gives you a detailed list of U.S. firms that have subsidiaries or affiliates outside the United States. Simply look up countries from Algeria to Zimbabwe and you'll be supplied with (1) the U.S. corporate headquarters for American companies in that particular nation, and (2) the addresses of those companies abroad. For example, look up Italy and you'll find that Abbott Laboratories (with headquarters in Chicago, or HQ Chicago for short) operates in Latina; AVON (HQ New York) has an office in Comasco; and Chiquita Brands Foods (HQ Ohio) employees can be found in Rome.

From the other side of the spectrum, Jeffrey Arpan's and David Ricks's *Directory of Foreign Manufacturers in the United States* (Atlanta: Georgia State University Business Press, 1993) lists large foreign companies operating in the United States by state, alphabetically, and by SIC code. When you look up California, for example, you'll get a list of foreign company locations in that state. Foreign corporations operating in the Golden State include A&M Records (HQ Netherlands), Calgon Corporation (HQ Germany), Canon Business Machines (HQ Japan), Lawry's Foods (HQ England), and Winchell's Donut House (HQ Canada).

Situation 3: Targeting or Cherry-Picking the Dominant and Growth-Oriented Companies in Your Area in Your New Job Search Campaign

Now, to complete our fascinating walk down fast and free Library Lane, let's discuss identifying companies that you'll want to pursue. This process takes more than ten minutes. Yes, it even takes more than an hour. But if you're beginning to feel as if you have a whole research department on your side, then your momentum is building to approach these winning organizations. That topic, however, belongs to the next chapter. Right now, let's do some cherry-picking of our own, and you'll soon see how this research foundation that you're building will support your self-marketing forays into the job market.

Personally, I would begin by photocopying the companies listed in the Annual Business Research Calendar profiled above. Those listings, more than anything else, personify the hidden job market. That's where the hiring is being done and is consequently where many recruiters or headhunters develop their hottest clients. There's no reason why you shouldn't tap into those very same informational resources!

There are two major works that profile four or five thousand major U.S. corporations and their divisions, subsidiaries, and affiliates:

☐ *Directory of Corporate Affiliations: Who Owns Whom—The Family Tree of Every Major Corporation in America* (New Providence, N.J.: National Register Publishing)

☐ *America's Corporate Families: The Billion Dollar Directory* (Dun's Marketing Services)

Both these works identify major U.S. ultimate parent companies (typically, companies that do $1 billion or more in sales) and display *corporate family linkage* of subsidiaries and divisions. That's the part that interests you. After all, IBM's corporate headquarters may not be in your backyard, but a subsidiary business may be. It would certainly make a unique impression to contact that organization and say, "I've done my homework in the library before making this call, and I learned in my research that your company, Mr. Employer, is a subsidiary of IBM. I'd love the opportunity to be affiliated with IBM and still have the advantage of working in a small-company environment."

Let's look at how these two books work. Both are broken down into various sections alphabetically, geographically, by SIC code, and so on. You're interested in the geographic sections. Locate your state first, then the nearest city to your home, and you'll find a listing of ultimate parent companies (in dark bold print) or subsidiaries or divisions of those parent companies (in regular type) that are all located in your area. For example, you could locate California in the geographic section and then find the smaller areas of:

La Mesa	Lodi
La Mirada	Long Beach
La Palma	Los Alamitos
Laguna Beach	Los Angeles

Once you've targeted companies geographically (in Los Angeles, for example), then follow the page reference to locate the organizations alphabetically. In the alphabetic section, you'll get the whole breakdown of the parent company and its subsidiaries. This is really helpful because you'll learn of companies that share the same corporate lineage and that you can pursue simultaneously.

Let's run through one example together: If you geographically looked up California—Woodland Hills, you'd locate a company called Malibu Grand Prix Corp. A page reference next to the company name would refer you to the alphabetic section of the directory. There you would see that Malibu Grand Prix is a subsidiary of the ultimate parent company Warner Communications. Now, scanning through the list of Warner subsidiaries on that page, you'd find four other local companies that are also subsidiaries or affiliations of Warner:

1. Panavision in Tarzana
2. Wolper Organization in Burbank
3. Discreet Records in Los Angeles
4. WEA Corporation in Burbank

Voilà! Five companies you should be pursuing instead of only one! Now that's working smart! Under normal circumstances, you wouldn't have known that these local companies were related to Warner Communications because they didn't share the Warner name. Well, congratulations, you're now in the know, and you're also in total control of your job search campaign! Again, this stuff isn't hard. The mysteries just need to be unlocked.

Keeping Your Research Facts Organized

Speaking of unlocking mysteries, you may be wondering how to categorize and organize all these wonderful facts without going into information overload. Well, as you might imagine, organization is the key to market research. Collecting it isn't enough; prioritizing the information so that it remains useful is the critical key. And, yes, I have a time-saving idea for you! The company research dossier that follows works just like an index filing system. (See Figure 1-3.) You can make multiple copies of the form or enter this form right into your PC database. Either way, companies can be sorted alphabetically, geographically, by size, software system, industry, or other configuration. It's a handy tool that accounts for big-picture items (like company size in terms of revenues or employees) as well as some of the more minor details (like the CPA, banking and law firms that service that company, and the number of employees at that particular location).

Figure 1-3. This company research dossier allows you to track winning organizations and your correspondence with them.

Company research dossier

Company: _____

Address: _____

_____

Telephone number: _____

Fax number: _____

Research source: _____

Industry: _____

Primary product line(s): _____

_____

Secondary product market(s): _____

_____

Corporate HQ: _____

Year founded: _____

Annual revenues: _____

Number of employees (local/overall): _____

Key executives: _____

_____

Law, CPA, Banking services: _____

_____

Local corporate affiliations: _____

_____

_____

_____

Figure 1-3. (*continued*)

Company research dossier

Local competitor organizations: _____

_____

_____

_____

Hiring official/title: _____

Initial contact date: _____

Date resumé sent: _____

Date of first interview: _____

Follow-up activities: _____

_____

_____

_____

Network leads/personal referrals/people in common:

_____

_____

_____

Notes:

_____

_____

_____

_____

_____

_____

_____

_____

Simply carry copies of this form into the library with you and jot down information on the companies you want to pursue. The other obvious benefit to keeping this information on a card in a recipe file box or in a PC database is that it leaves you with plenty of room for taking notes regarding your progress with that organization. You'll want to document your conversations with these employers faithfully as you begin your networking campaign so that you can customize your subsequent follow-ups. But that's a topic for further exploration in Chapter 2.

There are lots of other wonderful research materials out there that break down information according to industry, geography, size, and performance. Manufacturers' registers, service company directories, buyers' guides, and investor service registers are excellent resources. If I've piqued your interest and you'd like more insights, see Mary Ellen Templeton's *Help! My Job Interview is Tomorrow! How to Use the Library to Research an Employer* (New York: Neal-Schuman Publishers, 1991). Also, if you'd like to tap into one text that will provide you with broad sources of job-hunting information (specialty books, newspapers, magazines, and on-line database services), consult the *Job Hunter's Sourcebook: Where to Find Employment Leads and Other Job Search Resources* (Detroit: Gale Research, 1993).

For now, though, let's take these targeted companies and creatively approach them to set up some meetings!

Chapter 2

Your Very Own Marketing Plan: Networking Your Way Into the Hidden Job Market

Given the fact that this is the age of the knowledge worker, your ability to inform yourself about who the strongest companies are and what makes them unique will prove your resourcefulness and ingenuity. So now's the time to transform this library savvy into actual meetings with companies who either have bona fide openings or who are willing to talk with you on an exploratory basis. Let's discuss some refreshingly creative ways to set up successful company introductions.

Interviewing for Current *and* Future Openings

First, some definitions. A **bona fide opening** means that the company has an actual, current need for someone with your job title. For example, you'll hear something like, "Well, Janet, your timing is actually very good since we're looking for an executive secretary right now in our marketing department. Why don't we set a time to meet each other, and you can tell me more about yourself, and I'll tell you more about the opening." Wow, those calls are exciting! Understand, however, that they're pretty rare from a pure timing standpoint, so you should not count on them when planning your strategy. (After all, you don't want to research the strongest companies only to call and ask whether they have any openings. It's simply not a sophisticated enough presentation.)

It's more often the case that companies won't have an opening to fit your exact background at the time of your call. Even if they do, employers are predisposed to answer the question "Do you have any openings?" with a no, just as you're inclined to answer the question "Do you need to buy any insurance?" with a no. The phrasing of the question dictates a negative response simply by the way it's positioned.

But that won't stop you. You want to become a part of these superior companies even if it means waiting awhile for the opening to develop. We'll consequently assume that no opening exists at the time you make your phone call or send in your resumé. That will prevent you from hoping for miracles or planning your strategies around the misguided expectation that the ideal job is waiting for you at the exact moment of your call.

However, remember that strong companies want to be kept abreast of strong people regardless of openings. Therefore, present yourself to companies on a proactive basis and try to set up exploratory meetings with the companies you've cherry-picked. In doing so, you'll hope to hear an employer say something along the lines of, "Well, Janet, we really don't have any openings that would fit your background right now, but we may in the future. Our company often hires people that we interviewed several months before, and I'm very impressed with the research you've done on our firm. So come on in and we'll get to know each other so that when something becomes available, we'll be able to take advantage of the fact that we already interviewed you."

Does that really happen? Will companies meet with people months in advance for openings that don't yet exist? Well, yes and no. It sometimes does happen that companies hire people they interviewed awhile back, but it's usually not planned that way. Employers typically interview candidates only if there's a pressing need to fill a job opening. So how can you maximize this exploratory strategy?

First of all, realize that this technique works better for secretaries and administrative support staff than for other levels of corporate employees simply because there are more openings and more employees in the administrative support ranks. If you were a chief financial officer with ten years of progressive experience in the pharmaceuticals industry, setting up proactive, exploratory meetings would be tougher because there's only one slot you could potentially fill within most organizations. Therefore, it would all boil down to timing: if there were a problem with the current CFO, your attempt to meet with the company on an exploratory basis might work; otherwise, the strategy would most likely fail.

On the other hand, even if there were a thousand secretaries in a company, would a human resources practitioner meet with you if absolutely no openings existed? Probably not, because the HR person would most likely be busy with other areas of human resources management, not administrative support recruitment—unless there was something else brewing. In other words, there may be a new job in the works that isn't official yet but that will probably become official in the near future. Or maybe there's an administrative assistant who (they just found out) probably won't be returning from disability leave, or who's having problems with her boss and who needs to be replaced. The point is, you can't know the circumstances within the company! But you can be sure that if the company agrees to meet with you on an exploratory basis, there's probably an opening somewhere that you're well suited for, even if your interviewer isn't telling you about it up front.

Again, it may not be official yet: No ads were run, no word put out on the street. But the fact that you beat them to the punch, so to speak, is an outstanding coup on your part—a strategy based on the assumption that growing companies need excellent people at any given point in time. Furthermore, your chances of wasting time interviewing with a company that has absolutely no plans of hiring you are minimal because leading companies make efficient use of their time and resources. Staffing is one of the most critical areas for growing organizations. And your chances of good timing increase with more exposure. Timing has a lot to do with anyone's job search campaign. You're going to use that time element to your advantage by proactively approaching the strongest companies one at a time to set up your meetings.

Your goal in setting up exploratory meetings will be to meet with the companies you've chosen in advance regardless of openings. Then you'll let the numbers take care of themselves. It's often said that sales is a numbers game. The greater the raw volume of contacts you make, the better the chances that someone will have a need for your "product." So a hundred company contacts may result in three bona fide interviews along with four exploratory meetings. On the other hand, if you make only ten initial contacts, no interviews may come your way because your exposure was simply too limited.

What ratios should you expect in terms of attempted contacts to bona fide or exploratory interviews? There's no simple answer for that. It depends on labor supply and demand in your local marketplace as well as your skills, industry background, education, salary requirements, and so on. But remember that empowerment is the name of the game. And you're not only taking control of your job search campaign, but you're giving yourself a wonderful education in the process.

Sales 2000: A New Philosophy for an Old Discipline

I began Chapter 1 by saying, "Welcome to the world of sales." Well, it's true that job searching is a sales activity in terms of understanding how market research affects your campaign and realizing that meeting the numbers is a critical issue in getting to your next job faster. But it's not sales in the traditional, more pejorative sense of the word. Sales is changing today. No gimmicks, showmanship, or magic tricks are necessary. No "closes" to corner the other party into saying exactly what you want to hear. No pressure. It's simply a matter of people talking to people. If you get nothing else out of this book, let this one point sink in: Nobody wants to be sold by Slick Eddie anymore. We've become too sophisticated for that. The days of the proverbial used car salesman are over. Sales is transfiguring itself into ultimate customer service. And customer service always has the other party's best interests in mind. Every example in this book will be presented as a straightforward, honest, and communicative thought. Sincerity is the cornerstone of communication, and we'll faithfully apply that sincerity in speaking with employers. In short, be yourself. Show your humanity by asking for help, and you'll get sincere responses back.

Networking 2000: The Job-Finding Method That Will Produce 70 Percent of the Decade's New Hires

Networking is the buzzword of the 1990s and will remain the contact sport of the business world well into the year 2000. Why? Because it makes so much sense. Let's define it first, and then examine some of its more popular applications (based on your research, of course).

Networking is one of those employment-industry jargon words that has been buzzing around for about a decade or so. Networking is a skill to be developed and a sales technique based on mutual respect and information sharing. The philosophy of networking won't become obsolete once the word is no longer trendy in corporate America because the fundamental tenet of networking is to give to others by sharing your expertise without immediate payback in mind. (In theory, the payback comes later after you've established a relationship built on trust and goodwill.) Any approach that depends on relationship building and reciprocity will change the participant's style of doing business. It's an excellent way to do business.

Networking has many of the same advantages as library research: informed candidacy, reduced costs-per-hire, and the fact that it's a process that you can initiate on your own and use to directly affect your job search campaign. (We called that empowerment.) If there is a disadvantage to networking, it may be that the exercise of networking makes you a little uncomfortable: Networking is contacting the people your contacts know. It's an organized method of building an ever-expanding base of people whom you can help and who can help you. But you'll notice that we're talking about "cold call" introductions for the most part. Even if you have a name or a favorable recommendation to help you introduce yourself, you still have to make that introduction happen on your own. And the biggest selling challenge lies in making quasi-cold calls to complete strangers and getting results. That idea may make you a bit uncomfortable. Besides, you're thinking, what do I have to offer in return? Well, read on! You're going to develop your networking plan so that you can use it in different types of situations. Your goal will be to set up successful company introductions that you'll approach as pre-employment interviews. I'll help you map out how to set up successful company introductions on your own by phone or letter. You'll also learn how to qualify an organization to see whether its hiring official prefers you to pursue that company independently or with the help of a recruiting firm. (Although companies that refer you immediately to employment agencies may be potentially increasing their costs for hiring you, they aren't throwing their money away by referring you to that agency first. Instead they are allowing the recruiting firm to screen you properly by testing you and checking your references. This way, they save themselves the time of interviewing you if you're unqualified.)

If the idea of approaching companies on your own makes you a little uncomfortable, then working with a recruiter as a middleman will benefit your candidacy immensely. In that case, the company will already be predisposed to paying hiring fees, so you can allow the recruiting firm to be that favorable outside influence on your career that it's supposed to be. Finally, we'll discuss handling exploratory interviews with company hiring officials whom you're meeting with on an exploratory basis.

Reference Bridging: Three Things You Can Do to Strengthen Your Past References

Before you apply your research, there's one practical networking tool you need to focus on by making personal contacts. *Your past direct supervisors should be the first people you call when you begin a job search campaign.* That's because they'll be the first people your prospective employer or recruiter calls after having interviewed you. Past employers are the best sources for building an immediate network of employment contacts (beyond your immediate family and friends, of course). They know how you work, they understand what drives you and motivates you, and they've got their own networks of peers who might be able to benefit from the skills and experience you have to offer.

Equally important is the fact that these folks will be the first ones to pass judgment on you. If you don't take the time to reintroduce yourself to an old boss, you'll be approaching your job search campaign with a loose cannon on the deck of your ship! You'll be diligently working on your market research, customizing your resume and cover letter to meet the needs of a company you're hoping to meet with on an exploratory basis. Everything is going well when, all of a sudden, *boom!* The whole thing suddenly falls apart. No more telephones ringing, no more sharing of information you've developed in your research. Nothing.

What happened? It just could be that the prospective employer called one of your past references who said something negative about you. Oh, you'll never know that, because that company official would never tell you for risk of putting her company in legal jeopardy. And HR practitioners from your previous place of business know that there's a big legal danger that you, as past employee, might bring suit against your past company because a previous boss gave you a bad reference that caused you to lose out on a new job. But the scenario of deals falling apart because of a poor reference is certainly not uncommon.

Checking your references with your past supervisors makes good common sense. There are three crucial actions you must take:

1. Refresh their memories as to who you are, when you worked together, and where.
2. Ask them for suggestions about how you could have performed even better back when you were working together.
3. Find out who they could recommend who could benefit from your skills and experience.

Ah, this is working smart: Networking for job leads and clearing up your reference history all at the same time! This is an absolute must at the onset of your job search campaign.

Here's how I would go about gathering the information necessary to reconnect with past supervisors. First, find out where they are. That may take some fairly sophisticated detective work on your part if the person has now moved on to another company or another part of the country. But if it's possible, find that person! Supply a prospective employer with the new number of your past boss because it really looks good when a candidate has maintained contacts with bosses who have moved on to other ventures. (My gut reaction as a recruiter is that you probably had an excellent relationship; otherwise, the relationship would never have been maintained once you stopped working together.)

Next approach your past employer like this:

> Barbara, this is Paul Falcone. We worked together at XYZ Insurance between 1987 and 1989. I know it's been six years or so since we spoke, and I'm sorry we lost contact with each other. But, if you recall, you were transferred back to the corporate office in Ohio at about the same time I was offered a position with ABC Company, so I guess we both got kind of sidetracked with our own respective careers.
>
> Barbara, I had to do some pretty nifty research to locate you again, and I would really appreciate your help. I'm in career transition right now because ABC just went through a big layoff. I'm hoping that you'd agree to sponsor me, so to speak, as a

reference. I know that any recruiter or human resources professional I meet with will want to gain some insights into my ability to excel in the future via my performance in my past positions, and we always worked really well together. I enjoyed reporting to you, the direction you gave me was very clear, and I got rave reviews from you in all of my performance appraisals.

I would really appreciate your help with that, Barbara. Would you be willing to vouch for me as a reference?

Thanks. I have another question. As far as you can recall, were there any areas of my performance that I could have improved upon? I'm asking for two reasons: First, I'm interested in knowing what kind of feedback you'll provide a prospective employer. And secondly, while I'm in transition, there may be some areas that I can work on to improve my skills.

Oh, there is a third thing. I know you're still in Ohio, and you may have lost some of your contacts here in California. But I'm really working on building my network to get to my next position that much faster. Could you recommend anyone out here who could benefit from my skills and experience? I'd really appreciate the referral.

How's that? I covered everything I wanted to in one three-minute phone call.

This is critical for you because you'll always get a better reference from someone who you spoke with recently. As a recruiter, I could tell immediately during a reference check which candidates had done their homework in the reference-checking game. Either the employer said, "Paul Falcone? Gee, we haven't worked together for six years. I'm afraid I won't be able to tell you much," or I'd hear something like "Oh, yeah, I just heard from Paul. I was so sorry to hear he got laid off. You know, it's been six years since we worked together, but I gave him outstanding grades on all of his performance appraisals. I understand he's married now with two kids. Well, he's very responsible and will do well wherever he goes. What can I answer for you?"

Do you hear the difference? It's simply a matter of recontacting old contacts to build new bridges of communication. It works outstandingly well, and it will help you develop job leads and strengthen your achievement record all in one master stroke.

Applying Your Research to the Market

And now, the part you've been waiting for—setting up exploratory meetings with companies.

You'll have to make a couple of decisions at this point: whether to open your campaign with phone calls or mailed resumés, and whether to work with a recruiter.

Should You Write or Call?

Your first decision in the self-marketing process is whether to write or call the company where you want an interview. You can use either method depending on which one you're more comfortable with. Let's take a moment to explore the practical sides of each approach. If you write to the one hundred companies you're pursuing to announce your intentions of becoming a productive member of their organization, you'll be making a sophisticated and well-prepared entrance onto the scene. Your cover letter will compliment each organization's accomplishments (on the basis of your research, of course), and both your letter and resumé will show how you'll complement that company's mission (on the basis of your previous industry experience, for example). Bravo! A customized career-building approach better than any career counselor could have developed for you.

On the other hand, it's expensive to mail 100 resumés, cover letters, and envelopes if it turns out that many of those companies have no plans of hiring for the next six to eighteen months. What's an assertive, career-oriented individual like you supposed to do? Well, if you call those hundred companies first before mailing a resumé and cover letter, you might find out that:

- Three companies have plans for relocating out of state.
- Seven companies had layoffs and don't foresee hiring anyone new for the next year; and even if they did, they'd first rehire those who had to be let go. (This means that your chances of landing a new position in the near future are slim to none).
- Four companies have had staffing freezes under way for the past six months and expect those freezes to continue indefinitely.
- Six companies are very honest and up-front with you, saying simply that they aren't interested in your pursuing them, even though you've done your research and you respect those organizations. When they have an opening, they list it in the classifieds, and that's the only time they want to hear from people.

Congratulations! You've just developed some great information that cut down the expenses associated with your job search campaign by 20 percent, because twenty of those one hundred companies disqualified themselves as potential target companies for you. There's no use pursuing companies that close the door on you right from the outset. And now you can focus on the eighty companies that initially gave you a green light to pursue them. (It really works this way, folks. That's why sales will always be a numbers game.)

So to answer my original question: Yes, I believe that calling companies to get a feel for where they're at is a superior and more cost-effective approach than mailing resumés cold to every company on your list. That initial prequalification will go a long way toward channeling your energies in the right direction.

All right, you've now got a narrowed-down list of companies. What if the idea of introducing yourself to them makes you uncomfortable? Or what if you simply want to leave this part to a professional? You can still employ your market research even if you choose not to approach those companies yourself. You can't let that wonderful research go to waste!

Recruiter to the Rescue!

Guess what? You won't have to look too far! Contingency recruiters would give their eyeteeth for candidates who came in with lists of companies that they previously researched and where they would like to interview. That list would in effect become the recruiter's "daily planner." The recruiter would then have a list of companies that a particular candidate identified as a place she'd like to work. Wow! You don't realize what a gift you'd be giving that recruiter! Understand that recruiters try to get people out to the libraries to invest in their own careers. Most people don't do that legwork, though. They're too busy with other things.

If you provide your recruiter with a list of twenty-five or a hundred companies, probably two to fifteen of the those companies will already be existing agency accounts. The recruiter's job is therefore made much easier because she can simply call those client companies and explain that there's a candidate in the office who's researched that firm, is aware of the company's reputation, and would like to meet with that organization even if only on an exploratory basis. Now that's a strong marketing call! Think about it from the client's side for a moment: Suppose you were a human resources professional and your agency called you and said, "Paul, we've got a candidate in our office who's aware of your firm's reputation. She's gone to the library to research your company. She showed me the research, which is very impressive, and she's hoping I can coordinate a meeting between the two of you." I don't know about you, but I'd be very impressed! I'd also be very inclined to meet with this candidate even if I didn't have an opening, because anyone who admired my company that much would probably have a lot of potential to contribute. And voilà— your market research paid off handsomely with the help of the third-party agency setting up the meeting for you.

Now, that does pose one little problem. Namely, the cost-per-hire advantage is gone. The company will now have to pay the agency a fee to hire you because you're now officially considered the agency's "find." But realistically, the fee may be well worth it to the employer to locate someone who's that savvy and well informed. As we'll see in Chapter 5, agency fees for administrative support staff are fairly inexpensive, especially when compared to the fees for hiring senior management. And that's a big plus in your column in terms of offsetting the potential contribution you can make over the long term with a one-time, up-front hiring fee.

There's also one other big advantage that working through an agency can provide for you, which may help you mentally come to terms with the idea that your cost-per-hire will go up. Agencies often present candidates directly to the line management of a given company rather than only to the human resources department. As a result, you'd be opening up your chances of coordinating meetings with your target companies because the recruiter could present you both directly to your potential next boss and, if that didn't work, then to the human resources department. If, for example, you report to the vice-president of marketing at a large real estate developer, then other vice-presidents of marketing at competing real estate development firms would certainly have an interest in hearing about you. So a recruiter may call those marketing vice-presidents directly to try and coordinate meetings for you. The call might sound something like this:

> Ms. Vice-President of Marketing, I'm an administrative support recruiter, and I interviewed an executive assistant who works for one of your competing real estate development firms in downtown Los Angeles. I'm calling you directly to tell you about her because she understands the pressures of the marketing environment, she knows the protocol and vocabulary and key players in real estate, and most importantly, she's gone to the library to research your company. She's cherry-picked your company as a firm she'd be proud to become a part of, and I'm hoping that you'd agree to speak with someone who's shown that much ingenuity and commitment to her own job search process.

Again, put yourself in the shoes of that vice-president. Would your curiosity be aroused? Would your recruiter have at least painted a picture of you as someone who's more creative than your average employee in corporate America? And most importantly, would your chances for a meeting have increased dramatically by working in tandem with that recruiter? I believe you'll agree with me that you'd have to answer those questions with an overwhelming yes!

Let me anticipate one question that may have just risen in your mind: Wouldn't the employer tell the recruiter, "Well, if she knows who we are, and she's taken the liberty of researching our company in the library in advance, then why didn't she just call us herself?" A very logical question indeed. A very logical recruiter, in turn, would respond, "The two of us are working in tandem to maximize her career opportunities. It's more often the case that a lot of people aren't comfortable making cold-call presentations to companies about themselves, and that's typically because they feel as if they're bragging about themselves. Janet felt that if she did the legwork in researching the top companies of her choice, then I could do my job by coordinating the meeting with you." See, it's easy. And I hope that I'm now painting a picture for you of how to maximize the relationship with your recruiter! Believe me, your recruiter will love you for making her job so much easier, and companies will find it much harder to say no to you once you've piqued their curiosity via your research and admiration for that organization.

I have a question for you. Can you make calls directly to line-management decision makers (like the vice-president of marketing we talked about in our last example) to try to set up interviews for yourself? Unfortunately, no. Although that approach may work well for senior management (like a chief financial officer contacting a competitor firm's CEO directly), that approach would really be inappropriate for administrative support staff for two reasons. First, you'd have to get past the telephone screener (otherwise known as the secretary) whom you might ultimately be replacing, and—no doubt about it—that's cold. It wouldn't show much sophistication or human concern if you approached a vice-president of marketing asking for an interview to become her new secretary. The vice-president would say, "How did you get past my current secretary? Does she realize why you're calling me? And what gives you the idea that I need a new assistant?" No doubt about it, that's not a good sales strategy. Second, for a third-party contingency recruiter to suggest such an interview is business. For a candidate to try to coordinate that kind of a meeting directly is pushy. (That vice-president will be loyal to her existing secretary, after all, even if that person's performance is lacking.) Therefore, let recruiters do what they do best! Although an assertive job search campaign is commendable, don't go too far at marketing yourself lest you be perceived as desperate or overly aggressive.

Calling Researched Companies Yourself

Now let's address introducing yourself directly to targeted companies. Since you now know that you shouldn't go directly to departmental or line managers (the people you would actually report to within the company), then your options are limited to the human resources department. Suppose you've got a list of a hundred companies you want to pursue. You decide not to go through a recruiter because you've learned in advance that a particular company will not use a recruiting firm under any circumstances or because you want to learn as much as you can about job search and about yourself while going through this unique process. I know that's a big assumption on my part: If you need another job immediately and can't afford the luxury of considering this a learning process, then whisk yourself off to a recruiter you trust. You won't pay a fee, and you'll be playing strength to strength: your knowledge of the marketplace gained from your research and your recruiter's sales ability and knowledge of the employment process. Still, it's important to know how to handle a job search as a do-it-yourselfer in case there are no agencies in your area.

So you're a hardy soul and you've decided to make your own calls. Whom should you call, and, more importantly, what should you say? Well, each company handles administrative support recruitment a little differently. Larger companies typically have corporate recruiters who focus strictly on administrative support or nonexempt recruitment. (**Nonexempt** refers to the Fair Labor Standards Act of 1938, which defines what categories of employees qualify for overtime pay. Exempt employees like salespeople and managers, as a rule, do not receive overtime pay. Nonexempt personnel, on the other hand, receive time-and-a-half pay for any hours worked in excess of forty in one week, or eight in one day.) In other cases, human resources managers or managers of staffing and development handle all recruitment issues concerning both exempt and nonexempt personnel. In smaller companies, office managers may assume the responsibilities for administrative support hiring. All you have to do is ask the receptionist or someone in human resources, "Who's responsible for administrative support hiring in your company?" Get the exact spelling of that person's name and his exact title (so that if you send that person your resumé, you won't damage your chances of getting noticed by misspelling any names or titles). Then simply ask to be connected to that person.

If the person on the other end of the line, affectionately known as the "gatekeeper," is hesitant to give you anyone's name within the company (he'll say something like, "Please just mail your resumé to human resources. They'll call you back if there's any interest"), simply state that you've gone to the library to research the organization. You've customized a resumé and cover letter before initiating this call, and that you'd simply like the hiring manager's name and exact title to make your correspondence as professional as possible.

At that point, most gatekeepers will give you the name and title that you've requested. If, in some exceptional case, you sense that the other party is in a disagreeable mood or still won't divulge the information, then call back and speak to someone else. For example, if the receptionist won't provide information, call back and ask directly for human resources. Or, since your research will typically provide the names of the organization's three key officers, call back and ask for one of those bigwigs by name. You'll be put through to a secretary in the executive suite, and then you could simply ask that person for the name of the hiring manager. Request to be connected once you have the hiring official's name and title. Voilà! You're right back on track!

Once you're put in contact, ask that office manager or human resources manager something along these lines:

> Mr. Employer, I'm an administrative assistant with five years of experience working for a competitor commercial banking firm in the consumer lending area. Our company recently underwent a layoff, and I've taken the liberty of going to the library to research all of our competitors. I learned some wonderful things about your company, and I'm calling because I'd like your permission to send you a copy of my resumé. Can you tell me whether you're aware of any plans, say in the next quarter or so, of adding to staff in the administrative secretarial area? Also, do you recommend that I apply through a particular recruiting firm that you typically work with?

or:

> Ms. Employer, I work with another downtown law firm that also specializes in intellectual property law and patents. I've been here for six years and just learned that my boss, one of the original partners, will be retiring soon. Although my job is safe because they're planning on reassigning me to another partner, I'm thinking that now would be an excellent time to begin exploring some stronger opportunities with other law firms. I want to send my resumé to you, Ms. Employer, but I thought I'd better introduce myself first and see whether you had any particular advice before I mailed it out to you. Do you have any tips for me in terms of how you'd like me to proceed from here? Do you prefer that I register with a recruiting firm first so that that firm can set up the meeting?

or:

> Mr. Employer, I'm new to the Dallas/Metroplex area since my spouse was relocated. I've always been aware of your company's reputation, and I've taken the liberty of going to the library to research your company before initiating this call. My goal is to learn as much about your firm as possible so that I can deter-

mine where I can make the greatest impact as an executive secretary. And I'm calling because I'd very much like the opportunity to meet with you—even if only on an exploratory basis—to share my research with you and become part of your network. That way, when an opening surfaces, we'll have already met. I hope that at that point, I could be immediately considered as a candidate for the particular department that has a need. Would you consider meeting with me on an exploratory basis at your convenience?

In any case, this opening phone call will yield information about forwarding a resumé on your own or contacting an agency that the organization depends on for administrative support staffing. You may learn of particular bona fide openings immediately available. You'll definitely learn about a rough time frame till the next administrative hire will probably be made. And you may even land an exploratory visit to a company where you can share your research and get a chance to shine. All of this is worth the time and cost of making one phone call. And this way, when your resumé does arrive, it won't land cold on the desk. That employer will most likely remember you once your cover letter thanks the employer for her previous time over the phone.

Setting Up Exploratory Interviews

Your introductory telephone call probably will sound something like this:

You: Ms. Employer, my name is Paul Falcone, and I've been a branch sales secretary with the XYZ Credit Union for the past three years. I'm calling you because I've just learned that my present employer will be undergoing some staff reductions in the next three months, and I thought now would be a great time to expand some of my career alternatives.

I'm aware of your organization's reputation as a quality company that takes good care of your people. I've invaded the library researching you before picking up the phone today. And I feel I'm ready for greater responsibilities in my career. Coming from a competitor credit union, I'd hope to have some successful and creative ideas to share with you, and I'd like your permission to send you a copy of my resumé. Do you have any tips in terms of how I should proceed, or are there any recruiting firms that you typically deal with that could set up that meeting?

Employer: Well, Paul, we don't have any openings right now for sales secretaries, but I'd be happy to take a look at your resumé and contact
you when we have an opening.

You: Ms. Employer, that would be great. Could I make a quick suggestion,
though? I've always found that strong companies want to be kept
abreast of strong people regardless of openings. My approach to my
job search campaign is to be very proactive in terms of cherry-picking
the strongest companies in town. I've researched you in *Standard &
Poor's* and *Dun & Bradstreet*. I come from a competitor credit union
and have the same softwares that you use. (I understand that you're
an MS Word for Windows and Excel company.) And I'm hoping we
can meet for fifteen minutes so I can introduce myself. This way, when
an opening becomes available, we'll know each other, and I hope *I'll
be able to fill that need for you without your having to run an ad*. Besides,
I'd be happy to share my research with you if you'd like to see it. Would you
be open to meeting with me on an exploratory basis?

Great. Let's evaluate your approach. At this point you're probably
asking, "Gee, can I do that?" Sure, you can! It's a very humble and complimentary approach with an excellent strategy. You've already done your
homework in the library, which shows you've earned the right to ask for
the meeting. You set yourself up on a problem-to-solution basis by showing how an exploratory meeting with you now could save that company
time and money in the future when a bona fide opening surfaces. (You've
got to know the company, after all, before you can present yourself as a
solution.) And most significantly, you're now in a position to give something back—namely, your research—which is what networking is all
about. Obviously, the juicier your research, the more you have to offer!

See, it's not so bad after all.

If that employer does indeed invite you in to her office for an exploratory meeting even though no opening apparently exists, be prepared:
Your chances of landing a job offer are extremely high! This is because
there's got to be something brewing that the employer isn't telling you
about. Maybe a new position will be opening next month. Or maybe that
employer recalled that a new department will have to be staffed by the
end of the quarter. Or maybe you were just so nice and sincere in your
presentation that it would be a mistake not to schedule a brief fifteen-
minute meeting with you should something unexpectedly arise within the
company. The point is that if there were absolutely nothing available,
you'd still come up with a "thanks but no thanks" to your suggestion for
an exploratory visit. Instead, while you were sharing your philosophy of
job search with the employer, she thought of a place where you might fit.
So before you know it, you've got a fifteen-minute time slot tomorrow
morning.

Exploratory Interview Strategies

1. Never, and I do mean never, use what's known as the underpromise/overstay technique. Underpromise/overstay bases itself upon deceit: Tell the employer you only want fifteen minutes of her time, and try to stretch that out into a half hour or even an hour. Why is it so terrible? Because the first action this employer is observing is your commitment to time management, namely, her time management. If you keep rattling on beyond the fifteen-minute limit that you asked for, you become victim to the law of diminishing returns: The more you say (no matter how good), the more it's held against you. Remember that networking is an open and honest communication. Keep your word and your commitment, and let the brevity of the meeting leave the interviewer wanting more.

Does this mean that the meeting absolutely can't turn out to be an hour-long get-together? Absolutely not. But the employer must be the one to initiate the elongated meeting. After fifteen minutes, even if you're in a fairly deep conversation, interrupt the meeting with something like, "You know, Karen, I'm really enjoying our meeting, and I'm really grateful that you gave me the time to introduce myself. But my fifteen minutes are up, and I don't want to keep you one minute beyond our preestablished time. I hope that we can leave this meeting on a to-be-continued basis, but for now, I'd better allow you to return your attention to your work."

Wow! Who's in control here anyway? You are! You just demonstrated ultimate control, a commitment to time management, and sincere concern for that employer's time. You just gained big points in terms of reliability, follow-through, and goodwill. Well done.

2. It's up to you to do the entertaining. You invited yourself in for the interview, so don't expect the employer to interview you in the traditional sense. Once you sit in the chair in front of that hiring official, it's your responsibility to explain why you're there and what you hope to get out of the meeting. The five points you want to highlight in the opening moments of this exploratory interview are:

a. The minimum parameters of your responsibilities at your present/last job: namely, whom you reported to, the size of your company in revenues or number of employees, whom you supervised, and the nature of your primary responsibilities.
b. Your key accomplishments or achievements at a past company that could benefit this company (in other words, what you can do for this company).
c. Your needs as an employee and how this company could fulfill them. Be careful with this one: I don't mean a wish list of demands you have from your next company. Instead, I'm talking about in-

formed candidacy again. You need to discuss the fact that you're either pursuing a higher-echelon job in a similar company or a same-echelon job in a larger, stronger company.

d. Questions that you'd like the employer to answer for you.

e. An open-ended commitment to keep in touch by mailing or faxing (not calling, lest you be perceived as a pushy pest!) relevant information on the company, industry, or HR profession, which again is the essence of networking: giving back to the other party involved.

There is a litmus test for distinguishing your needs from the company's needs. Don't focus on what the company can do for you; instead, highlight how your personal needs can make a positive impact on that company. For example, turn "I like being kept busy and getting motivated" into "I enjoy finding work for myself and motivating the people around me to work together as a team." That way, you'll clearly show how your desire to succeed can be fulfilled by taking on the challenges that the company has to offer. Presenting yourself on a problem-to-solution level means solving the company's problems, not expecting the company to solve yours.

Let's run through this to see how it works. You've filled out an employment application in the lobby, and you're now being led back to the human resources manager's office. Once introduced, you're invited to sit down, and the manager says something like this. (Check how the bracketed letters correspond with those in the list on pages 39–40.)

Employer: It's really nice to meet you, Paul. It's very impressive to see people who have researched our company before making a presentation. I normally don't meet people unless I have an immediate need, but something may be surfacing in the near future that fits your background. What would you like me to know about you?

You: [a] Mr. Employer, I guess I'd just open up our meeting by letting you know that your organization has an excellent reputation as a quality company in the credit union industry. I worked as a branch secretary for ABC Credit, as I mentioned over the phone, for the past three years, and my primary duties have been to report to a staff of nine banking officers in the lending, mortgage, and credit areas. ABC only has a staff of nine people even though it carries $22 million in assets. I know that a credit union with $22 million in assets typically would have about fifteen employees, but we all pitched in to get massive amounts of work done on a daily basis.

[b] As a matter of fact, one of the achievements I'm proudest of is that I literally doubled the workload of the branch secretarial position. There used to be one secretary and one office administrator to

handle the workload before I arrived. When I came aboard, both the former secretary and administrator left for various reasons. Yet they never had to hire a second person to replace the administrator because I really enjoyed taking on lots of responsibilities and got all the work done. In my three years at ABC, the credit union grew from $19 to $22 million in assets by opening membership to noncompany members. Also, because I had worked for XYZ credit union before going to ABC, I made a suggestion to implement a membership fee schedule for various services like check writing and loan applications that brought in about $5,000 a month in increased service revenues. I got an Employee of the Month award for that.

[c] I guess the reason why I'm here is that I feel I could benefit a lot by working for your credit union. I'm looking for what I'd call a "same-echelon job" in a larger, stronger company. I definitely want to stay in the credit union industry, and I want to work for a company that's a real leader in the field. The *Los Angeles Business Journal* publishes an annual *Book of Lists* that profiles the top twenty-five companies in every major industry in Southern California. Your company ranked twenty-third in terms of assets under management, and I'd be proud to become part of a company that gets that kind of recognition in the press.

[d] If it's okay with you, I'd like to ask you some questions about what you look for in your administrative support staff and what you feel makes your company unique.

- ☞ The first thing I'd like to know is what two or three characteristics your most successful employees have in common.
- ☞ How would you describe the corporate culture of your credit union? In other words, what's the management style like? What's the pace of the office, and how do people typically get along with one another?
- ☞ What's the typical hiring process like once a bona fide opening exists within the company? Is there anything I can do in advance so that when something opens up, I'll be that much more prepared to capitalize on it?
- ☞ Finally, if you don't mind my asking, Mr. Employer, how long have you been with the firm, and what initially attracted you to the company?

[Note: This is a preview of the valuable interview questions in Chapters 6 and 7. For further suggestions on particular questions, jump ahead to those chapters.]

[e] Finally, Mr. Employer, my time's just about up. I really want to thank you for giving me an audience, so to speak. I've got my re-

search with me from the *Los Angeles Business Journal's Book of Lists*, and I'd be happy to leave you a copy of it for your PR files if you'd like. Also, I'd like to close the meeting by telling you that I'd really love the opportunity to become part of your company. I hope you'll consider me once an actual opening surfaces. May I ask for your permission to stay in contact with you—by letter or fax only—by keeping you abreast of any other research that I do on your company or the industry? That'd give me a great reason for staying in touch, and it'll obviously keep me in the forefront of your memory. Would that be okay?

Well, thanks again for your time and the information you shared. I really enjoyed our meeting.

Fifteen minutes and out the door. And you knocked his socks off! You were totally prepared to keep the conversation going by having the structure of the meeting all laid out beforehand. You knew how you wanted to sell yourself via your accomplishments. You articulated how your needs would be filled by joining that company. And you asked some great value-oriented questions that showed that you were sincerely interested in the company and its people. Note as well that this meeting format works exactly the same when a search firm sets up an exploratory interview for you, so you can use it in either an agency-generated scenario or an independent-contact situation.

Notice one thing you did not do: pushy sales. No "Are there any openings for me right now?" or "Is there any reason for not hiring me once an opening becomes available?" You never made that employer feel uncomfortable by forcing the issue. Instead, everything you did and said implied that you'd be proud to become a member of that company's team, but those implications were couched in a much softer, more sophisticated approach. You shared your research, complimented the company, presented yourself on a problem-to-solution level, gave your realistic expectations for your own career, and asked questions that focused on the emotional aspects of the organization and its people. Most importantly, you got a green light to continue the relationship.

Not bad for fifteen minutes of your time! The next step in your journey is to make sure that your tools—namely, your resumés and cover letters—are ready to present you in a favorable light. Once they're ready to go, you'll be 100 percent prepared to pick up the phone and maximize your networking campaign.

Chapter 3

Customizing Your Resumé to Meet Your Target Company's Needs

It takes only one trip to your corner bookstore or to the library to realize that a myriad of books have been dedicated solely to resumé writing. I've browsed through many of them myself, and I really like the advice that many of the newer ones give. (Of course, none of them targets the needs of the secretarial and administrative support marketplace the way this one does, but we won't hold that against them!) Still, I'm somewhat disheartened that the vast majority of job seekers haven't perfected their resumé-writing skills.

Your Resumé Is Your Ambassador

Many hiring managers may admit that if they've got the right resumé in front of them, they could care less if it were written in crayon. But that's a dangerous assumption for two reasons. First, those hiring managers would have to ferret out that resumé from among two hundred closely matched competitors, so the crayon effect wouldn't help too much. Second, when you hear statements like that, beware: They're usually not talking about administrative support folks but about professional-technical candidates who meet needle-in-the-haystack requirements, like "five years of mortgage banking and loan applications experience on an HP 3000 platform with MPE, Cobol, and Speedware." Sure, if you've got all that and the company needed to hire someone with that pedigree yesterday, then your resumé could have been written in crayon. But shy of that ideal scenario, the crayon routine would end up in the round files. So let's jettison the idea that the resumé as a hiring tool plays anything less than a critical role in your job search campaign.

I've often heard job candidates complain about corporate America's overreliance on resumés:

Resumés are only paper credentials that say nothing about who I am or what I'm capable of accomplishing. They're merely a menu of 'deselectors' that companies use to disqualify me from competing because:

I don't come from the right type of company.
My softwares don't match.
My education (lack of degree) makes me underqualified.
My last salary makes me overqualified.
If only they would meet me, then they'd know what I was
    capable of because I could prove it to them in person.

I'm sorry if you've ever felt that way, but those perceptions are wrong. First of all, anytime you see yourself rationalizing a situation as "me versus them," then understand that you're bordering on paranoia, and you're putting yourself into a victim posture. Second, understand that, as far as employers see it, the closer the match of any candidate to the technical nature of the job or to the company, the greater the chances of success. Success in the human resources practitioner's mind equates to increased output/productivity and reduced turnover. So you need to spend time in this chapter learning about how HR professionals perceive the resumé as a tool for screening candidates. Once you comprehend how human resources people get measured by their ability to recruit qualified talent within specific time frames, then you'll come to terms with your individual candidacy and realize that there's nothing personal about the rejection that goes along with job change.

Put the Law of Large Numbers on Your Side

Since a company isn't rejecting you, per se, but the pedigree or experience history you represent, then you'll come to realize that your only defense against the inevitable rejections that will come your way lies in the law of large numbers. The more companies you contact, the more rejections you'll develop—but also the more acceptances. So, to put another twist on how people have traditionally viewed the rejection that comes along with a job search campaign, *you want to increase the number of rejections you get!* That's because increasing the number of rejections is the only way to increase the number of acceptances.

With that happy thought in mind, let me briefly share with you a recruiter's nightmare story that happened to me not long ago. One of my clients was a leading investment banking firm that was relocating its mergers and acquisitions department back to the East Coast. This firm asked me to help find work for its displaced support staff. I happened to have an opening for a departmental secretary at a competitor investment banker in town, and I thought to myself, "Paul, this is your lucky day!

Now you've got three candidates from the premier Wall Street investment firm who are all available to pursue the opening with the number two firm in town." The resumés and references were impeccable, and all three had excellent people skills. I faxed the resumés to my client who had the opening for the departmental secretary position, and got a quick call back with a polite "Thanks, but no thanks."

There had to be some kind of misunderstanding. I couldn't have rubbed on a magic lamp and come up with three more qualified candidates from the choicest company in town. When I called my client to figure out what went wrong, I learned that the hiring manager wasn't looking for anyone with previous industry experience. Her plan for this particular hire was to bring in a secretary without previous investment banking experience who could be trained from scratch, which was certainly her choice. But didn't that just fly in the face of everything I'd learned in the search business!

The moral of the story is that you can't let one (or fifty!) rejected resumés get in the way of your successful job search campaign. You simply can't know all the ingredients in that particular search assignment or the company's past history trying to fill that particular opening. Because I was a recruiter and my client knew me, I got the scoop on why those three resumés weren't considered. But if you were the candidate in that situation, you wouldn't have received a call explaining the reasoning behind the decision. You would have merely received a polite "thank you for applying, but your background doesn't match our needs" letter. So again, remember the law of large numbers and let greater exposure increase both your rejections and acceptances. By playing a volume game, you'll let the ratios take care of the number of acceptances you generate.

Content: The Tools for Telling Your Story

Let's begin by examining how to phrase the content of your resumé, emphasizing wording. Later in this chapter, we'll address how to make your page layout most pleasing to the eye.

What Is a Resumé Supposed to Tell an Employer?

Resumé writing is a fun and creative process because it's uniquely you: It's an X-ray indicator of your self-esteem, the pride you take in your work, and your attention to detail. That one document represents the sum total of your achievements in the workplace, and it wraps those accomplishments up in a context outlining your broad duties, reporting relationships, achievements, and the scope of your responsibilities. A resumé is your calling card for career advancement, your advertising copy that sells the most unique product in the world, and your attempt at encapsulating your future potential on the basis of your past experience. In short, it's the most valuable credential you have.

You went to college to receive a four-year degree? That takes up one line on your resumé. You increased your company's monthly revenues by implementing a fee-for-service plan that awarded you the Employee of the Month designation? That takes up two lines on a resumé. Bilingual abilities ditto. The greatest achievements you've worked for all your life get only one chance to gain expression and benefit you by getting your foot in the door of greater opportunity. That's what your resumé is all about. It's the unique marketing tool that pays you back for all your work—but only if you treat it with the respect and utmost care it deserves.

How Do Employers Scan Resumés?

First let's take an official look at how employers are trained to screen resumés. The picture looks something like this: You're the human resources manager for your company, and you listed two ads in the Denver Post this past weekend—one for an executive secretary to the president, and one for a branch sales secretary. The mail clerk comes by your office every day at 10:00 A.M., noon, 2:00 P.M., and 4:00 P.M., each time dropping off a three-inch stack of resumés generated from the ad. Your mission in life? To get that job filled by weeding through those enormous piles of paperwork and separating out from the pack those three to six candidates who appear to be the strongest of the bunch. Ready, *go!* You've got twenty minutes before your next meeting!

Well, it's time for that human resources manager to put her recruiting training to work. Accurate candidate selection within strict time limits is an art as much as a science. What you need to keep in mind is that the average length of time an employer takes to review your (and everybody else's) resumé is somewhere between *twelve and thirty-two seconds*. That's right, your whole life's work gets evaluated in less than half a minute. It may seem unfair, but what else could that employer do if she's got over one hundred resumés to cut through for one particular opening? Besides, it's a worthwhile statistic that may help you keep the value of that resumé credential in perspective!

To be consistent, many employers look at resumé information in boxes or clusters. Here's how most recruiters review administrative support resumés:

What Employers Scan for

- ☛ Title (especially reporting relationships and departmental/functional experience)

- Longevity
- Company name-brand recognition/similar industry experience
- Software skills
- Education

The order of this cluster scanning may change, of course. Sometimes one factor (like specific software or industry experience) outweighs all other criteria in the selection process. But overall, this approach to resumé reading is valid across the board regardless of industry, discipline, or the part of the country you live in.

The article shown in Figure 3-1 appeared in the December 1992 issue of the AMA's *HR Focus* Magazine. It will give you some further insights into the sometimes daunting task of resumé evaluation. Looking at the whole process from the inside out—namely, from the human resources manager's point of view—will teach you to focus on achievements and avoid superfluous claims that have no factual support. Let's get more specific.

What Gets Disregarded Most on Resumés?

Now that you know what the employer *is* looking for when scanning resumés, let's focus on what sections of the resumé usually get skipped over in the selection process:

- Personal information and hobbies
- Summaries of qualifications or experience
- Objectives

Personal Information and Hobbies. At best, personal information and hobbies are harmless but useless little factoids that human resources professionals look right past. At worst, they can be so outlandish or politically incorrect that they bar you from being considered a serious candidate even if everything else on your resumé looks great. For example:

Examples of Unnecessary Personal Interests and Hobbies

- Single, raising rescued dog and cat
- Silent-movie buff, teach needlepoint
- Enjoy bicycling, tennis, water sports, and war games
- Blissfully married, 5'8", 180 lbs., excellent health

These probably won't kill your candidacy on the spot, but any employer would consider such information extraneous at best. Of course, you're providing ammunition that could be used against you in a discriminatory

Figure 3-1. When you write your resumé, keep in mind the main factors managers evaluate.

A Manager's Guide to Screening Resumés

Screening resumes is no fun. Even the most tolerant of managers might be tempted to throw out the whole stack

BY JOAN F. BURROW–Few managers today can get by without having to sort through a stack of resumés as part of the hiring process. Unfortunately, the pile usually looms large and grows with each day's mail delivery. To make matters worse, time is not on the side of most managers. Many complain that every time they pick up a resumé from the top of the stack and read about halfway down, something interrupts their train of thought. The phone rings, someone stops by for a "quick" question, or an emergency erupts. In turn, the resumé gets tossed back on the pile. This cycle can continue for days until even the most tolerant managers are ready to throw out the whole stack of resumés.

Rx for Resumé-mania

The following tried-and-true suggestions can help managers overcome "resumé-mania."

• **Be ruthless.** Begin by screening resumés. Don't read every resumé; that can take hours. (Think about the amount of time wasted wading through three pages of a resumé, only to discover on the last page that the person lacks the required degree). Instead, skim the resumé and look for the most basic of criteria, such as education and years of work experience.

• **Check for stability.** Look first for the year that an applicant graduated from college and then read your way toward their present position. In the margin, mark in pencil the number of years that the candidate has spent at each organization. (Pencil is preferable over ink because the resumé may become part of a permanent personnel file.) Beware of an applicant who has changed jobs every two or three years. Such employment instability could signal performance difficulties or other undesirable traits.

• **Examine job title progression.** Look for levels of increasing responsibility throughout an applicant's career. Good employees either move up within an organization or move out. To avoid underhiring or overhiring, first determine how much experience the available position would require.

• **Critique overall appearance.** How does the resumé look visually? Was care taken in its presentation and reproduction? Are there spelling errors? Don't waste time on sloppy or carelessly written resumés.

• **Make a decision.** After screening the resumé, make a decision. Determine if the applicant is a "yes," a "no," or a "maybe." A "yes" means that the applicant warrants further consideration; a "no" signals that there's no longer a need to proceed any further. Managers who might be ambivalent about a resumé—either because they are too tired to make a definite decision on it or the resumé is structured in a nontraditional format—should create a "maybe" stack. This way, if the stack of potential job candidates runs low, managers can refer to their "maybe" stack. This method also avoids allowing one resumé to hold up the entire screening process.

These steps require concentration and discipline. With a little practice, however, managers can whip through an ominous stack of resumés quickly and be on their way to the next project in record time.

Joan F. Burrow is a vice president with Hannahan Associates, a Cincinnati-based healthcare recruiting firm.
Source: Joan F. Burrow, *HR Focus,* December 1992.

fashion; for example, employers are not allowed by law to question your marital status or physical condition. References to your personal health, marital status, or year you were born are never recommended because they provide information that the employer, by law, shouldn't have. (We'll discuss discrimination issues further in Chapter 6.) And what if the employer just went through a messy divorce? Do you think your advertising that you're blissfully married will win you any points? Again, the rule in resumé writing is that if the information isn't going to further your candidacy, don't mention it.

Are there ever any reasons to list your hobbies or personal interests? Probably only if those outside interests directly relate to the particular company where you're applying. For example, if you're applying for a position with the Red Cross, then listing that you're a member of their Gallon Donor Club might come in handy. But other than that far-out occasion, avoid all mention of personal interests.

Summary of Qualifications or Experience. The qualifications summary section on the resumé usually boils down to a lot of fluff with no real-world application. Unsubstantiated claims that have no factual back-up waste the reader's time. Again, picture a human resources professional wending his way through 170 resumés. Probably 70 percent of those resumés include a qualifications summary section.

Examples of Unnecessary Qualifications

- Skilled planner and decision maker
- Conscientious and hard-working team player who produces quality work and gets along well with others
- Innovative and resourceful contributor to the corporate team; adept at managing a wide range of activities; effective at communicating with all levels of staff and management
- A big-picture strategist with initiative and enthusiasm
- Good leadership abilities; dedicated to the task at hand
- Ability to prioritize, delegate, and motivate; responsive and creative in problem solving
- Dedicated to quality improvement and cost containment; proven record of dependability with increasing responsibilities
- Highly developed written and verbal communication skills

Snore! This is cannon fodder. These claims say and do nothing to further your candidacy because they're unsubstantiated. Companies don't hire people on the basis of those people's perceptions about themselves. Instead, companies hire people whose industry background, skills, and reporting relationships are similar to those of the job at hand. So I suggest that you jettison the qualifications summary section of the resumé because it simply gets passed over by the reader.

Are there ever any reasons to list qualification summaries? Only if you want to emphasize certain specific, factual aspects of your experience, or licenses and certifications you hold that make you more qualified for the job at hand. For example, if you're a senior-level executive secretary applying for a position reporting to senior or executive management of *Fortune* 500 companies, then you might write:

> Extensive administrative support experience at the highest executive level of *Fortune* 500 companies; executive travel experience with both commercial and corporate flights; board of director meeting preparation and attendance, corporate minute taking . . .

Other valid examples could be:

- More than six years of experience in the financial services industry with a focus on marketing and training
- Current Series 7 and Series 63 licenses
- Bilingual abilities: Spanish (fluent), French (working knowledge)

Again, list only factual information that shows the depth of your experience or emphasizes your background in a given industry. Otherwise, it shouldn't be included on the resumé.

Objective. A third section of the resumé that an employer usually overlooks is the objective. Here are what typical objectives sound like:

> Seeking a position in which to utilize my organization skills and communication abilities to their fullest potential

> To secure a position where I will be able to utilize my full knowledge and experience

> To locate a position that will be challenging and will offer me opportunity for further advancement

Or worse,

> Seeking a sales or administrative position that will utilize my diverse background, training, and experience in a stable position with growth potential

Now think about it for a moment. Do these things really say anything? After reading about a hundred of these objectives, you would come to the heavy conclusion that all those people want jobs. Okay, the objective actually tells you a little more than that: All those people out there want *good* jobs. Other than that, most people's objectives say nothing at all.

But objectives aren't benign little factoids like the qualifications we looked at earlier. Objectives can really hurt your candidacy by pigeon-holing you. Here's how: Let's look again at some of the examples on page 50. My first criticism of most of the objectives I see is that they focus on the candidate's needs rather than the company's needs. Remember, you're not going to seem very attractive to a potential employer if everything you write focuses on what you want. The sale, so to speak, lies in convincing the company that you could benefit it. So if you were to use an objective (and I obviously highly recommend against that in most circumstances), you should at least turn the phrasing around to show the benefits you have to offer the organization, not what you expect from that company. For example, turn:

> Seeking a position in which to utilize my communication and organization skills to their fullest potential

into:

> Seeking a position in which to utilize my communication and organization skills to my next employer's benefit by streamlining procedures and increasing the work flow

Similarly, you can adapt this strategy to the next selection on page 50 accordingly, turning:

> To secure a position where I will be able to utilize my full knowledge and experience

into:

> To secure a position where my knowledge and experience will benefit my next employer by increasing productivity and decreasing expenses

You get the idea. Sell how you can contribute and where you'd like to make a difference. Presenting your goals any other way assumes that they owe you a job, a challenging place to keep you busy every day, and a guaranteed future. They don't. That's your responsibility.

The final example in that list of sample objectives is a killer: "Seeking a sales *or* administrative position that will utilize my diverse background, training, and experience in a stable position with growth potential." Ouch! You mean you don't know whether you want a sales job or an administrative support position? Well, if you don't know, the employer isn't going to tell you! "Pick a career—any career—and stick with it" is the employer's rationale to that objective statement. You're dead in the water before the employer's had a chance to look at anything you've accomplished. Remember how we said that most resumés get between twelve and thirty-two seconds for review? Not this one: Two to three seconds is all you get to be screened out. Beware of indecisiveness on a resumé! You can't be everything to everyone, so pick a plan and stick with it.

Are there any occasions where an objective statement is necessary? Yes, but only when you're changing fields. For example, if you've been an accounting clerk for the past two years since you entered the workforce, and now you want to become a secretary, then an objective statement would be necessary to sell your desire to change over from accounting to administration. Otherwise, an employer looking at your resumé would see two years of accounting work and assume you're a candidate for the accounting department. Without that objective to clarify your desire to make a change, your resumé would be misunderstood. Of course, it's a tough sell to make a transition from one area of work to another, and a short statement on the resumé alone won't sell your idea. You'll need to address your desire more thoroughly in your cover letter. But we'll get to that a little later on in Chapter 4.

How Many Resumé Versions Do You Need?

What if you're pursuing two career paths simultaneously (for example, sales and administration)? That's fine, but you need two separate resumés. *It's a critical mistake to mix and match functional objectives on the same resumé.* There's no set number of resumés that you need to have when looking for a job, but you'll usually need more than one. Better yet, if you happen to have a computer, you can customize every resumé for the job at hand. If that luxury isn't afforded you, then two or three resumé versions emphasizing various aspects of your experience will suffice.

Let's look at a brief example. You have ten years of secretarial experience in total, but for the past three years you've been in commercial property sales and leasing. You got your real estate license when you made the transition into sales and you won a Rookie of the Year Award at your present real estate company. Now you've reached a point where you're questioning whether sales is the long-term field for you. You miss the nine-to-five routine of working in a nice office and letting your boss worry about all the pressures associated with commissions. Maybe it would be nice to settle into an administrative support role again. On the other hand, if someone made you a really solid offer to continue in sales, then you'd pursue that as well.

In such a case, your *first* resumé needs to be geared to your administrative support background. You'd probably want to dedicate a lot of room in your cover letter and in your resumé's objective statement to your desire to make a functional change from sales back into secretarial work. Your longest job descriptions would focus on the secretarial work you had done in the past before moving over to sales three years ago. As a matter of fact, you'd probably want to downplay your job description and achievements in the past three years so as to dedicate more room on your resumé to your secretarial experience. I'd recommend possibly omitting your Rookie of the Year award and your current valid real estate license. Those might function only as detractors that could take away from your goal of moving back into administration.

On your *other* resumé, in comparison, you'd focus mostly on your achievements in the past three years. You'd highlight your Rookie of the Year Award in boldface type and list your valid real estate license at the top of the page. You might address your branch ranking, sales dollar volume, average monthly percentage in excess of quota, and the like. On the other hand, you would want to reduce your secretarial past to brief footnotes without spending much time addressing duties and accomplishments because they have very little relevance to your sales audience. Remember, you're not misrepresenting anything by overemphasizing some things and de-emphasizing others. You're simply selling key areas of interest to your respective audiences.

What Gets the Most Attention on Resumés?

Now that we've addressed some of the most common mistakes people make in writing their resumés, let's address what employers really want to know about:

- Exact titles
- Reporting relationships
- Primary duties and degrees of responsibility
- Key accomplishments
- Company descriptions

Exact Titles and Reporting Relationships. Your first mission in developing your position descriptions after providing your exact title will be to articulate your reporting relationships. The goal here is to put your experiences and responsibilities into some kind of context or perspective. You specifically want to name both the *title(s)* and *number(s)* of people that you support(ed). For example,

Reporting directly to the partner-in-charge of the management consulting department, kept a department smoothly running during three transition periods.

As executive secretary in small corporate headquarters, assist chairman, president, and vice-president of finance with. . . .

Performed diverse administrative and secretarial duties for president of largest savings and loan institution in San Joaquin Valley.

Served as corporate administrative assistant to chairman of the board and chief executive officer.

As assistant to the executive vice-president and chief credit officer for international banking, trading, and securities. . . .

Support president/CEO and vice-president of business affairs with. . . .

Provided word processing support to president, three managing directors, four vice-presidents, and six associates for one of the largest real estate investment firms in northwest Arkansas.

Responsible for all administrative/clerical functions of this small public accounting firm whose clientele consists largely of real estate developers and other real estate–related businesses.

Primary Duties and Responsibilities. Next you'll want to provide a detailed description of your primary duties and the scope of your responsibilities. Don't make the mistake of merely listing generic job functions like typing, phones, and filing. Everyone does that! The challenge here will be to paint pictures with words so that the reader/employer will truly get an accurate feel for your style of support. Remember as well to employ action verbs to keep your prose moving along. For example,

Created own correspondence and worked from Dictaphone; *tallied* monthly project and office expense reports; *coordinated* travel arrangements and hotel accommodations for twelve account executives; *set up* office filing systems and customized Paradox client database.

Formulated key proposals and brochures using Microsoft Word for Windows and Aldus Pagemaker. *Coordinated* word processing assignments for entire corporate staff, including president and chief financial officer, board of directors, controller, area managers, and director of suite operations.

Assisted in the design and development of a database for defense team of three law firms located in New York; Washington, D.C.; and Texas. These firms represent an individual in multiple-issue, complex litigation including interrelated federal and state civil and criminal cases.

Scheduled internal appointments, meetings and telephone conferences as well as luncheons and speaking engagements outside company. Made extensive and complicated travel arrangements with corporate jets and commercial airlines as back-up. *Performed* many personal duties for vice-chairman, including personal checking accounts and expense logs.

Assisted the general counsel with the company's name change nationwide, which entailed extensive research in each state to determine its respective requirements. Duties included keeping all records of board meetings and resolutions and assisting with various mergers and sales of subsidiaries and county operations.

Providing one-on-one administrative support to vice-president of human resources; responsibilities include *scheduling* off-site training seminars for sales staff, *editing* company newsletter, and *translating* personnel documents into Spanish.

Post cash and sales reports; *reconcile* month-end bank statements; *prepare* related payroll reports such as federal and state quarterly reports, W-2s, and 1099s; *make* journal entries for general ledger and financial statement purposes; *batch* and *code* invoices; *run* cash requirement and aged trial balance; *file* duplicate copy of checks with original invoice by alphabetical order.

Describe your responsibilities with zest! Your activities have to be put into the context of your level of involvement and authority. To assist you in developing your ideas further by putting fresh insights into some tired phraseology, rely on these actions verbs to move your writing along:

assist	compose	coordinate
broaden	consolidate	create

design	increase	provide
develop	initiate	purchase
edit	maintain	reduce
eliminate	manage	revise
evaluate	negotiate	save
expand	organize	simplify
generate	plan	streamline
handle	prepare	supervise
identify	proofread	train
implement		

Key Accomplishments. A third area of concentration on your resumé, and in many ways the most significant, will be the focus you put on your achievements. Accomplishments are what the resumé-writing game is all about. One of the greatest sales trainers I know, Peter Leffkowitz of The Morgan Consulting Group in Kansas City, made the uncommon insight that employers are not so much interested in what you do between nine and five; rather, *they're interested in the results you achieved for that company by having worked from nine to five.* Few statements will revolutionize your understanding of how to present yourself to a company more than this one!

Your achievements allow you to stand out among your competition. They elevate your status to exceptional employee capable of adding value to a company beyond the call of duty. Not everyone reading this book will have concrete and quantifiable accomplishments to bring with pride to an employer's attention. After all, we can't all be Employee of the Month or Employee of the Year. Still, you'd be surprised how you'll be able to weave patterns of achievement into your resumé even if no lofty achievements come to mind right off the bat.

There are two types of achievements: the traditional, hard-core accomplishments that get marked down in your employment file and give you public recognition among your peers; and the softer, less obvious kudos that will also further your candidacy handsomely. The first type, the **hard achievements,** are fairly obvious:

Examples of Hard Achievements and Recognitions

Earned Customer Service Representative of the Month Award for five months during a two-year period

Received Night on the Town Award for participating in voluntary company activities

1993, 1995 Top Gun Award for outstanding sales support

Recipient of the Employee of the Year Award for overall outstanding performance

Best Supporting Employee in the Office Services Department

Those are easy enough to identify and list. But what about soft achievements? How do you identify and list them? So-called **soft achievements** fall into four categories:

1. Promotions
2. Lateral moves to gain greater exposure to your field
3. Demonstrations of increased responsibilities and creative accomplishments
4. Volunteer work within the company

Again, these achievements may not have put your picture on the cover of the company newsletter, but they certainly indicate patterns of accomplishment that will most likely be repeated in the future.

Examples of Soft Achievements and Recognitions

Developed and wrote procedures for the property tax unit that resulted in more accurate payment of impounded property taxes. The company increased revenues previously lost on late payment penalties.

Promoted to a newly created position developed because of record-breaking growth in corporate revenues.

Publicly recognized for outstanding contributions to company volunteer programs including annual blood drive and City of Hope walkathon.

Served as temporary office manager during supervisor's leave of absence.

Within nine months of entering department, I was placed in charge of two major accounts, and I raised on-time deliveries from 62 percent to 81 percent.

Provided support to senior vice-president of finance and administration when needed.

Where do these accomplishments spatially belong on the resumé? As a general rule, if you wish to list concrete achievements and awards, list them in a separate section on the resumé under the title "Awards" or "Special Achievements." They'll stand alone rather handsomely and need no further explanation. If, on the other hand, your accomplishments fall under the soft recognition category, then weave them into the body of your job descriptions. That way, they'll have a logical tie-in to the events surrounding them, and they'll add much greater impact to your resumé by revealing the immediate results of your activities.

Company Descriptions. Finally, I believe that company descriptions enhance most resumés by providing a context or framework for your responsibilities and achievements. Most people don't work for IBM, Disney, AT&T, or General Motors. Far more people work for Johnson, Roe & Smith; The Metropolitan Consulting Group; Harbinger & Associates Management Consultants; or Vanguard LTD. In those cases, even if you present your qualifications, achievements, and reporting relationships in great detail, one question will constantly nag the reader: *What kind of company is this?* What industry is the company in? Is there any relationship to what we do here in our company? Are we talking large company or small?

Obviously, without reference to the company's background, there will be a lot of question marks surrounding your background. Remember that ambiguity in resumés will many times be interpreted against you! That's just the nature of the beast when employers have thirty seconds or less to get to the right candidate. So remove any final doubts or question marks right from the start. That kind of attention to detail will be highly valued by the prospective employer. (Yes, it can knock you out of the running as well if your background isn't right. Maybe your company is too big or too small, or maybe it's in an unrelated industry. But don't look at it that way: If your company background is wrong, you'll just be delaying the inevitable by trying to get around that information. In that case, you'll be better served by accepting the rejection up front and then moving on to other opportunities.)

Here are examples of company descriptions that will put your employment experience into a workable context for the resumé reader:

Regenfogel Industries, Chicago, Ill.
A 200-employee, two-plant division of Watering Hole Inc., producing electronic and electromechanical controllers for irrigation systems.

H₂O Solutions, Erie, Pa.
An eighty-employee, $12MM sales and marketing division of Watering Hole Inc., selling irrigation products and turnkey systems in 100 countries worldwide.

Plastics-R-Us, Brooklyn, N.Y.
A six-plant, 400-employee nationwide manufacturer of injection-molded containers for the dairy, soft drink, baking, and waste management industries.

Pills Galore, Phoenix, Ariz.
An $8 billion, *Fortune* 100 publicly traded manufacturer of pharmaceutical products worldwide.

We-B-Jammin Inc., Atlanta, Ga.
Corporate headquarters for a fifteen-store, retail division of a family-owned music publisher and wholesaler.

Smith and Austen, Philadelphia, Pa.
Small public accounting firm whose clientele consist largely of real estate developers and other real estate–related businesses.

Ajax Furniture Rental, Cody, Wyo.
Vertically integrated, nationwide furniture leasing, retail and manufacturing company with forty-eight showrooms, sixteen warehouses, and two manufacturing plants. Company sustained over 18 percent annual growth from $1.9MM to $31MM between 1986 and 1995.

This feature is definitely optional, but it's always helped me as a recruiter to gain a frame of reference for a candidate's duties and achievements. Putting your functional experience into a particular business framework makes most sense if you work for a company whose line of business isn't evident from the name of the organization alone.

But what if you work for a bank? That's pretty clear to a prospective reader or employer, isn't it? Well, yes and no. If you're not continuing your career in the banking field, then some prospective employers might not know the difference between commercial, investment, and mortgage banking. A brief, one-line description may come in handy in that case. As a matter of fact, even if you're pursuing another position in the same industry, don't necessarily assume that other bankers will know your company. For example, you might want to qualify and quantify the companies where you've worked:

A leading Wall Street investment banking firm recognized by Forbes in 1994 as one of the fastest-growing companies in America; XYZ Bank serves the institutional banking community almost exclusively, with retail banking limited only to very high-net-worth individuals.

A ninety-employee, owner-operated mortgage brokerage firm that writes A–D paper for conventional, fully amortized fixed and adjustable rate mortgages as well as hard money loans.

Largest commercial banking firm in the Ohio Valley, which increased assets under management from $9B to $13B between 1992 and 1995.

A short description of company details also gives you a chance to sell your companies' achievements via dynamic growth patterns in staffing, increased revenues over a period of time, or media-recognized achievements. Try this—you might end up liking your resumé a whole lot more if you can prove that you've worked for winning companies!

Form: Stylistic Alternatives

Up to now, we've really focused on the content of the resumé: how to word your reporting relationships, achievements, and company descriptions. Now it's time to take a look at the other side of the aesthetics coin—namely, form. Everything from the weight of the bond paper to typing fonts and printer accuracy make your resumé stand out from the other 175 pieces of mail on the human resources practitioner's desk. How unique can you be without going overboard? When does the resumé pass beyond that fine line of being "too creative"? Will chronological or functional resumés suit you best as administrative support person?

Paper, Printing, and Margins

My first pieces of advice cover the most noticeable aspects of resumé preparation: the quality of the "ad copy." There are certain hard and fast rules about resumé writing that will never steer you wrong. First, use white or off-white (pearl or light gray), high-quality, acid-free, 100 percent cotton, 24 lb. **paper.** I know that seems like a mouthful, but any stationery store will be able to provide you with that premium paper because it's standard fare in the printing business.

Next, have the resumé **laser typeset.** (A Bubble Jet or DeskJet Printer will provide near-laser copy, and that's also good enough for the untrained eye.) Again, if you don't have a PC at home, then take advantage of the full-serve laser typesetting or self-serve desktop publishing services provided by a local copy center.

Finally, leave one-inch **margins** all around the page. There's got to be enough white space left on the page so that the resumé data don't overwhelm the reader. After all, no one wants to sit down and read wall-to-wall words. It's too hard on the eyes, and it will hurt your chances of getting the reader's full attention (even for only fifteen seconds!) away from the other 175 resumes on the desk.

Another reason why leaving white space on the outer corners of your resumé makes so much sense is that the document becomes more *scannable.* Employers are looking for specific answers to particular issues (like reporting relationships, softwares, educational histories, and the like), and the extra space within the margins is simply more inviting. That space, more than anything else, makes your resumé user-friendly.

Length

What about the **length** of a standard resumé? Well, ask three people and you'll get four opinions: "Long copy sells." "Keep it short." "No one reads the second page." There is no hard and fast rule. One page is the safest and most practical length, and two pages is maximum, no matter how many accomplishments, volunteer activities, or particular qualifications you have. Once you go past a second page, you put your candidacy in jeopardy: No matter how significant the information, you're lacking the ability to condense or crystallize it. That misuse of form could end up hurting you a lot more than any benefit statements in the content.

Verb Tenses

Next remember that the **verb tenses** that you use have to match the time frame in which you held those positions. In other words, describe your present position in the present tense:

> *Provide* departmental secretarial support to eight engineers. *Coordinate* travel arrangements and *schedule* hotel accommodations. *Generate* bids and proposals and *compose* correspondence using Microsoft Word for Windows.

Describe past positions in the past tense:

> Formally *documented* office policies and procedures in company handbook. *Updated* office automation systems and *was* instrumental in converting a manual accounts payable system to Lotus 1-2-3.

Remember that, all else being equal, your present position's description will usually be longer than your previous job descriptions since it is most relevant to your current capabilities.

And speaking of verb tenses, do you remember the term **parallelism** from your freshman English composition class? Parallelism means that the verbs in a given paragraph or story maintain the same tense endings. For example, job description paragraphs beginning with past tense verbs must continue to employ the past tense throughout:

> *Coordinated* all preparations for loan committee meetings, *prepared* minutes and *maintained* corporate records, and *assisted* in publication of company newsletter.

Similarly, if you begin your current job description in the present tense, be consistent in applying present tense verbs throughout:

> *Answer* a ten-line Merlin phone system with thirty-six extensions. *Greet* clients and vendors and *provide* direction to our various departments and delivery areas. *Sign* for employee deliveries and overnight Federal Express shipments. *Catalogue* new loan applications and *file* retrievals.

Of course, you might feel that this is bordering on being picayune. But believe me, mixing verb tenses is one of those things that could really throw an employer off, especially if she was an English major! It's frustrating to the reader because it lends an unnatural feeling to your prose:

> *Provided* word processing support for risk management and legal departments. *Plan* company activities for employee appreciation day. *Assisted* other secretaries with overflow work from engineering and MIS departments. *Process* staff security clearances.

See what I mean? The tense keeps shifting and throwing the reader off. Mixing and matching doesn't work when it comes to verb endings! Avoid this common pitfall, and you'll enhance the quality of your writing. Besides, since it is especially important that secretaries have impeccable writing skills, your resumé serves as your first work product. Give it the opportunity to shine!

Bullet vs. Paragraph Formats

Finally, a stylistic approach all your own: the bullet or paragraph form of job descriptions. **Bullet formats** use a visual advertising technique to capture the reader's attention. They permit concise, staccato-like statements of fact, which move the reader along and, most importantly, enhance your resumé's scannability. Anything that makes information on paper quicker and easier to decipher will be appreciated and win you points. The bullet format for job descriptions typically looks something like this:

Bullet Formats That Accent Specific Resumé Highlights

- Prepare and analyze statistical reports for clients, including:
  —Claims expense
  —Cost savings
  —Weekly sales activities
  —Utilization review
- Assist in the continual development and translation of brochures and educational materials for distribution to Spanish-speaking enrollees
- Identify trends to assist account managers and sales executives in selling expansion business

If there's a limitation to bullet formats, it's that they don't allow transition phrases to tie everything together. The **paragraph format,** in comparison, has a smoother flow and pace. Ideas lead into one another more gracefully and present a more complete picture of your responsibilities. For example:

> Provided administrative support to Academic Dean of the College of Letters and Sciences. Handled queries by phone and in person from students, faculty, staff, and the public. Typed accreditation reports and collected data from departmental chairs for annual faculty planning meeting. On occasion, assisted university ombudsman with faculty audits.

> Began as an entry-level receptionist and was promoted to secretary and quality control analyst within three years. Responsible for proofing all certifications done by outside processors. Assist customers and buyers with order tracking and tracing, shipment preparation, and rush order processing. Currently oversee two major clients that account for $800,000 in annual business revenues.

Chronological vs. Functional Formats

The choice of a chronological versus a functional resumé format is critical, and it plagues many administrative support candidates. That's because many human resources practitioners have been trained to regard functional resumés as devices to hide job-hopping and large gaps in employment. Understanding this presumption as a prejudice, you should realize that using the functional format puts two strikes against you right from the start. Still, there are times when the functional format is preferable to the chronological format, so let's discuss the two.

First of all, some definitions. A **chronological** resumé uses your dates of employment as the key structuring mechanism. Your employment history unfolds from job to job in a reverse chronological format, meaning that you start with your present position and work your way backward. How far back do you need to go? As a rule of thumb, ten years of your most recent work history will suffice. There's no need to go back to what you were doing in the 1970s. That experience is far too outdated to have a significant impact on your present abilities. Besides, going back too far can actually hurt your chances of surviving the cut because it could intimidate an employer who's significantly younger than you.

The actual dates of employment should include your months and years of attendance. It's not enough to simply list years. "1993–1995" could either mean three years of employment (January 1993 to December 1995) or two years of employment (December 1993 to January 1995). In addition, employers appreciate the months of your employment history because it more easily accounts for any gaps in your employment. Those gaps won't be held against you, but they should be fully explained. A typical chronological format looks something like Figure 3-2.

The vast majority of employers will agree that they prefer chronological resumés because they clearly and succinctly reveal what you've been doing at various companies. There's no place to hide when you're using a chronological format—everything is neat, clean, and readily available for the reader's scrutiny. It's a logical and practical format that, under most circumstances, is by far the more accepted and desired style of resumé construction.

When to Use a Chronological Resumé Format

- ☞ Each position you've held has led to greater responsibilities or job titles (for example, from receptionist to staff secretary to executive secretary)
- ☞ You are staying in the same field or industry and the next step in your career is apparent (in other words, if you've got four years of administrative support experience and you're applying for a similar type of position)

Of course **functional,** or **skills-based, resumés** have a place as well. However, they have much more limited application. Functional resumés structure informational data in functional clusters of experience, not in chronological blocks of time. If chronological resumés reveal longevity

Figure 3-2. Sample format of a chronological resumé.

Doris Ann Panico
123 Main Street
Jamestown, NY 11012

EXPERIENCE

4/92–present   ABC Company, Jamestown, NY

Administrative Assistant

Assist regional vice-president of acquisitions by establishing and maintaining logging systems for construction projects and capital expenditure requests. Coordinate travel arrangements, hotel reservations, and boardroom meetings. Supervise annual sales incentive award presentations. Manage accounts payable and receivable.

2/87–4/92   XYZ Company, New York, NY

Tax Secretary

Reporting to two principals of this CPA business management firm, coordinated audit engagements and organized records, summaries, and findings. Assisted in preparing monthly financial reports and quarterly budget reports, including cash flow statements and balance sheets.

---

and promotability through the ranks, functional resumés show skills and abilities. However, functional resumés strip away the context of those skills and abilities from the time or place where they occurred, ultimately frustrating the reader. Such resumés usually look something like Figure 3-3.

As you can immediately see, the professional skills listed have no connection to either ABC Company or XYZ Company. Because those skills stand alone and in no relation to your work assignments, the resumé reader wonders whether your office management skills were part of both jobs or only one. And if they were part of XYZ, then it's been a fairly long time since you've been responsible for office management, which means your skills may be a little rusty. Again, this format is ambiguous, and as we've said before, in the interview game, ambiguity will typically be interpreted against you.

By emphasizing skills and abilities and de-emphasizing the time frames within which these accomplishments occurred, functional resumés, also known as skills-based resumes, best serve you if:

Figure 3-3. Sample format of a functional resumé.

Doris Ann Panico
123 Main Street
Jamestown, New York 11012

PROFESSIONAL SKILLS

Office Management

- Coordinate work schedules for clerical support staff
- Act as vendor liaison with suppliers of corporate services
- Evaluate subordinates' performance and assist in determining salary adjustments

Executive Assisting

- Arrange business travel and hotel reservations
- Manage executives' diaries and accurately screen incoming telephone calls
- Schedule executive committee meetings and ensure that senior management's reports are delivered on time

Document Preparation

- Type 60 WPM using word processor or electric typewriter
- Advanced software skills on well-known applications, including WordPerfect 6.0, Lotus 123, Microsoft Word for Windows, Excel, Aldus Pagemaker, and Harvard Graphics

Dictation/Transcription

- 80 WPM vocal dictation (Gregg shorthand)
- Dictaphone

EXPERIENCE

4/92–present ABC Company, Jamestown, N.Y.
              Administrative Assistant

2/87–4/92 XYZ Company, New York, N.Y.
           Tax Secretary

☛ You have frequent gaps in your employment and want to de-emphasize dates.

☛ You have a multi-industry or multifunctional career history (meaning you've moved from auto sales to telemarketing to bookkeeping to zoology).

☛ Most of your work has been temporary.

☛ You're planning a career change.

A multifunctional career path would probably look too jumpy in chronological form and lead the reader to believe that you're not sure what you want to do. So instead of listing your jobs chronologically, you cluster your skills and abilities into the body of your resumé and then add the company/date details almost as an afterthought.

Who else benefits by employing the functional format? Students and people returning to the work force. Here's how. Students whose only work experience includes two three-month internships at a public relations agency really can't employ a chronological resumé format because there's not enough critical mass to build the resumé. So instead of showing two jobs with three months of experience at each one, students typically can lump the skills and experience they've gathered from those internships into the body of the resumé, and then briefly list the companies at the bottom of the page.

Similarly, candidates who are rejoining the ranks of corporate America after a ten-year hiatus while raising the kids might logically employ a functional format to sell skills and experiences gained through community and school involvement, home businesses, and any leadership roles assumed.

Don't Let Promotions Confuse Your Reader!

One final issue of form worth mentioning before we move on. *When could promotions and the assumption of increased responsibilities critically wound your career?* When you account for those promotions improperly on your resumé! Many outstanding candidates have done themselves a terrible injustice because they documented their internal company movements as if they were jumping from company to company. Here's how it works: Remember that employers typically spend somewhere between twelve and thirty-two seconds reviewing a resumé. If the dates of your employment appear to be too jumpy, you might immediately get disqualified from consideration. But what if all those dates represent movement within the *same* company? Well, sorry, it's too late! The format you used looked as if you were jumping around too much from company to company, so the employer, in his haste, assumed you lacked stability.

What to do? The solution is simple: Put your big dates of employment

Figure 3-4. How to document the dates of your promotions.

7/89–present   ABACUS COMPENSATION CONSULTANTS
                New York, N.Y.

$22MM management consulting firm with fourteen offices nationwide, which specializes in designing benefits and compensation plans for small to medium-sized companies primarily in the financial services arena

Junior Staff Accountant   (3/94–present)

Reporting directly to the assistant controller, in charge of accounts payable, accounts receivable, job costing, and client billing. Tally cash receipts and bank reconciliations. Assist controller with journal entries, financial statement analysis, and general ledger posting.

Accounting Clerk (7/89–3/94)

Responsibilities included batching and coding invoices. Circulated invoices for payment and entered invoices by batch. Prepared cash requirements and trial balances for approval by vice-president of finance. Delivered checks to controller for signature. Assisted customers and vendors with invoice inquiries. Promoted to junior staff accountant position upon controller's recommendation.

---

in the left-hand margin next to the company name; put your small dates of internal company progression in the right-hand margin next to your job titles. That way, the resumé reader will easily and quickly recognize your promotions within your companies. (See Figure 3-4.)

Sample Resumés

Remember to review Chapter 10 before finalizing your resumé. There are some important commonly asked resumé questions and tips in that section. For now, we'll close this chapter by reviewing a few different styles of resumés. (See Figures 3-5 through 3-9.) After that, we'll move on to another tool of the trade that will allow you to stand out on paper and build a unique case for your candidacy: the cover letter.

Figure 3-5. The "got it all" resumé.

Nina Sam
261 Dorset Street
Brooklyn, New York 11236
(718) 555-4321

EMPLOYMENT HISTORY

2/91–present   Johnson Industries, Brooklyn, N.Y.
$31MM national manufacturer of alarm systems and security hardware components with 330 employees

Senior Executive Secretary

As senior executive secretary to the CEO, chief operating officer, and president, coordinated and directed corporate events and was responsible for authorizing and arranging all company travel and supplier visits to corporate headquarters. Set up board of trustees meetings along with monthly high-level management meetings. Supervised reception desk and secretarial services. Served as administrator of in-house voicemail service for approximately 90 employees. Oversaw installation of company-subsidized cafeteria. Approved all billing and invoices for forty locations nationwide.

3/87–2/91   Lake Placid Drinking Water Corporation, Lake Placid, N.Y.

Fortune 1,000 international bottler of carbonated water beverages recognized as one of the leading companies to work for in America

Administrative Assistant

Reporting directly to the vice-president/general manager of an organization of 1,200 employees, coordinated special events planning and assisted with annual budget preparation. Created new business materials such as brochures, newsletters, graphics, invitations, slides, and overheads.

11/85–3/87   U.S. Army, Heidelberg, West Germany

Traffic Accident Investigator/Military Police Investigator for on- and off-base military personnel and dependents. Processed traffic citations, responded to accidents, and conducted witness interviews.

Figure 3-5. (*continued*)

TECHNICAL SKILLS

WordPerfect 6.0	Type 65 WPM
Lotus 1-2-3	Gregg shorthand 80 WPM
Microsoft Word for Windows	Dictaphone
Microsoft Excel for Windows	Harvard Graphics

LANGUAGES   German (working knowledge)

EDUCATION   B.A. in English, Brooklyn College, Brooklyn, N.Y.

PROFESSIONAL AFFILIATIONS AND CERTIFICATIONS

Certified Professional Secretary,
Professional Secretaries International

Figure 3-6. The "progression through the ranks" resumé.

Pam Shelby
123 South Ardmore Street
Fort Smith, AR 75601
(501) 555-0000 (H)

EMPLOYMENT HISTORY

9/91–present   Adams County Federal Bank, Fort Smith, AR
   Commercial banking firm with $2.5 billion in assets

   Legal Secretary, Legal Department (4/94–present)
Provide administrative and secretarial support to assistant general counsel
with preparation and follow-up of files, pleadings, and branch trade
agreements. Prepare Securities Exchange Commission reports regarding stock
ownership by directors and officers. Generate ongoing reports of pending
cases with FSLIC/FDIC relating to insurance claim matters and litigation. Provide research support to general counsel as needed.

   Executive Secretary, Investor Relations Department (9/91–4/94)
Reporting to senior vice-president of investor relations and strategic planning,
coordinated road trips for speaking engagements as well as retreats for chairman and senior management. Maintained department operating expenses
and reported and reconciled variances. Promoted to legal department upon
legal department supervisor's recommendation.

4/89–9/91   Bank of Oklahoma City, Oklahoma City, Oklahoma

   Commercial banking firm with $750MM in assets

   Secretary
Supported vice-president/district manager of asset-based lending department. Typed correspondence, reports, proposal letters, and security agreements. Assembled expense reports and budget proposals using Lotus 1-2-3.
Ran daily computer back-ups.

11/87–4/89   Lumber Emporium, Springdale, Arkansas

   Salesperson
First full-time position out of school. Hired as inventory analyst and promoted
to salesperson.

ACHIEVEMENTS   • Received Employee of the Month Award in January 1994

• Customized a database retrieval system at Adams County Federal Bank to
streamline internal reporting requirements for FDIC/FSLIC that saved the bank
approximately $3000/year

Figure 3-6. (*continued*)

SKILLS   Type 70 WPM, Fastnotes 60 WPM, Macintosh Microsoft Word for Windows and Excel, Claris Works

LANGUAGES   Spanish (fluent), French (working knowledge)

PROFESSIONAL MEMBERSHIP   National Association of Legal Secretaries

Figure 3-7. The "I worked my way through college" resumé.

Marlene Velasquez
13579 Windsor Court
Nashua, New Hampshire 19843
(603) 555-4141 Home
(603) 555-2628 Work

EDUCATION

> Boston College, Boston, MA
> Bachelor of science, business administration
> Major: Accounting
> Degree expected: June 1996

EMPLOYMENT HISTORY

1/94–present BANK OF NEW HAMPSHIRE, Nashua, New Hampshire

New Accounts Representative
Part-time position to help finance my college education. Catered to customers' individual financial needs. Accurately recorded customers' personal information in order to set up their checking or savings accounts. Applied cross-selling techniques to inform clients of the many financial products and benefits that the bank offered.

6/92–9/92   Easterner's Bank, Nashua, New Hampshire

Teller
Full-time summer position to finance education. In a high-activity environment, worked effectively with a staff of 15 co-workers. Handled high volumes of customer transactions with speed and accuracy. Issued money orders, travelers' checks, new account applications, and withdrawals. Verified customer signatures, closed accounts, and coordinated incoming and outgoing wire transfers of international funds. Reconciled large sums of cash, checks, and transaction totals on a daily basis.

6/90–9/90   ABC Electronics, Nashua, New Hampshire

Manufacturer of electronic components used in aerospace and airline industries.

Systems Support Clerk
Full-time summer position while in high school. Responsible for computer reports and microfiche retrieval. Maintained log of inventory parts. Ordered missing items from on-line catalogs.

Figure 3-7. (*continued*)

COMPUTER PROFICIENCY

        Basic and C++ computer languages.
        Software: MS Word for Windows, WordPerfect 6.0, Quattro
            Pro, FoxPro
        Hardware: IBM PC clones, Macintosh
        Operating Systems: DOS, Windows

ORGANIZATIONAL MEMBERSHIPS
        Alpha Beta Gamma sorority
        University Accounting Society

Figure 3-8. The job-hopper's resumé, which needs a strong cover letter to explain reasons for leaving.

Dave Tolle
666 Calle Arbor Road
Phoenix, Arizona 85250
(602) 555-3165

EMPLOYMENT HISTORY

8/94–present MERRILL LYNCH PIERCE FENNER AND SMITH
          Phoenix, AZ

    Sales Assistant/Registered Representative
Reporting to two top-producing stockbrokers, responsible for generating income on dormant accounts, placing cold calls, and posting trades. Coordinate account deposits and withdrawals and new account transfers for equity, government, and corporate bond trades. Calculate realized/unrealized gains and losses and account balances. Scored third highest on Series 7 exam in company history.

7/93–8/94   BEAR, STEARNS & CO., INC.
          Mesa, AZ

    Investment Research Coordinator
Organized and presided over weekly investment committee meetings that entailed setting agenda, analyzing offering materials, and recording minutes. Prepared marketing material on proprietary products as well as products from outside syndicators. Presented due diligence orientation material to newly registered representatives during quarterly administrative training seminars.

2/93–6/93   SMITH BARNEY SHEARSON
          Sun City, AZ

    Office Assistant/Student
Reporting to branch sales manager, reorganized complete filing system, ordered office supplies, maintained inventories, and coordinated new account deposits. Handled billing, bookkeeping, and telephone screening. Maintained extensive files for 12 brokers to meet auditor requirements.

EDUCATION

Arizona State University, bachelor of arts degree in political science
    Cum Laude, Dean's List, Honor Status

Figure 3-8. (*continued*)

PROFESSIONAL CERTIFICATIONS

National Association of Securities Dealers: Series 7 and Series 63 Registered Representative

COMPUTER SKILLS

Proficiency in Quotron, ADP, Microsoft Excel, Quattro Pro, Monroe Bond Calculator, Shaw Data, Keeptrax, Brokers Ally

Figure 3-9. The "I've had only one job" resumé.

Tony Epifanio
777 South Ardmore Avenue
San Francisco, CA 94109
(415) 555-1346 (H)
(415) 555-9731 (B)

EDUCATION

    Gonzaga University, Santa Clara, CA
    1994 Two years completed toward bachelor of arts in economics
    3.3 GPA

EMPLOYMENT

6/94–present NATIONWIDE MUTUAL INSURANCE COMPANY
San Francisco, CA

    Claims Adjustor
Reporting to regional claims manager, investigate, evaluate, and negotiate property and liability claims in order to arrive at equitable settlements with attorneys, claimants, and other insurance carriers. Record witness statements over the phone, trace automobile license identifications, and order Department of Motor Vehicle SR-1 reports. Maintain $5,000 claims settlement authorization and coordinate a monthly open-case volume of roughly 120 files. Received Top File Closer recognition six times in a department of 20 adjustors.

ACADEMIC ACHIEVEMENTS AND ACTIVITIES

    Recipient of Economics Department book award in 1994 for academic excellence

    Gonzaga University Wind Ensemble and Concert Band

    Currently enrolled in the University of San Francisco's insurance certification program

TECHNICAL SKILLS

    CRT data entry experience, 10 key by touch, type 35 WPM

Chapter 4

Classified Ad Response Strategies and Winning Cover Letters

Your resumé is your most compelling credential. Still, there is an inherent limitation with resumés in that they don't quickly and neatly match your qualifications to the employer's immediate requirements. Cover letters to the rescue! These tools in your employment arsenal allow you to dovetail your resumé to the company's particular needs. Consequently, they function as calling cards introducing you and bringing particularly relevant areas on your resumé to the reader's attention.

Reasons for leaving and salary data don't belong on a resumé. However, they need to go somewhere, and the cover letter's the place. I'm not implying that every cover letter you compose needs to include these details if they're not specifically requested in an employment ad. There are even circumstances where no cover letter is perfectly acceptable. However, if you've been caught up in a wave of layoffs that make you appear to have spotty longevity, or if you're changing career paths (say, from accounting to secretarial support or from customer service to commission sales), then you'll probably do well to make a case for yourself in the cover letter.

Also, I personally believe that all cover letters should include your most recent salary. As we'll see in Chapter 5, your current salary represents your market worth to a prospective buyer. Salary is, after all, a function of supply and demand, just like everything else. In providing pay information up front, you do run the risk of getting screened out faster. On the other hand, if you're "at market" in terms of balancing your years of experience with your current pay (in other words, you're not grossly under- or overpaid) and you're right in the middle of the employer's salary range, which could be very wide open, you'll probably be screened in a lot faster. Besides, if you're not at the right dollar level, you're only delaying the inevitable. You'll most likely be screened out later on down the line, after you've invested more time and hope and energy, for something that's really out of your control.

Let's first take a look at the anatomy of a job ad, and then I'll show you how to tailor your cover letters to sell your strengths to match the company's needs.

An Introduction to Classified Ads

Published classified ads represent the largest major source of concentrated information about available jobs in your local marketplace. They are a cost-effective source for companies seeking to identify high volumes of qualified applicants for specific openings. Furthermore, human resources people can tailor these public bulletins to reveal as much or as little detail about their companies as they like in order to protect corporate identity (**blind ads**). Similarly, ad writers might opt to provide next to no details about the particular position's requirements (**sparse ads**) so that they could choose the most befitting resumés without allowing candidates to doctor up their resumés or customize their cover letters.

Relying exclusively on ads represents a very passive approach to staffing and development because the classifieds won't always produce the exact product that the company needs at that given moment. Ads are a "buckshot" mechanism for attracting a large volume of related applicants, not a "rifleshot" approach to quickly locating individuals with the proper industry, functional, and educational pedigrees. You can almost picture the employer who has placed an ad sitting at his desk waiting for the mail to arrive, hoping to find that one resumé that meets his needs. If that resumé isn't in the employer's mail basket, then he's got to wait until the next mail delivery to sort through that new batch of resumé applications.

Why Do Some People Do Better With Ads Than Others?

Let's get right to the heart of the matter. Why is it that some people find all their jobs through the classifieds, while others never seem to have any luck with them? What's the key to success in exploiting this job search medium? The answer can be found in two words: hard qualifications. Ads are written in black and white, and that's pretty much how you have to respond to them. If you've been a secretary to a purchasing manager at the Plaza Hotel in Manhattan, and you happen to be responding to an ad from the Waldorf-Astoria for a secretary to its purchasing manager, you can bet that you'll make it right to the top of the pile.

Similarly, if a company has a desperate need for a Macwrite and Macpaint graphics expert, and your word processing experience speaks for your advanced Mac abilities, you're a finalist. And of course, you need to combine these hard skills with the softer qualifications of longevity, education, career progression, and the quality of the resumé itself.

So what will lessen your chances of benefiting from classified ads as an employment tool? Well, if you jump a lot from company to company, show negative progression in your functional responsibilities (meaning that four years ago you were an office manager, most recently a secretary, and currently you're applying for a receptionist job), or have a low-quality resumé with typos and coffee stains, then you'll most likely not excel in this arena of job search. In other words, networking and recruitment firms may be stronger options for you because your resumé alone, without you personally available to help sell the product, fails to generate a buy signal in the prospective employer. Cover letters can also help you enormously under such circumstances, but we'll get to that topic shortly.

Why Do Ads Provide Such Limited, Sketchy Details?

Have you ever wondered why ads have such sketchy and incomplete details? The most practical reason is that those details cost companies lots of money. A major metropolitan paper charges about $300 to $500 an inch for classified ad space, so any space saved is money in the bank. Also, many employers believe that they'll maintain an edge if they keep the information short and neutral so that candidates will have no way to bias or influence the reader beyond what's written on the resumé. This way, the employers can more easily choose the most qualified resumé that has the strongest potential fit for their immediate needs. Either the experience, skills, longevity, education, and appropriate reporting relationship are already there or they're not. ("I've always wanted to work in the hotel industry" or "I'm more than willing to take courses at night to learn Macintosh" distract from the employer's task of locating people who already have those skills or industry background.)

Why Don't All Employers List Their Salary Ranges in Their Ads?

You might think it would make sense to weed out those candidates who wouldn't end up accepting the job even if it were offered them because the salary was too low. Well, it's not so much that companies don't want you to know what they're paying. Most quality employers aren't going to lowball you, after all, by making you an offer 25 percent below your last position's salary, so there's no need for secrecy from that standpoint. Instead, companies don't want their competitors to know what their going salary ranges are. Companies guard their pay data pretty tightly in corporate America, and plastering salary ranges all over the newspaper for your various openings isn't a good move from a human resources standpoint.

It's also possible that some current employees are actually making less than the salary being offered for the new job. Not that the company wouldn't plan on remedying that kind of situation immediately. It's just that something could have slipped through the cracks, and then the HR department could have a calamity on its hands. Furthermore, if XYZ Corporation advertises its pay rates all over the news, search firms could use that information to recruit its people away. If XYZ pays below market or if the agency is conducting a search for a competitor company that pays higher starting salaries, then that pay information XYZ provided in good faith in the newspaper could be used against it as a leverage point to entice people out of its organization and into the arms of its corporate rival across town. Ah, the world of employment! It is complex, isn't it?

The Anatomy of a Job Ad

Let's spend a moment looking at the structure of a job ad to understand its purpose. Ads obviously come in all shapes and sizes depending on the amount of information the employer wants to provide along with the cost of the ad. There is a definite relationship between the quality of the ad and the quality and quantity of the response an employer generates. Large layouts that provide critical detail into the nature of the position and the company attract the largest volumes of qualified candidates. That's because (a) people feel more comfortable responding to qualified openings with verifiable organizations, and because (b) they will spend extra time pursuing leads that provide more detailed information against which they can match their own personal qualifications. All else being equal, the more information available, the larger the target candidates have to shoot at in order to build a case for themselves. It follows that, statistically, the weakest responses come from blind ads that don't reveal a company's identity or the nature of the job.

Here are some samples of ads listed in the *Los Angeles Times* on a warm summer Sunday in Southern California. Which ones would you be most inclined to respond to?

> ☐ **Sample Ad 1:**
>
> We Need a Secretary We Can Count On!
>
> ABC Accounting Practice is seeking a secretary who enjoys handling a variety of administrative responsibilities in a challenging, stimulating, team-oriented environment.

The essential skills include good organization and detail orientation, effective communication skills, professional attitude along with strong typing and proofreading capabilities. Solid word processing experience is necessary.

Forward your resumé along with salary history to: ABC Accounting, 342 South Main St., Los Angeles, CA 90071

☐ **Sample Ad 2:**

Use Your Creativity and Talent in Newly Created Position

We're eight years old and never had a layoff! Prestigious high-tech leader in the South Bay seeks talented individual for sales administration and support. Prepare proposals, presentations, correspondence, and plan meetings and travel. Outstanding compensation, benefits, and continuing education await the right candidate with Word for Windows, Excel, and a strong desire to grow. Fax or mail your resumé to: High Flyers, Inc., 721 Pacific Coast Highway, Manhattan Beach, CA 91731

☐ **Sample Ad 3:**

Junior Secretary

Reports to admin asst who in turn reports to Exec. VP of Marketing. Proposal typing (min 50 WPM), sched. mtngs, gen. clerical, WP 5.1, Excel. Multi-task oriented, fast-paced, flex w/ teamwork attitude. Health benes. Mail resumé & sal to P.O. Box 80041, Los Angeles 90076

☐ **Sample Ad 4:**

Secretary-Executive 65 WPM/shrthand pref. WordPerfect 6.0, Excel & database literate. Salary commensurate with exp. John (213) 555–7901

☐ **Sample Ad 5:**

Secretary needed immed. Xlnt pay; No exp. (310) 555–0975

Your gut reaction to the question I posed above is fairly predictable: You'd most likely first pursue the companies that offered more creative environments, tuition reimbursement, and a team-oriented environment. Once you made your way through those first choices, and only if time allowed, you would pursue the blind ads that provide no company or position information. And by all means, watch out for any ads that say things like "excellent pay—no experience." The two are mutually exclusive!

What characteristics do these ads share? Most classified ads have four distinct sections. The first three are all optional; the fourth section with response instructions is common to all (even though that may be all that you get with certain sparse, blind ads):

- The *enticement* lead-in (the "draw" or "attractor," so to speak)
- The *requirements* section
- The *responsibilities* portion
- The *administrative* follow-up instructions

The *enticement* portion of the ad functions as the appeal or draw mechanism that is meant to elicit your immediate attention and entice you to respond to it above the other hundred-some-odd ads on the page. Lead-ins look like this:

HIGH FASHION RETAIL ENVIRONMENT!

NEWLY CREATED POSITION!

WE NEED AN ADMIN ASST WE CAN COUNT ON

FORTUNE 100 SERVICE CO AND WORLDWIDE LEADER IN ELECTRONIC COMPONENT PRODUCT DISTRIBUTION

LET YOUR CREATIVITY AND TALENT COME ALIVE!

Fine. If the company is willing to spend some extra money to showcase its pride and uniqueness, that's great for it and great for you.

The *requirements* section typically focuses on the hard skills necessary to qualify for the position. However, the requirements section often provides lists of fluffy adjectives as well to describe the ideal personality of the prospective new hire. So you can expect to find these components in a typical requirements section:

- Technical skills (Word for Windows and Excel, WordPerfect and Lotus)
- Functional or departmental orientation (management information systems, sales, accounting, human resources departments)
- Reporting relationships (to vice-president of finance, sales manager, acquisitions editor)
- Fluff claims

Remember that hard skills are the key to classified ad response. This is where you'll spend most of your time in preparing your cover letters. One note of special interest: Do you remember how I said that filling your resumé with subjective, personal evaluation adjectives like "hard-working, creative, multi-task oriented, willing to work with the team to accomplish the task at hand, and a 'can-do' attitude" were a waste of time? They say and do nothing to further your uniqueness because they are unqualified, superfluous claims. Well, guess what: you'll (unfortunately) see a lot of these very same fluff claims in classified ads. So we'll discuss how to incorporate them into your cover letters by removing the fluff factor yourself and redefining the organization's real needs.

The *responsibilities* portion of the ad can also be important in determining the hard factors that will be considered in the selection process, although they're usually not as critical as the requirements listed. Responsibilities listed often include:

- Word processing and spreadsheet composition and creation
- Travel arrangements
- Telephone screening
- Filing and general office duties

As you can see, however, these topics are usually very broad. Their usefulness to you as a focusing tool in writing cover letters remains, consequently, somewhat limited.

Finally, the *follow-up instruction* section provides specifics regarding the timing and method of your response: mail, call, or fax. At face value, this seems simple enough, but allow me to share with you some of the more common mistakes that candidates make at this stage. First, I have seen job strategy books advise that "if it says to call Monday between 10 A.M. and 12 noon, call at 9:45 to get a headstart on the competition." I've also seen recommendations from authors that "even if it says 'no phone calls,' you should still call before 8:00 or after 5:00 (when the hiring official will more likely answer her own phone) to introduce yourself personally." I strongly disagree! Now remember that this is one human resources manager's perspective only. Still, I believe that following instructions is critical when initially presenting yourself to a company. Taking a shortcut right off the bat is a telltale sign that you're a compromiser when it comes to getting the job done, and that strategy could hurt your candidacy a lot more than help it.

Tracking and Evaluating Classified Ads

Now that you know how the ads are constructed, you need to formalize your response mechanism. Sometimes drawing information out of an ad is difficult because the copy is so condensed and cramped on the page that all the ads start to look and sound alike after a while. So why don't we delve into your job search tool box to build a device that will help crystallize the information you'll need to respond properly to that ad? The worksheet shown in Figure 4-1 will take you through a quick exercise that will force you to separate the company's "keys to hire" from the fluff. It will also help you make inferences about a particular job when little or no information is given. Furthermore, it will serve as a follow-up tool later on for tracking your results.

You know from reading Chapter 3 on resumé writing exactly what companies want to know about you: exact titles and reporting relationships, technical skills, scope of responsibility, and patterns of achievement. You've now got to extrapolate that knowledge into the active job-finding process. So let's briefly apply sample ads 1 through 3 earlier in this chapter to your evaluation worksheet to help you ferret out the true keys to hire. (See Figures 4-2 through 4-4, which utilize condensed versions of the evaluation worksheet to track applicable information.) Again, after going through these exercises a number of times, you'll figure out how best to present yourself to each organization on a problem-to-solution level.

As you can see, there isn't much to go on directly from the ad, so your extrapolations have to guide your response. There is a chance that your second-guessing the employer might be somewhat off the mark, but it's a calculated risk you've got to take to construct the most effective cover letter response. Besides, you're always much better off providing concrete examples of your work experience than simply parroting back empty con-

Figure 4-1. The classified ad evaluation and tracking worksheet.

Company Name: _____

Address: _____

Title of Position:

_____

Reporting Relationship/Direct Supervisor:

_____

Department/Division:

_____

Qualifications (Keys to Hire):

• _____

• _____

• _____

• _____

Responsibilities:

• _____

• _____

• _____

• _____

Software Systems: _____

Salary Range:

_____

Date Resumé Sent:

_____

Date of Follow-Up Contact from Company:

_____

Corporate Officer Who Filed Response:

_____

Figure 4-1. (*continued*)

___

Date of Initial Company Interview:

___

Creative Follow-Up Agenda:

___
___
___

[Clip ad—or a copy of it—here]

___

Figure 4-2. Worksheet filled out for sample ad 1 (We Need a Secretary We Can Count On!)

___

Company Name: ABC Accounting Practice

Address: 342 South Main St., Los Angeles, CA 90071

Title of Position: Secretary

Reporting Relationship/Direct Supervisor: unknown (appears to be a multiple reporting relationship)

Qualifications (Keys to Hire):

   • variety = deadline pressure & juggling of multiple activities

   • challenging/stimulating CPA environment = well-educated, independent managers looking for staff assistants who will need little structure and supervision

   • organization and detail orientation = complex spreadsheets to track data like royalties, earnings, and financial ratios

   • word processing & proofreading capabilities = solid language skills

Date Resumé Sent: 7/23/95

___

firmations about how "I am a very task-oriented individual and have excellent communication skills and excel in an environment that thrives on teamwork and shared responsibility."

Your challenge, consequently, will be to develop concrete examples of how you've dealt with deadline pressure, complex spreadsheets, multiple bosses, and light supervision with little structure or feedback. Your cover letter might therefore state:

Figure 4-3. Worksheet filled out for sample ad 2 (Use Your Creativity and Talent in Newly Created Position).

Company Name:	High Flyers, Inc.
Address:	721 Pacific Coast Highway, Manhattan Beach, CA 91731
Title of Position:	[Secretary] or [Administrative assistant]

Qualifications (Keys to Hire):

   • High-tech company = complex and detailed product line, technical orientation of employees, emphasis on research and development, competitive pressures to rival global competitors, innovative solutions to customer needs

   • Sales administration = working with sales engineers who are talented not only in a technical discipline but who also excel in a sales and marketing environment; heavy proposals in a deadline environment; ultimate customer service to respond to customer inquiries; profit and loss responsibility to generate revenue to make the company profitable

Responsibilities:

   • Prepare proposals, presentations, and correspondence = generating high volume of quality graphics in the bidding process to win contracts, preparing slides and overheads for sales presentations, and creating macros and templates that can be easily customized for rapid turnaround times while still lending correspondence a personalized and customized feel

   • Meeting and travel planning = regional sales force that covers large territories and most likely needs to book reservations quickly and with last-minute notice; also, sales travel plans are likely to change or even be cancelled at the last minute

Software Systems: Word for Windows and Excel

Date Resumé Sent: 7/23/95

Date of Follow-Up Contact from Company:

Creative Follow-Up Agenda:
Ad mentions "strong desire to grow" (but leave this out at this point since it would be premature to talk about growth!)

Figure 4-4. Worksheet filled out for sample ad 3 (Junior Secretary).

Company Name: None given
Address: P.O. Box 80041, Los Angeles, CA 90076
Title of Position: Junior Secretary

Reporting Relationship/ Direct Supervisor: Report to the administrative assistant who in turn reports to executive vice-president of marketing

Qualifications (Keys to Hire):

• Reporting to an executive secretary = not having an ego problem supporting another member of the administrative support staff, taking direction from a peer, filling in as the assistant to the executive vice-president in the administrative assistant's absence, and handling all the clerical busywork that the administrative assistant doesn't want to do; balancing priorities between the executive vice-president's needs and the administrative assistant's direction

• Type 50 words per minute

• Multi-task oriented, flexible with a teamwork attitude = realizing that changing priorities will be the norm; company is probably looking for someone who gives service with a smile, never says no to even the most menial of chores, and who finds work to keep busy when things are slow; no "I don't do windows" attitude!

Responsibilities:
• Proposal typing
• Schedule meetings
• General clerical

Software Systems: WordPerfect 5.1, Excel

Date Resumé Sent: 7/23/95

Working for the past four years for three top-producing account executives in a stockbrokerage made it necessary for me to prioritize the workloads of multiple supervisors, adapt to constant deadline pressures, and compose complex spreadsheets for investment performance tracking. Furthermore, the pace of the office dictated that I work very independently with little structure and formal feedback from my direct supervisors.

Nice work! Your cover letter addresses the concrete and emotional aspects of your work experience and thereby complements your technical resumé presentation. That's just the balance you need to strike between the cover letter and the resumé to customize your response to this employer's individual needs.

Notice how you've extrapolated or developed your impressions of the employer's qualifications and responsibilities in a stream-of-consciousness fashion. There are no right or wrong answers in these exercises. The key lies in putting the listed requirements into some kind of real-world scenario based on your understanding of the industry (high-tech manufacturing), function (sales and sales engineering), and probable corporate culture (well-educated, technically oriented workers) of this particular company. Once you've given some thought to what those real needs could be, you then have something concrete to present back to this company. And voilà—you end up selling real solutions to real problems despite the employer's lack of concrete detail!

Another challenge in this instance (using the same candidate from the stock brokerage as an example) will be to segue from a financial services orientation to a manufacturing/high-tech line of business. I don't recommend starting your cover letter with "Although I've never worked in the manufacturing/high-tech industry," because that will only give the employer an immediate reason to reject your resumé. Instead, match strength to strength by pointing out the similarities of your businesses. For example,

> Assisting three top-producing stockbrokers in my last job required a thorough understanding of complex and changing product lines. The competitive pressures of our industry forced us to develop innovative solutions to our customers' needs. I also believe that I am particularly well suited for this position because I understand the pressures associated with working in a revenue-generating unit with full profit and loss responsibility. Sales brochures and slide presentations needed to be produced with very little advance notice, and the travel plans I made could be changed or cancelled at the last moment.

Do you see how you can build a case for yourself based on the functional similarities of sales even if you come from a totally different industry? Well, it's likewise the case that even if you've never worked in sales but come out of another discipline or department within the high-tech manufacturing arena, you could sell your understanding of the corporate culture, the key players in the business, and the pressures common to your industry to target your qualifications to the organization's needs. Remember, all employers buy solutions to their problems, and even though you'll rarely fit a job head-on, your ability to recognize that company's needs and speak to your role as part of the solution will allow you to stand out from your competition.

Now, how might you respond to sample ad 3 in your cover letter?

> Technically, I believe that I am thoroughly qualified for this position because I have over three years of advanced WordPerfect 5.1 and Excel experience, and I type 60 words per minute. More importantly, I understand the pressures and the protocol of reporting to a senior administrative support professional. I am more than willing to accept direction from the administrative assistant to the executive vice-president of marketing, and I would view that situation as an opportunity for excellent administrative training. I enjoy handling the clerical busywork that keeps an office running smoothly, and I believe my references will vouch for my attitude of never saying no.

Again, although your resumé may indeed show that you have previous experience reporting to another secretary, reemphasizing your willingness to handle the clerical busywork, take direction from a peer (albeit senior peer), and look at that situation not as a necessary evil but as an opportunity for growth and learning will overcome any doubts the employer might have about your willingness to function as "another secretary's secretary."

When Is It Appropriate to Leave Out a Cover Letter Altogether?

There are three situations in which it's perfectly acceptable to pass on including a cover letter. The first situation occurs when there's so little information in the ad that attempting to customize a response would be a futile exercise. Either your resumé has what they're looking for or it doesn't. Your cover letter in that case would add very little pertinent information that could help sway an employer in your favor. As a rule of thumb, if you believe that very little effort was invested on behalf of the employer who listed the ad (as is the case in sample ads 4 and 5), then you, as the respondent, should match that effort (or lack of effort, I should say). Let the resumé fly on its own. This is a hit-or-miss exercise, so don't expend effort trying to persuade or convince an invisible audience.

The second situation (and the most common) occurs when the cover letter is used to provide fluff about yourself. Unfortunately, this scenario is all too common. The majority of cover letters I've seen go on and on about the individual's work ethic ("I am a very hard worker and would like the opportunity to prove my skills to you"), attitude ("I take pride in my work and in learning new fields of interest"), or personal desires ("I very much want to join the ranks of a stable company where hard work, initiative, and achievements are recognized"). I've seen many two-page cover letters say absolutely nothing about what I'm looking for in my search as the manager of human resources. The hard facts are simply nowhere to be found; the opinions run rampant.

My advice in this instance is simply to skip the cover letter. Because it does nothing to further your candidacy, it wastes time. And although these kinds of "fluff" letters are most likely not going to knock you out of the running, they take time to put together. If you don't have enough information to address the company's needs, save yourself the inconvenience of writing any letter at all.

The third instance in which no cover letter is perfectly acceptable is when prewritten, generic cover letters get routinely attached to the resumé. That's a big time waster. Many candidates use boilerplate typewritten cover letters to introduce themselves where everything is filled out except the line "Dear _____." Then on that line they write in the employer's name in blue ink. I hate those letters! I guess that's because I see so many of them that I can't help but think that people who use them should have realized that those extra pieces of paper take up space and waste my time.

Instead of filling in a prewritten form letter, simply clip the article you're responding to and attach it to your resumé so that the employer can immediately reference the job you're applying for. Another alternative would be to write in the title of the position you're applying for at the top of the resumé's first page. Often a human resources manager has three or five openings simultaneously advertised in the same newspaper. So receiving a cover letter that simply says "This resumé is in response to your recent advertisement" adds no value whatsoever to your candidacy. Even when you're customizing a response letter to an employer's ad in the *Chicago Tribune,* you need to reference the particular job you're applying for. Again, don't assume that the one ad you're responding to is the only one that this company has listed in the *Tribune.* It's a minor point, I know, but it's appreciated by employers and recruiters alike.

Decoding an Ad's Post Office Box

Before we leave these job ad examples to explore writing successful cover letters, there's one more issue that has to be explored—one you've been itching to get to since you picked this book up off the shelf! Look back at sample ad 3 for a moment, and you'll see that a post office box and zip code were provided rather than a street address. Companies often use post office boxes to maintain their anonymity. That's obviously not always the case, since an organization can simply list its street address and leave out its name to get the same result. Or can it? By listing a street address, a company could actually be tracked down by a determined job seeker with the help of a local librarian.

Many libraries carry what are known as reverse directories. A reverse directory does exactly what its name implies: rather than listing the name of a company followed by its address (which is in normal directory fashion), reverse directories list the address first followed by the companies at that location. Here's how it works. Let's assume you see an ad that omits the company name, yet lists the address 3500 Wilshire Boulevard, Suite 1470. Well, here in Los Angeles, you'd probably grab a copy of the Haines Directory and locate "Wilshire Blvd." alphabetically. You'll then come across pages and pages of Wilshire Boulevard addresses beginning at 1 Wilshire in downtown Los Angeles and moving west across town toward the beach. When you land at "3500 Wilshire Blvd.," you'll see every suite in that building listed like this:

> 1449 DR. JOHN H. SHORT, DERMATOLOGY
> 1458 NEBRASKA MUTUAL LIFE INSURANCE COMPANY
> ☛ 1470 SMITH AND SMITH ADVERTISING

There it is! You've identified the company within ten minutes of stepping into the library. To make sure that the directory listing is up to date, you could simply call the company.

So, to avoid overly curious job candidates with a nose for library research, companies use their post office boxes so that reverse directories become a dead end. However, most people (employers and job candidates alike) don't realize that post office boxes can be decoded under certain circumstances. Here's how it works. Let's look again at our ad:

> P.O. Box 80041, Los Angeles, CA 90076

If this happens to be a public post office box, then the post office has to tell you whose it is when you call. The first step in deciphering the box is to locate the post office that handles that particular zip code. Simply call your local post office and ask which branch of the post office handles zip code 90076. Some post offices offer a local customer service phone number dedicated to matching zip codes to their corresponding post offices. That comes in handy when you've got a large number of blind ads that you want to decipher at the same time because you can identify all the post offices you need in one phone call.

Once you know which post office handles zip code 90076, call that office and ask to speak to a box clerk in the zip code information department. When that clerk picks up the line, all you have to say is, "Please let me know which company has P.O. Box 80041." You'll immediately be given that company's name and street address. It's that easy!

If you've seen multiple ads running using the same box, you might want to pursue that company a bit more aggressively and actively. Having the identity of the company might allow you to refocus your approach to that organization by researching the company in the library, contacting the employer over the phone to set up an exploratory meeting, and following up with the firm after your initial contact. We will cover all these areas thoroughly before you reach the final chapter of this book.

When is a post office box impossible to crack? When it's a private newspaper or trade journal box number. When employers run ads, they have the choice of using their own (public) boxes or paying a fee to use the newspaper's (private) box. Newspapers won't ever divulge a company's identity for fear of breaching client confidentiality. The way I see it, if the company was so intent upon not having its identity revealed that it purchased a post office box from the newspaper running its ad, then James Bond himself probably couldn't crack it. So respect the organization's need to keep its identity top secret at this point, and respond to the blind ad along with everyone else.

When and How to Answer an Ad

Before we move away from ad responses, let's cover two more issues: determining when is the best time to submit your resumé and cover letter, and responding to an ad by fax.

First, a quickie quiz: When should you respond to an ad, whether by mailing or faxing your resumé or by calling? Is it:

- ☛ Immediately after reading that new ad in the paper?
- ☛ One week after the ad came out?
- ☛ One month after the ad came out?

The answer: Yes to all of the above! How's that for a helpful and definitive response? The important thing to remember is that the bulk of the responses arrive on an employer's desk about three days after the ad is published. So the response time you choose is more of an issue of personal choice than anything else. If you feel comfortable being among the first considered, then mail your response immediately. If you'd like to avoid the three-day-after rush that clogs the employer's desk, then wait a week. And if you really want to allow your resumé to stand out from the masses of other responses, wait several weeks or a month. That way, your resumé will probably have very little competition for the position. However, it's obvious that the longer you wait to respond, the greater the chances that the position will have been filled by the time your resumé arrives. So again, let your intuition be your guide when it comes to sending that response off in the mail.

On the other hand, you bought this book for some timely and concrete advice, so I would recommend responding to an ad immediately after it was published. I believe that for administrative support positions (which fill a lot faster than senior management and technical jobs), timing is of the essence, and wasted time means lost opportunity. The only time I can see responding to an ad three weeks to a month after it was run is when you really want to join a particular company and you're willing to expend the extra effort to get noticed. After all, the position may have been put on hold a few weeks ago, and now there's a renewed sense of urgency to fill it. The human resources manager is about to run another ad in the paper when, out of the blue, your resumé—a very qualified resumé with a well-strategized cover letter—lands on his desk. In that case, it's probably worth an hour of the employer's time to bring you in for an interview before paying another six hundred dollars to run a new ad. It is a bit of a long shot, I admit, but I'm also aware of candidates who relied on this strategy very heavily in their job search campaigns and developed excellent job leads and offers because of it. Still, I wouldn't recommend making this your only classified ad response strategy. It's simply too limiting for my taste.

On to our next point: faxing resumés to employer's classified ads. Many companies request faxed responses because it saves two or three days in the selection process. The reason why, statistically, the bulk of classified ad responses arrive three days after the ad was published is because it takes the mail about that long to get your letter there. Looking at it backward for a moment, that means that the majority of ad responders mail out their letter the day the ad was written. Add two to three days of mail travel time, and Wednesday turns out to be the big day of the week when employers receive resumés for ads run the previous Sunday.

Not so when it comes to faxes. The majority of ad responses land on the employer's desk on Monday when faxing is the desired medium of transmission. So faxing saves an employer two to three days when trying to fill openings that are particularly immediate. I bring this up to remind you, then, that if you don't want your resumé arriving with the throngs of others that are being launched for that very same position, then wait till Wednesday or so before submitting your fax.

I also surface this issue for a more practical reason: Please put your name on all the pages of your fax transmission. Remember that faxes arrive backward—that is, they come across the employer's desk in reverse order. You put your fax cover sheet into the machine on your end first, followed by your cover letter (page 2) and resumé (page 3). That very same fax cover sheet indeed arrives first at the employer's office, only to have your cover letter and resumé land on top of it! So the employer ends up with a stack of backward documents. If names are missing on any of those pages, your transmission could very well become mixed in with other documents, and all your hard work will have been for naught.

Sample Cover Letter Responses

Now it's time to put it all together. Tailoring cover letters entails repeating the ad's requirements (either listed or implied) and showing how your experience and achievements match that company's needs. There is no particular prescribed length or order for cover letters. Just remember that if employers spend an average of twelve to thirty-two seconds reviewing resumés, they probably spend half that time scanning cover letters. So make your point quickly! Also, if you have a computer to aid you in writing your cover letters, use the bold, italic, and underline features to call attention to your main points of interest.

The salutation immediately sets the tone of your letter. "To Whom It May Concern" is trite, hackneyed, and impersonal. I would avoid it like the plague! What's even worse is "Dear Gentlemen" or "Dear Sirs." I would guess that at the administrative support recruitment level, both in contingency recruitment and human resources management, 80 percent of the people you'll be dealing with are women. Ergo, "Dear Sirs" won't ingratiate you or make you a favored candidate from the onset of your job search campaign.

Also, our working women give the United States an important source of well-developed brain power. Today more small businesses are founded by women than by men. And roughly 35 percent of today's medical, dental, law, and business school degrees will go to women, up from about 5 percent in the 1960s. With this encouraging trend in mind, don't you think that "Dear Gentlemen" is a bit of an anachronism? I'd replace it simply by "Dear Manager of Human Resources" or "Dear Staffing Manager." They'll know from that salutation that the reason you're submitting a resumé and cover letter is to be considered for a position.

Following are several cover letters that I feel incorporate the candidate's strengths with the company's needs and requirements. Notice how the job titles are all in boldface or italics to ease the employer's job matching process. Also notice how the respondents get to the heart of the matter immediately and emphasize their own achievement profiles, thereby pointing out areas on the resumé that deserve further attention.

Sample Cover Letter 1

Dear Human Resources Manager:

This letter is in response to the *Administrative Assistant to the President and CEO* classified advertisement in the *Arizona Republic* on Sunday, July 24, 1995. In that ad, you outlined your requirements that were very appealing to me since I have over ten years of experience reporting one-on-one to an executive vice-president of marketing. The individual I currently report to is the number two person in the corporate pyramid in terms of strategic decision making and planning. Since she is currently considering retirement, I feel it would be in my best career interests to consider new employment opportunities.

I currently earn $34,000 a year. My next logical career move would be to increase my reporting relationship to a president and CEO. Furthermore, I am thoroughly familiar with pressures and protocol involved in representing the office of an executive-level manager. My **responsibilities** include acting as a liaison between the executive office and the Phoenix business community, including newspaper reporters, university deans, the office of the mayor, and outside counsel.

As an executive/personal assistant to the executive vice-president at Williams Foods, I saved the company $5,000 in printing costs by developing a computer graphics procedure that created camera-ready artwork for recruitment advertising, company announcements, and invitations. For bringing in-house a procedure that formerly had to be farmed out to a printing company, I was rewarded with an **Employee of the Month** designation last October.

In closing, I would like to suggest that we meet soon to discuss your specific needs in greater detail. I can be reached from 8:00 A.M. to 6:00 P.M. Monday through Friday at (310) 555–7901. Thank you for your consideration.

Sincerely,

Sample Cover Letter 2

Dear Hiring Official:

Please accept my resumé for the **office manager** position listed in this Sunday's *Arkansas Gazette*. I have over eleven years of office administration, accounting, and supervisory experience, and I understand the processes and protocol that constitute the information flow in a busy office.

Sample Cover Letter 3

Dear Director of Human Resources:

Are you looking for a legal secretary who is:

- *Experienced with contracts?* Broker/dealer registrations, initial public offerings, powers of attorney, dealer and warranty agreements, clearing authorizations, SEC filing requirements
- *A technical expert?* WordPerfect 6.0, Lotus 1–2-3, Harvard Graphics, Microsoft Word for Windows and Excel, Paradox, dBase IV, Aldus Pagemaker
- *An experienced and certified legal assistant?* Five years of securities law with one of the nation's largest and most prestigious law firms, two years of in-house legal experience with an institutional investment banking firm, and the Accredited Legal Secretary designation from the National Association of Legal Secretaries

If so, then look no more! I am searching for a full-time position with Goldman, Susskauer and Rabinowitz because I am aware of your reputation in the field of securities law and feel that I could make an immediate contribution to your firm. My most recent salary is $38,000. Please contact me at (718) 555–2921 to schedule an interview if my skills and experience appear to complement your present staffing needs.

Sincerely,

Sample Cover Letter 4

Dear Mr. Witkin:

Please accept my resumé for the **customer service representative** position. I learned of the opening through Nanette Duff Sullivan in your marketing department. She recommended that I immediately send you my resumé.

Upon reviewing my resumé, you will notice that the majority of my work experience has been in the field of accounting and payroll. I strongly desire to make a transition out of the accounting field because I have come to realize that my greatest strengths lie in dealing with people. I am consequently seeking to enter the customer service area immediately.

As an accounting and payroll specialist, many of my daily duties revolved around the customer service function. I was responsible for reconciling and tracking employee time cards, aging accounts receivable, and coordinating collection calls for past due accounts. In each of these situations, I was often faced with challenges that required technical expertise and excellent communication skills to solve customer problems.

My greatest achievement, however, was in the field of collections, where I managed to increase my department's average collection percentage from 62 percent to 79 percent. I became the top collector in my area, and I believe that was because of the patience and trust I displayed toward our customers along with the willingness to help them help me resolve their outstanding balances.

I am currently earning $14 an hour. I believe that my work in the accounting area has a direct bearing on your customer service position. I look forward to hearing from you, and I thank you very much.

Sincerely,

Once again, you'll notice that these model letters can take very different (and creative!) forms depending on your personality and degree of self-expression. The key is to customize your approach to meet the company's present needs. *Form letters are out!* The job search process is too personal and intimate an experience to not involve yourself by investing your energies and enthusiasm into the details of the process.

Does every cover letter need an individualized response, though? What if you're mounting a massive ad campaign and don't have a computer to assist in the letter customization process? Here's what I would advise: If it's at all humanly possible, tailor your response to the company's particular needs. One of the main focuses in this chapter has been on identifying an organization's real needs by extrapolating ideas from the written ad. Selling yourself to a company on a problem-to-solution level will allow you to stand out as a refreshing rarity!

On the other hand, totally leave out a cover letter when you're dealing with sparse and/or blind ads where the company's given you nothing to aim for. Remember, a cover letter isn't a formality that you must include.

It's necessary only when it will strategically help you build a stronger case for yourself by adding an individualized, personal touch to your resumé.

Finally, if you don't have access to your own personal computer, it's probably worth it for you to invest some money at the local copy center that should provide you with a Mac or IBM computer for between five and ten dollars an hour. The cost to print one page begins at one dollar per page and then decreases depending on the number of copies you print. It may sound expensive, but there's a trade-off between volume and quality here: If the quality of your response is significantly enhanced, then the quantity of your responses will fall because you'll land your next job that much faster. In my opinion, that's an excellent trade-off! After all, anything that gets you to your next job faster will offset the extra initial investment involved.

They say that if the only tool you have is a hammer, then everything starts to look like a nail. If, on the other hand, your only tool in writing cover letters is a typewriter, then you still need to take the time to customize your responses as much as possible. You'll find, however, that after customizing two or three tailored broadcast letters, you'll actually be creating an adaptable template that will help you automate the writing process and adapt it to new situations. So typewriter or word processor, if you're going to take the time to write a cover letter, customize it as much as possible to that company's needs!

If you'd like more information about classified ad response strategies and creative cover letters, see Kenton W. Elderkin's book *How to Get Interviews from Job Ads* (Dedham, Mass.: Elderkin Associates Management Consultants, 1989).

✷ ✷ ✷

With your research, resumé, and cover letter tools in hand, you're ready to meet the employer face to face. Let's continue to Chapter 5 to meet both the human resources professional and the contingency recruiter (or "headhunter"), the human players in the job search process.

Chapter 5

Inside the Heads of Contingency Recruiters and Human Resources People: One-Upmanship for the Executive Administrative Assistant

Now we have the opportunity to read the other guys' handbooks. Employment agency recruiters and human resource interviewers share a lot of the same tasks such as interviewing and reference checking. Yet in many ways they're cut from a different cloth. Let's investigate the mind-sets of the two most significant outside influences on your career.

Agencies and the Changing Labor Market

How the employment agency business developed and how it functions today reveal a lot about the hiring process. Over the past four decades (when the recruitment business evolved into the multibillion-dollar industry that it is today), the agency-company-candidate triad adjusted itself to accommodate changes in labor market demand. (See Figure 5-1.) Candidates can make their way to the hiring authority on their own or with the help of an employment agency. Agencies typically have more openings in tighter labor markets marked by lower levels of unemployment.

Situation 1: A Loose Labor Market

In recessionary business markets, marked by high rates of unemployment (also known as a **loose labor market**), employers have a big advantage in finding people on their own because jobs are in high demand and people are in high supply. This type of marketplace has been in place since the final quarter of 1990, when most economists agreed that a severe recession began. Many predict that it will remain in place throughout the decade as American business redefines itself in a post–Cold War, post–baby boom economy.

Figure 5-1. The candidate-company-agency triad.

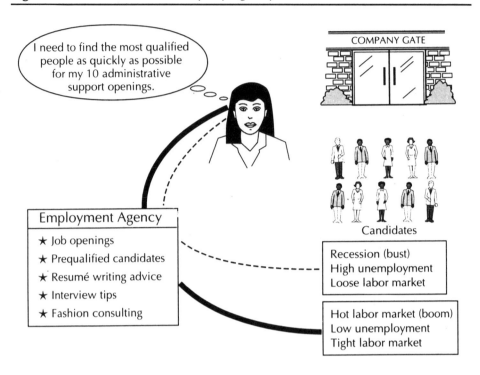

Situation 2: A Tight Labor Market

In a **tight labor market** marked by low unemployment, contingency agencies play a more dominant role because there's a high demand for people and a low supply of them. Agencies' services are needed more to scout out scarce talent, and companies consequently have a much easier time justifying fee-paid hires.

In either situation, you'll have to walk a fine line in balancing your individual job search with external labor market forces. I believe that the recessionary business mentality described in Situation 1 will remain the dominant scenario throughout the 1990s. This recession isn't so much a cyclical downturn as much as a repatterning of the U.S. corporate fabric in light of increased global competition, the specter of increased taxes as means of deficit reduction, and the inadequate demand for consumer loans because of the baby bust generation's decreased demand for residential real estate. These factors stall economic growth and make jobs scarce.

How Agencies Work

After many years as a professional contingency recruiter and search industry trainer, I'm surprised at the basic lack of understanding that most job applicants have regarding how agencies function and what they can and cannot do for you. Everyone, to be sure, has a general idea that agencies somehow bring people and jobs together. But agencies don't really define themselves as companies that find jobs for people. They see themselves more as staffing partners with their client companies. Generally, I believe that being presented to an employer on a recruiter's recommendation is more advantageous than finding the employer yourself and interviewing cold (without a recruiter's endorsement or preparation). However, there is one situation where going through an agency may lessen your chances of landing a job: when a cost-conscious company is comparing you to an equally qualified candidate who doesn't have an agency fee attached to her resumé.

I'm obviously a big believer in the benefits an agency can offer: I've made a living by providing a critical service to corporate America in terms of quickly identifying superior staff. Most companies, at any given point in time, will justify paying a recruiter's fee for the luxury of getting pre-screened, prequalified candidates for a particular high-need job opening. But until you, the candidate, understand what motivates the commission sales recruiter and the cost-conscious human resources practitioner—the two first-line screeners who can open or close doors of opportunity for you—you won't be able to maximize the career opportunities they can offer you. Learn to sell to their needs and you'll establish yourself as a savvy, well-informed job candidate.

Understanding how employment agencies work and learning what motivates human resources people is the best place to begin. Let's start with a brief history and the structure of the search business. We'll cover human resources management a little later in this chapter.

APF vs. EPF Agencies

Employment agencies first began sprouting up in the late 1940s. They followed on the coattails of the executive search business that came into being shortly after World War II, when America was rebuilding itself and there was a severe shortage of executive management. The first clerical agencies functioned as **APF**, or **applicant-paid fee** organizations. Applicants (most of whom did not want to wade through pages and pages of classified advertisements to find a job) registered with personnel services that matched them up with jobs listed by employers. After being hired, applicants paid the agency a fee of approximately 60 percent of the first month's salary. (For example, a secretary earning $350 a month might have been charged $210, which she paid to the agency over a period of three months.)

Because applicants paid the fee, those applicants were considered the agencies' clients. The function of an employment agency was to find work for individuals. What drove those early companies' marketing efforts was simply matching applicants' and companies' needs as closely as possible. Back in those days, it wasn't uncommon to see recruiters placing three or four people a week (as opposed to three or four people a month, which is more often the case today).

As the economy boomed in the 1960s, an even greater shortage of labor hurt U.S. companies and put a premium on locating talented human resources. This time, in an effort to find the best people quickly, companies assumed the costs associated with employment agencies because it was a relatively inexpensive, viable option for locating qualified employees. The **EPF**, or **employer-paid fee** agency, was born.

Because of increased government regulation affecting the labor marketplace in the 1960s civil rights movement, new restrictions were placed on American companies in terms of equal opportunity and affirmative action efforts and other hiring practices. Companies' selection procedures became more complex, and those increased demands trickled down to affect agencies' recruitment practices. This increased regulation necessitated a new level of sophistication in the employment marketplace in light of increased employee rights, which in turn made recruitment a more challenging business with far fewer numbers of agency placements than before. Because of those increased client company and regulatory demands, agencies raised their fees to 20 to 35 percent of a candidate's annual salary, the structure that we see today.

You'll still run across APF agencies, but their marketplaces are more typically found in outlying areas where there are few companies and lots of people. With few openings and large pools of local talent, it makes sense for agencies to charge candidates for career guidance in locating scarce jobs. APF agencies are also typically seen in metropolitan areas in situations where back-to-the-workforce employees or recent college grads—people with relatively little recent work experience—are willing to pay recruiters a fee for help in the job placement process.

But since the 1960s, the EPF shift has been here to stay, and with it came something of a change in agencies' responsibilities. Since companies footed the bill, they became the client in the relationship. Candidates became more like scarce inventory or a valuable product that recruiting firms marketed. And even though there has always been and will always be a shared kinship between agencies and candidates, personnel agencies focused less on finding people jobs and came to identify themselves more as staffing partners dedicated to maximizing their client companies' corporate development. Agencies today provide solutions to their clients' needs by finding people while helping those people with individual career counseling.

Contingency vs. Retained Search

The search industry as a whole mushroomed into a multibillion-dollar service industry by the late 1960s and early 1970s. Two recruitment methodologies developed side by side and filled different niches in the head-hunter's arsenal. **Contingency recruitment's** premise was that if an employment agency could locate exceptional people, refer them to client companies, and get them hired, those agencies could earn a fee for their services. The payment was contingent upon the company actually hiring the candidate referred by the agency.

Today the telephone (rather than the classified ads in the local newspaper) has become the symbol of the contingency recruiter's trade. Telemarketing allows recruiters to actively source (call into) their clients' competitors to locate the best people. Although agencies still run ads to attract qualified applicants, depending on the classifieds is much too passive in a marketplace with incredibly high demands. Advertising has lost some of its significance as recruiters attempt to attract employed people who are not actively seeking better jobs to explore opportunities with that agency's clients.

In line with the more complex services offered by agencies today, much more is expected regarding testing and familiarity with employment laws. Agencies have become sophisticated suppliers of people and services. Agencies nowadays align themselves with their exclusive executive search brethren in that they find themselves searching for administrative candidates with fairly specific industry or software backgrounds.

Agency terminology has changed a lot in the past few years as well. Applicants became known as "candidates." Employment agencies became "placement firms" or "search firms," and the counselors within those agencies called themselves "personnel consultants," "account executives," and/or "staffing specialists." What drives contingency recruiters' marketing efforts nowadays is that they can keep their clients abreast of exceptional talent on a proactive basis, regardless of whether a company has an opening. The best recruiting firms attempt to set up exploratory meetings between candidates and clients once an exceptional applicant has been identified. Again, agencies align themselves with their clients as extensions of the company's recruitment department, not only as organizations that find jobs for people.

Retained search, in comparison, is a much more exclusive game. Retained recruiters, sometimes called headhunters, target six-figure ($100,000 or more base salary) candidates for their clients. If, for example, a chemical processing company is looking for a chief financial officer with an MBA and a plastics manufacturing background to become part of a

Figure 5-2. Target search, the recruitment method used by executive search firms, otherwise known as headhunters.

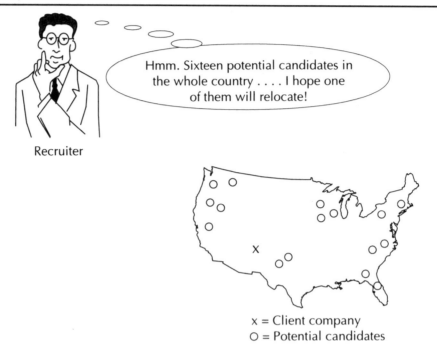

Recruiter

x = Client company
O = Potential candidates

$200 million company with 1,200 employees, a retained recruiter would bid for the business and begin the search.

Of course, there might be only fifty qualified people in the whole country who fit those qualifications. That means that a great deal of time would have to be spent researching competitor organizations across the nation just to find out who and where those people were. Then the fifty targeted individuals would have to be approached and qualified in terms of their willingness and ability to do the job, fit the client's corporate culture, and potentially relocate. (See Figure 5-2.)

This process is obviously not cost-efficient on a straight contingency basis. Far too much time and money would have to be expended to research and identify potential candidates. So the idea of a retainer developed. A company could pay an executive recruiter a fee in installments to accept the search. The headhunter gets paid to conduct the search regardless of the outcome. That retainer fee in essence covers the cost of the research and overhead that goes into identifying and approaching qualified candidates.

Since retainer fees are typically 33 percent of the candidate's annual base pay, retainers could range anywhere from $25,000 to $1 million (although fees of that size are rare). It probably sounds like a lot considering that the recruiter gets paid whether the client hires a candidate or not. But don't fool yourself: It's a very tough and competitive business, and headhunters don't stay in business very long if they're unable to fill the vast majority of their executive searches.

Target Search vs. Continuous-Cycle Recruitment

Retainer search is "exclusive" not only in terms of the size of the fees or the calibre of the executive candidates, but also in terms of the intensity of the search. Extensive research and sophisticated databases are necessary to target the right candidates. Because companies identify very specific backgrounds that potential candidates need to qualify for their job openings, executive recruitment techniques have become known as "target search," a.k.a. "looking for a needle in a haystack."

This contrasts dramatically with the other end of the search and placement spectrum, known as continuous-cycle recruitment. Contingency recruiters, or employment agencies, work on a volume basis. They develop job openings with client companies in horizontal market niches—that is, they focus on placing similar types of candidates across different industries. Administrative support recruiters, for example, place administrative secretaries and other nonexempt staff members in financial services, manufacturing/high-tech, and nonprofit organizations. That's because candidates' skills are often transferable across industries.

Employment agencies achieve economy of scale by placing a large volume of candidates into a large volume of openings with their client companies. It's a brokerage business where candidates with like skills, knowledge, and abilities are referred to companies with like needs. (See Figure 5-3.)

Contingency agencies, therefore, don't usually coordinate target searches for secretaries with very specific backgrounds. (At most, the candidate may need prior mortgage banking experience or expertise in the Windows operating environment.) Instead, they search for a general profile of a successful candidate who will meet the majority of their clients' hiring requirements. This is important to understand because most people make a big mistake when speaking with an agency: They focus either on a particular job they read about in a classified ad or, when being recruited, on the particular job the recruiter is presenting rather than attempting to find out more about the types of search that are the agency's specialty. It's a similar error to call a residential real estate broker wanting to know only about a house on the cover of this week's flyer. That house may be sold by the time you get that flyer, or it may be too expensive or in the wrong neighborhood. Because both businesses are brokerage, volume operations, it's more important to ask about what the agency (or real estate brokerage)

Figure 5-3. Continous-cycle recruitment, the recruitment technique used by employment agencies.

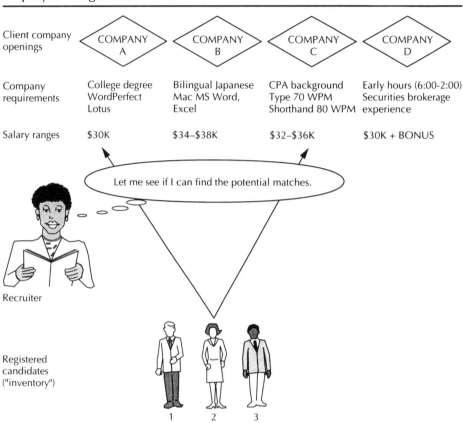

specializes in to see whether that agency is the right type of organization to help you.

Most administrative support recruiters look for four general characteristics in potential candidates:

1. *Longevity in past employment.* Longevity ultimately assures a future employer that a candidate will become a long-term member of the team. It also provides the company with a long-term return on investment for the training and hiring costs that will be incurred.
2. *Promotability* through the ranks. Progressive demonstrations of increased responsibilities show that you know how to make yourself more valuable to a company over time.
3. *Technical skills.* The ever-increasing benefits of technology save time, increase the work flow, and virtually do away with external costs like typesetting and printing.

4. *People skills*, personality, and bonding ability. Eighty percent of most hires is determined by how the employer and candidate get along.

As far as an agency is concerned, once you meet these general criteria, you will most likely be able to provide a solution to a client company's problem. There are general kinds of problems that companies try to solve through people: saving time, producing revenue, or redirecting and streamlining the work flow. Bear in mind, however, that administrative support recruiters usually don't know where they're going to send you while you're sitting in their office or interviewing with them over the phone. Therefore, recruiters spend most of their time focusing on the solutions you have achieved for past employers that you can in turn bring to their clients. So the recruiter's questioning format focuses on what makes you stand out from your peers. For example:

"What's your greatest strength?"
"What have you done in your present position that you are most proud of or that you feel was particularly creative?"
"What's the strongest comment a past employer would make about you on a reference check?"
"What have you done in a past position to save time or to save your company money?"
"What have you done to increase revenues for the organization?"

Again, the idea here is to put together a menu of achievements that can be presented to a potential employer depending on that particular company's needs at the time.

Recruiters are trained to look for the positive in people's backgrounds. That's what they have to sell; it's what justifies the fees they charge. On the other hand, recruiters need to make sure that you're not your own worst enemy in terms of answering tough questions that will surface during an interview. So additional types of questions they ask may go something like this:

"Where do you see yourself in five years?"
"What's your greatest weakness?"
"Who was your least favorite boss and why?"
"Which of your past employers would give you the weakest reference and why?"
"Give me three adjectives to describe yourself."
"Give me an example of a time when you had a serious disagreement with your boss. How did you handle the situation?"

You get the idea. If finding out how you will provide a solution to a client's problem is the offense, then ensuring that you know how to steer clear of dangerous questions is the defense. It's the recruiters' lean, mean strategy for simultaneously representing you and providing staffing solutions to their clients.

How Much Do Agencies Charge Companies?

You should know how much you cost if a firm hires you through an agency. As mentioned earlier, there can be a disadvantage in having a price tag attached to your resumé if you're competing against an equally qualified candidate who doesn't have a fee for hire. However, this too is debatable: Once a company has determined that it will use an agency, it may solely focus on hiring the best person for the job, regardless of the fee involved.

Agencies today charge companies 1 percent per thousand dollars of your annual salary. For example, a $20,000 annual salary costs the employer 20 percent of $20,000, or $4,000. A $30,000 candidate costs 30 percent, or $9,000. Contingency recruiter fees typically reach a maximum of 35 percent, so that a $50,000 candidate would cost an employer $17,500 (35 percent of $50,000). These fee structures can be negotiated, especially in a high-unemployment marketplace.

Recruiters typically offer a thirty-day free trial period and a sixty-day probationary period so that a client company isn't penalized if a candidate leaves in the first sixty days.

Agencies' Responsibilities

The purpose of a recruiting firm is to identify exceptional candidates, interview them, test them, and check their references. These areas must be thoroughly covered for the agency to earn its fee. Recruiting firms act as middlemen bringing qualified people to clients in a timely manner. That's why they're paid by companies. Why they're an excellent, free source to you lies in the fact that they have job openings and know their companies' profiles, and they can help you with resumé preparation, interview techniques, and salary negotiations. Understand, however, that the decision to hire a candidate belongs strictly to a company. The decision to accept or reject a job offer on the basis of its own merits belongs solely to you. Once you accept the company's offer, the recruiter's job is done. (See Figure 5-4.)

Figure 5-4. The employment agency's contractual responsibilities to a client company.

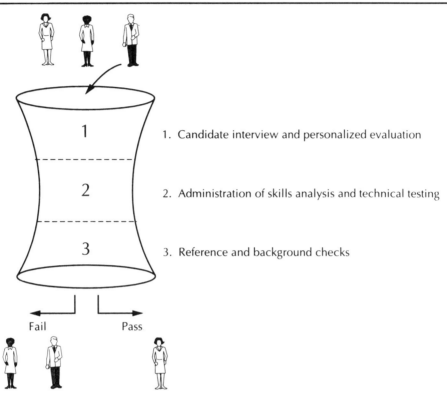

1. Candidate interview and personalized evaluation

2. Administration of skills analysis and technical testing

3. Reference and background checks

Fail   Pass

Cost-per-Hire: The Human Resources Practitioner's Orientation

Let's now meet the other first-line screener who can open or close doors of opportunity for you: the human resources professional. HR practitioners and contingency (agency) recruiters have very similar functions (for example, interviewing, skills testing, and reference checking) but very dissimilar attitudes and business philosophies. It's a reciprocal relationship: If agencies screen people in to make placements, then human resources executives focus on keeping their costs per hire as low as possible and reducing turnover primarily by avoiding questionable hires.

Comparative Costs-per-Hire

Employment agencies are the most expensive means of adding to staff. The average fee per placement that an administrative support agency in Los Angeles receives is roughly $4,000. The average cost of running a twenty-eight-line, two-inch classified ad in a major metropolitan news-

Figure 5-5. Relative costs associated with hiring support staff in a typical metropolitan area.

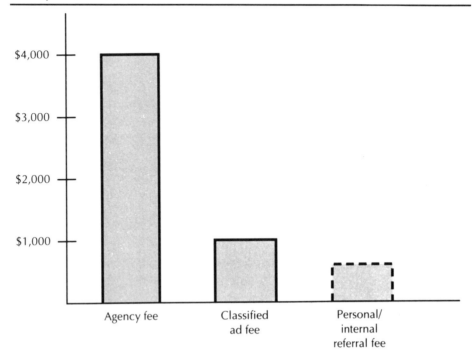

paper runs somewhere between $600 and $1,000. There is no guarantee, however, that one ad will find the right person; multiple ads can increase this cost immensely. Internal employee referral programs yield a minimal cost-per-hire of roughly $500. Many companies award an employee who refers a new hire with a $500 or $1,000 gratuity for the referral. It builds employee morale and lets people feel they have more of a stake in their company's success. (See Figure 5-5.)

Since agencies are the most expensive way to hire new people, HR people often rely on them only as a last resort after other, less costly avenues have been exhausted. This too depends on the particular company. Many firms, even in a recession, insist on using agencies to interview only the most qualified candidates right from the start and save time through quality staffing.

Screening Out Questionable Hires

Human resources is a staff function in corporate America. Staff jobs like human resources, accounting, and purchasing support a company's core business, whether it be selling widgets or coordinating leveraged buyouts. As opposed to line jobs that create revenue—sales and marketing functions are line jobs because each job is a profit center—staff jobs focus on decreasing costs or saving time. One of the key ways in which HR practitioners seek to decrease company costs is by minimizing turnover.

The contingency recruiter's orientation is sales, a line job. "When in doubt, do," they believe. Recruiters live to make placements and make placements to live.

The HR professional's orientation is to carefully select only those job candidates who have the greatest chances of success in the company. They are trained to look for the match between the candidate's personality, skills, and experience and the company's corporate culture and technical needs. Consequently, human resources interviewers are expected to keep an eye out for:

- Any inconsistencies in your presentation
- Incompatibility factors (technical, emotional, or of corporate culture) that may hinder your performance once aboard

And rightfully so: Most have been burned by people who interview like Dr. Jekyll and then perform like Mr. Hyde once on the job. Most have unfortunately experienced the consequences of candidate misrepresentation of employment dates, salary history, education, and other such employment misdemeanors. Understand, therefore, that their sole mission in the recruitment and selection process is to guard the gate and maximize their organization's use of its human resources.

As a result, the strategy for passing human resources' evaluation is to take a conservative and circumspect approach to interviewing and not give human resources a reason to screen you out. Human resources performs screening interviews that size up your suitability in terms of technical skills, personality, and reference information. However, remember that human resources usually doesn't make the final decision to hire! The personnel department typically recommends candidates to the line departments that do the actual hiring. The screening interview is consequently not the place to razzle-dazzle the employer. That comes later when interviewing with the department head who will be your direct supervisor.

Because HR practitioners identify themselves as people who save costs for their company, they keep a focused eye on the bottom line: the cost-per-hire. As mentioned earlier, that is simply the total cost of hiring new employees in a year divided by the number of new employees. (See Figure 5-6.)

Human resources' mission to reduce costs goes beyond the up-front fees that recruiters charge. When a company adds an employee to its payroll, it risks:

Figure 5-6. The cost-per-hire figure is a barometer of human resources' efficiency and ability to decrease company costs.

I. Company hiring process

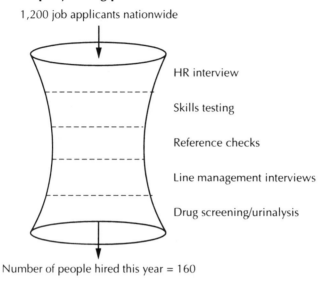

1,200 job applicants nationwide

HR interview

Skills testing

Reference checks

Line management interviews

Drug screening/urinalysis

Number of people hired this year = 160

II. Costs associated with hiring (not including on-the-job training)

$39,000 Agency/search fees

$33,000 Classified ad fees

$9,000 Internal referral fees

$81,000 Total recruitment costs

III. Cost-per-hire calculation

$$\frac{\$81,000 \text{ costs}}{160 \text{ people}} = \$506.25 \text{ per person}$$

- Recruitment fees to be spent on finding a new employee
- Training and orientation costs
- Payroll taxes
- Unemployment insurance
- Benefits coverage and benefits administration
- Workers compensation exposure
- Wrongful termination exposure

Figure 5-7. Payroll is typically the number one expense on a company's operating statement. (*Note that the order of raw materials, overhead, and advertising may vary from industry to industry.)

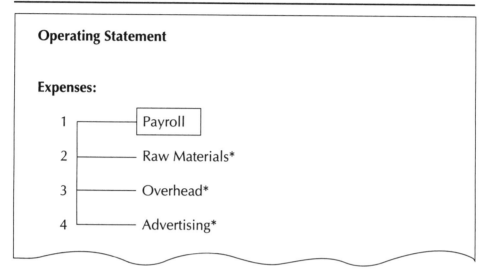

Operating Statement

Expenses:

1 ——————— Payroll

2 ——————— Raw Materials*

3 ——————— Overhead*

4 ——————— Advertising*

Ouch! The high costs of turnover can wreak havoc on an organization's bottom line.

Payroll is the number one expense on a company's operating statement. (See Figure 5-7.) That's why companies are so quick to lay off in an economic downturn. Labor must constantly be adjusted to keep tempo with sales. Accordingly, one poor hire equals a lot of negative exposure, which is not good for a staff department trying to decrease costs. (Even though individual departments have the ultimate say in the decision to hire people, excessive turnover problems are often blamed on human resources, whether this is really fair or not.)

If I'm making human resources practitioners sound like a bunch of IRS auditors ready to find skeletons in your closet, I'm exaggerating to make a point. They're expected to test, reference-check, and generally evaluate all administrative prospective hires. Evaluating people is more art than science, and it's always a tough call because the HR manager is constantly balancing intuition or gut feelings with objective, factual criteria. Having concrete, scientific evidence like test scores and reference information sure helps, though. Knowing the pressures HR managers face to reduce costs associated with turnover should help clarify what they look for in initial evaluations.

So let's tie all this together: When you've set up an interview on your own or through a friend and are about to begin your meeting with the human resources department of the company of your dreams, feel good about the fact that your chances for hire go up when your particular cost-

Figure 5-8. Pie chart of the three marketplaces for finding your next job.

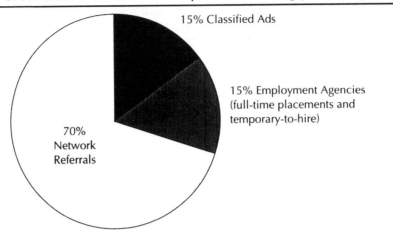

15% Classified Ads

15% Employment Agencies
(full-time placements and
temporary-to-hire)

70%
Network
Referrals

per-hire goes down. (And the cost-per-hire in this case, again, is zero. Bully for you!) In Chapter 1 you learned to build your network and learn to maximize the golden resource of job search: your local library. Continually try to get in front of new companies via exploratory meetings and informational interviews.

On the other hand, when you're about to meet with the human resources department of the company of your dreams, and you've been referred by an agency (which, again, has a fee attached to your resumé), act the part! Companies will pay fees only for the strongest candidates in town. Just the fact that you're talking with the company via an agency referral means you're on the top of the charts! Let your attitude reveal your sense of accomplishment by having developed a job interview based on a contingency recruiter's recommendation.

Even if your individual cost-per-hire goes up in this case, bear in mind that average contingency fees for administrative support staff range from $2,500 to $10,000. That's not a heck of a lot of money for most larger companies, especially if you're exceptionally qualified for the job. The interview preparation that an agency provides, along with the identification of companies you might not otherwise have heard about, makes an agency a wonderfully logical choice for your job search campaign. However, to be totally effective in the employment game, you've got to utilize all three marketplaces: agencies, classified ads, and your network of past employers, co-workers, and friends. (See Figure 5-8.)

The Third Member of the Hiring Process: You

Understanding what human resources practitioners and contingency recruiters look for gives you the perspective to see the bigger picture of recruitment and selection. But unless you can articulate your own needs and goals—what you want out of a job or affiliation with a specific company—then a powerful element of the interview will be lost. The criteria you use in selecting your next company reveal how you see yourself fitting into a particular environment and making an impact on that organization.

Be Clear About What You Want and Can Contribute

First of all, understand where you'll be wanted most and where you can make the biggest impact. Companies will primarily be attracted to candidates with exact industry (field) and job (function) backgrounds. If you come from a competitor, you're wanted. If you're switching industries or will somehow need an extended training period or learning curve, you'll lose some of your edge to the competition. Conversely, if you're interviewing for a presidential assistant spot and have provided one-on-one executive secretarial support to a CEO/president, you'll logically be one up on a competitor who has been reporting to a different functional head, such as a chief financial officer or executive vice-president of marketing.

Keep in mind, however, that the size of your present organization weighs heavily in the decision-making process. For example, a secretary to a president in an organization with thirty employees and $8 million in revenue most likely will not qualify for an assistant position in a corporation with 1,200 employees and $300 million in revenue. The moral of the story is that if you're interviewing for a job in a different industry or in a company of a substantially different size than your present one, you must be prepared to articulate that you're aware of the discrepancy along with why you want the job, and why you're especially well suited for it.

Following is a brief checklist of typical criteria that you might use in selecting another company:

- Industry preference.
- Salary and location.
- Title or functional responsibilities.
- Departmental function. (Would you be better off working in sales and marketing, human resources, or finance?)
- Reporting relationship. (Do you prefer one-on-one relationships or multiple reporting relationships? Do you tend to get along best with certain personality types or people trained in certain professions?)
- Company size, either in terms of number of employees or annual revenues. (Do you like *Fortune* 500 companies because they offer name-brand recognition and may have better benefits and higher compensation than smaller businesses? Or do you prefer a smaller, more entrepreneurial type of environment because the lines of

command are typically more fluid and employees are expected to handle a larger variety of tasks?)
- Pace/personality of the office. For example, do you prefer:
  —A moderate, controllable, and predictable pace?
  —A faster pace with variety and deadline pressure?
  —Hyperspace, a frenetic environment that vibrates with energy?
- Why you want to leave your present position.

You must formulate definite answers to these questions before any interview because most employers will directly or indirectly ask you, "What are you looking for, and why do you want to work here?" Also refer to pages 197–202 for a discussion of how to decide whether it's really time to leave your current job.

Explaining what you want is a difficult task because you do not want to be so specific that you screen yourself out of a job. However, there's more danger in playing it safe and saying you're flexible to anything and everything the company wants. You need to be as agreeable as possible, but you'll maintain your edge if you're definitive about showing that you know what's important to you. (Of course, the ideal match happens when your needs coincide with the company's needs. Unfortunately, it's likely that you won't know their hidden agenda unless you've got an inside contact.) Therefore, hammer out your own personal needs before you go in. Obviously, the more you learn about a company beforehand, the greater the probability that you can match your needs to theirs. Library research or an agency can certainly help with that.

The key to expressing your wants is to show yourself as an *objective, third-party evaluator* of your career progression. People either give the impression that they control their careers or are tossed about like a cork on a wave, passively willing to accept whatever happens to come their way. The following are examples of meshing personal needs with company goals:

Ms. Employer, my goal has always been to provide one-on-one, executive-level support to a president of a *Fortune* 500 company. Up to now in my career, I've been a key administrative assistant to executives at the senior and executive vice-presidential levels. I see this as an opportunity to increase my reporting authority to the presidential level. I believe that my experience, technical skills, and education have prepared me for this level of responsibility.

Mr. Employer, I have a multiple reporting relationship to the vice-president of finance and chief financial officer at my present company. I've been there two years, and although I'm very grateful for the trust my bosses have placed in me and for all that I've learned, I believe that I can make a greater impact in a sales and marketing environment. My degree was in English with a minor in speech, and I really feel that I would excel and add more value to an environment that is less numbers-driven and more people-oriented.

Ms. Employer, I've had a one-on-one reporting relationship to the owner and president of a medical-device manufacturer with thirty employees. I believe that pharmaceutical, biotech, and medical manufacturing companies are in an exciting field with constant changes due to new technologies. But, *looking objectively at my career,* I know I need to be part of a much larger company with higher brand-name recognition. That's my goal. I'm here because I want to provide one-on-one support to the senior vice-president of research and development in your organization. I'm familiar with the pressures and terminology common to the medical manufacturing environment. I've researched your company, I'm aware of your reputation, and I'd love the opportunity to become part of your team.

You get the idea. Know where you've been and where you're going. Put yourself in your potential employer's shoes. Give thought to who your toughest competition will be, and plan your strategy accordingly. Self-awareness is a very impressive trait. It shows mature business judgment and objective evaluation skills. It's one element that will separate you from your peers.

Now that you understand what your first interviewers are looking for and you've thought through your own motives for seeking a new job, let's move on to the interviewing stage.

Part II

The Game Plan: Putting Your Knowledge and Tools to the Test

Chapter 6

You Can Be the Shining Star in the HR "Screening" Interview

Thorough preparation for an introductory meeting with a company's human resources representative entails some hard work on your part if done properly, but can be a creative and rewarding process if you have a consistent, tested strategy—a blueprint for maximizing the information-gathering and self-marketing processes that are part of every interview.

The postrecession 1990s have toughened us all. Those of us without jobs learned how difficult it could be to land one (a very humbling pursuit), while those of us with jobs learned to increase our productivity and work lots of overtime to keep them. As mentioned earlier, jobs will probably remain scarce throughout the decade as the fabric of the post–Cold War, global economy repatterns and redefines itself to adjust to the new demands and technical innovations we're seeing today. Supply and demand dictates that stiff competition will remain the law of the land.

As a result, you'll need an edge to remain competitive. Knowing how to field sophisticated interview questions and how to formulate high-gain questions for employers (that is, questions that knock their socks off!) will enable you to make a unique impact. Employers, remember, are honing their questioning skills to get below the surface of traditional interview responses. Their new reality is to gauge how well you'll actually perform on the job, not just how well you respond to interview questions. Turnover and retraining expenses have forced employers to strengthen their interviewing skills. This chapter will introduce you to an interview preparation methodology that will help you justify your candidacy in light of employers' sophisticated questioning techniques.

This interview preparation strategy covers four areas:

1. The T account approach to research and information gathering: separating the company from the job
2. Questions to expect from human resources interviewers
3. Questions to ask interviewers during the meeting
4. Miscellaneous issues such as salary negotiations, discussing your

reasons for leaving past positions, and closing the interview by asking for the job

The T Account: Separating Company From Position

The essence of the T account is to have all your information laid out neatly in the shape of the letter "T" on one piece of paper before the meeting begins. It's the ultimate organizer. It distinguishes company characteristics from job details and sets you up to ask analytical interview questions. (See Figure 6-1.)

The left side of the T account focuses solely on company information. As you might guess, the more thorough your understanding of the company and the role it plays within its industry, the more you'll stand out from your competition. Spend at least thirty minutes in the library researching the company's history, demographics, and market niche. For example, it's no longer the case that a bank is a bank is a bank. The recession hit financial services extremely hard. California's Bank of America/Security Pacific merger made large banks the key players in the field. That left small banks with less than $2 billion in assets prime targets for takeover. To maintain their independence, small banks began to specialize in niche markets serving particular clients. It's critical, therefore, to understand where a particular company fits into the whole picture of its overall industry. However, if you're not aware of how the particular company fits into its industry, it's okay to ask the interviewer because it's an excellent and insightful business question.

The right side of the T focuses on the position: its title, reporting relationship, and duties. Be sure to quantify the reporting relationships above and below you. Ask about the exact titles and number of people you'll report to. Distinguish between straight-line and dotted-line reporting relationships. Straight-line relationships imply direct and immediate supervision. Dotted-line relationships have to do with occasionally reporting to your boss's boss or other key executives on an as-needed basis.

Similarly, quantify the exact numbers and titles of workers you will supervise. What will be the nature of that supervision? Daily assignments of work? Proofing and signing off on subordinates' assignments? Shared authority with an office manager or administrative supervisor? Will you write annual performance appraisals?

Primary duties are the basic job descriptions, or the essential job functions that human resources has on file. Again, quantify the proportions of work that the job entails by breaking down tasks into percentages or ratios. For example, what percentage of the day will you spend handling administrative duties (travel and business arrangements, personal affairs,

Figure 6-1. The T account interview organizer. You should research checked-off items before your meeting.

Company	Position
Company name:	1. Title:
Address:	2. Department:
Cross street and interview parking:	3. Supervisor(s)/reporting relationship(s):
Human resources contact/ interviewer	4. Reason position open:
Name: Title: Telephone number:	5. Primary duties:
✓ Industry:	
✓ Primary & secondary product lines:	
✓ Product markets:	
✓ Key accounts/clients:	
✓ Year founded:	6. Secondary responsibilities:
✓ Headquarters city:	
✓ Sales volume:	
✓ Number of employees Entire corporation: This location:	
Hours:	
Overtime? Exempt or nonexempt pay scale?	7. Key(s) to hire:
Software systems:	

special projects, corporate functions) versus secretarial duties (word processing, telephone screening)? How often is your boss away on business? What type of and how much decision-making authority will you, as assistant, have in your boss's absence? Many of these specifics will be more thoroughly answered in your interview with the immediate supervisor later on. However, human resources can provide you with an overall picture of the position's responsibilities that can serve as a means for comparison to the department's feedback.

The keys to hire comprise those elements that the company hopes to find in the ideal candidate. Often the company is strictly looking for the opposite of the incumbent's characteristics. When an individual is being replaced because of poor performance, interviewers keep a sharp eye out to avoid those same problems in the new hire. Understanding what the company likes least about the last person on the job defines how you should sell yourself. However, asking an interviewer that question may seem a little awkward. Instead, you can figure out the keys to hire by asking, "If you, Ms. Employer, could change anything about the background or skill level of the person who last held the position that could have made that individual more effective, what would it be?" Keys to hire additionally are emotional qualities that help an individual's personality mesh with the organization's culture. You can draw out this information by asking, "If you could match the ideal candidate's personality to fit this company's corporate culture, what would that individual's personality be?"

Questions to Expect From Human Resources Interviewers

As discussed in Chapter 5, human resources practitioners are trained to conduct screening interviews that screen people out. Recall that if poor hires are made, the human resources department suffers because responsibility for new hires falls into its lap. Human resources professionals are intent on identifying what could go wrong. Their questions will bait you to volunteer information about yourself that could harm the company. Beware! (See Figure 6-2.)

Meanwhile, let's look at some specific questions that you are likely to be asked. Many interview questions have multiple versions, so you should recognize them in disguise as well.

"What's your greatest strength?"
"Why should we hire you?"
"What makes you stand out from your peers?"

Figure 6-2. Human resources' typical questioning hurdles.

This one seems easy. It is. It's an opening stratagem to get you talking freely. *Watch out*—its purpose is to lead into the next question (which is much tougher): "What's your greatest weakness?"

First let's open up the greatest-strength question. The primary over-sight interviewees make is to respond with lists of adjectives to describe their nobler traits, such as hard-working, intelligent, loyal, and a people person. Adjectives are nothing but unproven claims. They waste time and delay getting to what the interviewer really wants: concrete proof of how you'll fit in and what you're likely to contribute. Following are examples of well-developed responses that avoid adjective lists and that are based in reality:

> I'd have to say that my greatest strength is my organizational forecasting ability. I think I have a sixth sense for staying one step ahead of every project I'm on, and that's helped me tie together multiple projects in a smooth fashion. For example, . . .

> My boss would say my greatest strength is that I never get flustered under pressure. We worked under constant deadlines, yet I really seemed to thrive when the heat was on. I somehow become more efficient and effective when under the gun. For example, . . .

> I guess I'm most proud of my promotability through the ranks. In my five years at XYZ Company, my bosses asked me to assume greater responsibilities three times. In my last position, I was responsible for reporting one-on-one to the CEO, attending board meetings and publishing the minutes, and supervising two clerical staff people. It could get pretty hectic at times, but I always managed to balance my responsibilities. For example, . . .

> My greatest attribute is my lightning work pace. Money management firms buzz with energy. Each person's decision has incredible financial impact. Time is money. I really look forward to coming to work every day because the adrenaline rush I get keeps me totally stimulated and into my work. Working for this company would be ideal for me for that reason.

> Hands down, anyone I've ever worked with would say my greatest strength would have to be my software skills. I'm admittedly teased by co-workers for being a Mac nerd. I've done practically everything there is to be done on Microsoft Word and Excel. My production levels are really high for that reason. And that's one reason why I would love this position. Just give me my Mac, and my creative juices come to life.

Notice two things about these responses: First, these answers always avoid filler adjectives. Second, the answers are either based in reality ("For example, . . .") or they strategically convince the employer that you're right for the job ("That's why working for this company would be ideal for me").

"What's your greatest weakness?"

"Who would give you the weakest reference and why?"

"What one area do you really need to work on in your career to become more effective on a day-to-day basis?"

"No one's perfect. Is there any reason why your competition for this job might have one up on you?"

Warning: This query is always one of the biggest knockout factors! I learned the value of this question the hard way. Denise was one of the strongest executive assistants I'd ever met. Technically she was a dynamo. Her personality brightened up the room when she walked in. It so happened that, in the course of our interview, she identified one of our client companies as a place she'd love to work. Was she surprised when I told her we had an opening in that company that seemed to fit her perfectly! She researched the firm that afternoon, called a friend of hers who worked there to get the scoop on the opening she was applying for, and bought a new suit just for that interview. I saw myself as the recruiter's version of a knight in shining armor getting my candidate her ideal job and solving my client's problem by presenting a superstar.

Well, you guessed it—Denise never made it past the first round of interviews. Here's what my follow-up phone call from the employer sounded like:

> Paul, we're not interested in Denise at all. You were right about her image and personality, and I was impressed by the fact that she researched us in the library. But you won't believe what she told me! Apparently, her greatest weakness is that she has a "low tolerance for stupidity." It totally threw me when she said that. Talk about an arrogant remark! That kind of attitude would never fit into our company.

Granted, no one is perfect, but this isn't the time or the place to bare your soul and come clean. Your strategy when answering this question is to steer clear of the snare. Here are some paradigms that will keep your neck out of the noose:

> If I had to work on anything at this point in my career, I'd say it would have to be delegating work to others. Not that I don't

trust other people to do their jobs well. I just feel that if I don't do it myself, it won't get done the way I like it. Don't get me wrong. That's given me more pressure on occasion. But it's one of those personality quirks that I have to make a conscious effort to change.

I don't feel I have any major flaws, but I am somewhat of a neat-nick. I have to cross every *t* and dot every *i* and read everything twice before it leaves my desk. Maybe it's an insecurity, but I can't bear the thought of redoing work, or, heaven forbid, having a key executive in another organization receive a letter from my boss with a grammatical error or typo.

There may be some disadvantage in this in that it slows me down a little bit, but I've never been known to be slow at any-thing. So I guess that you can argue that it's a fault or an imper-fection, but from a day-to-day operational standpoint, it helps more than it hinders.

My greatest weakness is that I tend to be very impatient about my own performance. I've always been my own toughest critic. I love the feeling of being on top of my game—being the one that people come to in order to get problems solved. I realize, however, that in any new work environment, it will take time to learn the ropes and the who's who in the organization. I'll just have to learn to be a little more patient with myself.

In reviewing these answers, you'll notice that weaknesses are really *strengths in disguise*. Not delegating too much work to others and being overly critical of your own performance are ideal character traits of any successful employee. As with the greatest-strength questions, greatest-weakness questions need to be rooted in reality. Not delegating work to others *can* pile your work up at times. If you cross every *t* and dot every *i*, it *may* slow you down. Therefore, you should end each answer by over-coming the weakness you named. For example, the fact that you've never been known to be slow at anything ensures the employer that you're really not too slow to get the job done.

Many exceptional candidates have disqualified themselves by re-sponding that they have no weaknesses. *Unacceptable answer!* Remember that interviewing is to a certain extent a game to see how deftly you land on your feet. By having no weaknesses, you're refusing to play the game. That's a tactical error you need to avoid.

Many critics argue that interviewing, consequently, is becoming more and more of a practiced and rehearsed art. Books like this one are faulted for teaching people to act rather than be honest. I agree with that observation to a point. However, the realities of today's economy simply don't allow for admitted mistakes. Also, critics should not underestimate the significance of the game itself. American cultural values place a premium on ingenuity, creativity, and wit. The interview game, consequently, maintains its own significance despite outside influences (like tips from contingency recruiters and instructional texts) that may blur reality.

"Where do you see yourself in five years?"

This question is a known showstopper and one of HR's most often asked questions.

Fatal Responses

"In five years, I'd like to be in my manager's shoes."
"In five years, I still want to be doing the same job I'm applying for right now."
"In five years, I want your job, Ms. HR Manager, because I think human resources is a really exciting field."
"Five years from now, I hope to own my own business."

If it seems as if anything and everything you answer is wrong, you're learning the danger of this question. It's a mistake to name a title other than the one you're applying for. After all, since human resources focuses on costs-per-hire, they need to know that you're planning on making a long-term commitment to the job at hand. As soon as you name a job title other than the one you're applying for, the interviewer questions your commitment level. On the other hand, you might not want to state that you want to be an administrative assistant (or accountant, customer service representative, etc.) for the rest of your life, lest you be perceived as a person with underdeveloped career goals.

The key to addressing long-term goals lies in not mentioning any job titles at all! Instead your answer should emphasize your commitment to assuming greater responsibilities as your supervisors get more comfortable delegating work to you. For example,

Mr. Employer, I have a track record of assuming more and more responsibilities on my past positions as my bosses had become more confident with my abilities. I see myself taking on that same role in your company. Right now, I believe I can make the greatest impact in an organization by using my administrative and secretarial skills. That's where my total focus lies. Where it leads me in five years, I hope you'll eventually tell me. But I want you to know that I'll be open to adding value to your organization in whatever way you see fit.

Ms. Employer, if I am hired as the executive administrative secretary to the CEO, I'll be as far up the corporate ladder as my function will allow. So I won't interpret your question in terms of other positions within the firm. Instead, I'll share with you the fact that I've always enjoyed my work and the relationships I've developed over the years. I continually upgrade my skills through night classes. I belong to a secretarial networking group. And I have a very healthy, happy home life. In short, I believe it's my responsibility to complement the CEO in all her dealings. And as my references will testify, I'll continue to find new ways to do my job more efficiently and add value to the organization.

Proofing these answers, you'll note that the respondents do not make the mistake of naming a title other than administrative secretary. The candidates stress, instead, that their focus is on excelling at the job at hand because their skills and abilities can make the greatest impact there. Finally, they intimate that they would welcome greater responsibilities as the circumstances warrant. Voilà: an open-ended, nonlimiting response to a query meant to entrap you!

"Which was your favorite job and why?"
"Who was your favorite boss?"

At first glance, these should seem simple enough to you. However, the key to answering the questions lies in matching tasks you've handled in the past with the present position's requirements. Take the case of Dorothy. When the question about favorite jobs came her way, she mistakenly mentioned a past job that was extremely creative and got her out of the office a few hours a week. She had worked for an international company that entertained foreign dignitaries, and she had been responsible for giving corporate tours of the company's solar energy plant. Granted, those may be reasons why that particular job stood out in Dorothy's memory. However, because the job she was applying for didn't offer these nontraditional perks, she ended up selling her love of tasks that she wouldn't be handling on the new job. She weakened her case because the company felt that she was overqualified—in other words, they couldn't offer her the glamour she was accustomed to and felt she wouldn't be stimulated in their environment.

It's much wiser to sell your love of a past task that you'll also be handling on the new job. In case this question surfaces before you have a chance to gauge the particular tasks of the job at hand, focus your answers on more generic issues like the personalities of the people you've worked with, the amount of trust your supervisor(s) placed in you, and the opportunities to assume greater responsibilities. Hold off on giving exotic answers because they may make the interviewer see a red light that flashes, "overqualified; needs a lot of variety or else gets bored."

> *"Which was your least favorite position?"*
> *"Who was your least favorite boss?"*

Again, be careful with questions that invite you to criticize or censure a boss's performance. This question baits you to complain about the person to whom you should be most loyal. Steer clear of it by revealing your objective business evaluation skills, as opposed to how you were personally affected by the situation. Personal interpretations force you to defend your actions. Objective evaluations, on the other hand, remove you from the action; they place an impersonal distance between you and the goings-on of others. They reveal your ability to separate the forest from the trees—that is, your business maturity that allows you to objectively evaluate a situation rather than irrationally react to it. For example,

> If I had to objectively critique a past employer's performance, I would first want to say that I enjoyed working for all my past supervisors immensely. Objectively evaluating the various reporting relationships I've had, I would say that working for Jane Stewart, the executive vice-president of sales at XYZ Company, had the most challenges. We worked very well together, but there were occasions where Jane could have been somewhat less reactive and a bit more proactive in her dealings with others. She actually prided herself on putting out fires. My style, on the other hand, was more proactive. I enjoyed preplanning and forecasting potential problems before they arose. All in all, I think Jane and I balanced each other well. We made a very successful team.

In other cases where you're asked to identify your least favorite position, address issues that were beyond your control.

> My least favorite position would probably have to be my last one only because the layoff came so suddenly and unexpectedly. I really loved my job and the company, and I was planning on

making a career with them. My resumé will show that I'm not a job-hopper. I hope I never have to go through another layoff again.

Two positions ago, while I was at XYZ Company, the firm relocated twenty-five miles farther from my home. I enjoyed my work, I respected my boss, and I really felt that I was part of a family. However, four months after the move, I realized that the extra travel time simply added too much to my day. I decided to look for work elsewhere.

My least favorite employer would probably be ABC Company because there were no benefits. I originally accepted the job because it was a first position back into the workforce after ten years of staying at home with the kids. I was covered under my husband's plan. But I believe a company that provides long-term incentives and benefits coverage is really dedicated to making employees long-term members of the team. [Use this only if you know the organization has such plans in place, of course!]

The Neglected but Critical Art of Filling Out an Employment Application

Human resources practitioners are trained to build a case for a particular candidate. Issues that they silently think about during the screening interview but don't necessarily voice to you include accounting for the salary progression in your career, the changes in industry and reporting relationships you've made, and your reasons for leaving past positions. If a candidate was making, for example, $35,000 a year two jobs ago, $32,000 on the last position, and $28,000 on the present position, there's either a serious problem with the marketplace, or else that person may not be capable of progressively assuming heavier responsibilities. If a candidate leaves the service industry because she feels manufacturing would have more challenges, leaves manufacturing one year later to get into the medical/pharmaceutical field, and now wants to explore work as an administrative secretary in a nonprofit organization, there's a good chance that she has a nondefined career path. In other words, there's too much risk that she will be off and gone on another adventure in the near future. If a candidate leaves one company for the chance to report one-on-one to an executive, leaves that company to work as a group secretary, and is interviewing for a one-on-one reporting relationship again, HR interviewers will question why she is pursuing a relationship that she worked so hard to get out of in the past.

The best way to prepare yourself for this silent interview analysis is to prepare explanations to account for various important threads running through your career, such as reasons for leaving, salary progression, industry preferences, job titles, and reporting relationships. Figure 6-3 will reveal anything that noticeably stands out. Jot down your answers and think about how an interviewer would view them.

Is each reason the same (for example, no room for growth or more money)? If so, that might give off a selfish perception of what's important to you in your career. Are these circumstances out of your control (layoff or corporate relocation) or have you orchestrated your own moves (desire to report one-on-one to a chief corporate officer or looking for increased responsibilities and a heavier workload)? Are these explanations defendable and do they reveal positive and healthy career progression, or might they indicate a low tolerance for making long-term commitments? (More about reasons for leaving a little later.)

Salary history is another major issue you'll face when filling out an application. There's nothing wrong with taking a salary cut. You must, however, be able to explain the circumstances surrounding your decision.

Similarly, don't underestimate how interviewers weigh your decisions of having chosen particular industries. Account for why you changed industries. For example, do you prefer services to manufacturing? Is there a reason why you left investment banking for a Big Six CPA firm?

Even more significant than industry choice is your functional career path: the titles you've held on past jobs. Titles can overqualify you. If you left one company as a secretary to become an administrative manager and are interviewing for a secretarial opening again, you may be considered overqualified for the job. Sell why you want back into the secretarial function (for example, "I enjoy working independently and being responsible for myself rather than overseeing others' workloads").

Do you prefer one-on-one reporting relationships to multiple reporting relationships? How would you compare working one-on-one with the vice-president of finance at ABC Company to your experience reporting to two human resources officers at XYZ Company? Is splitting up your time among three executives troublesome, or do you prefer multiple tasks because of the variety? Good questions. And bear in mind that HR will try to read your body language as well as your spoken responses in interpreting your answers.

If you ever wondered why employment agencies and companies ask you to fill out their internal application forms even though you have your own resumé, it's because their forms bring out these issues much more clearly than a resumé does. Interviewers are initially trained to look at the four salary boxes on the application to account for salary progression, to view the industry boxes and supervisor's title boxes for changes in reporting relationships, and to analyze the reason-for-leaving boxes to iden-

Figure 6-3. Worksheet for analyzing your job history the way interviewers will.

A. **Reason(s) for leaving:**

Present position: _____

Past position 1: _____

Past position 2: _____

Past position 3: _____

B. **Salary progression:**

Present position (base plus bonus): $ _____

Past position 1: $ _____

Past position 2: $ _____

Past position 3: $ _____

C. **Industry experience:**

Present position: _____

Past position 1: _____

Past position 2: _____

Past position 3: _____

D. **Functional experience/job titles:**

Present position title: _____

Past position 1 title: _____

Past position 2 title: _____

Past position 3 title: _____

E. **Types of reporting relationships:**

Title of past supervisors/departments

Present position: _____

Past position 1: _____

Past position 2: _____

Past position 3: _____

tify what motivates you to make job changes. That orientation to follow the boxes represents a comfort zone to many interviewers. Besides, a lot of the information requested on an application isn't even addressed on a resumé (like salary progression, reasons for leaving, and names of supervisors who can verify your employment).

Reasons for Leaving

By far the most important lines on an interview application are the reason for leaving each past job, or motivation for change. This factor, more than any other, reveals your values and goals. It serves as the link in your career progression. The best reason for leaving centers around circumstances out of your control. For example, layoffs and corporate relocations are neutral reasons over which you have no say. When you leave a position for your own personal reasons, however, the way to address this issue when filling out an application becomes significant.

One of the most popular answers I see as a corporate recruiter today is "no room for growth." When I ask candidates about this response, many seem to take pride in the fact that they've outgrown their positions or companies. People wear this response like a badge proving the growth and personal development they've undergone. They couldn't be more off the mark! No room for growth, from an employer's perspective, translates into bored, tired, and uninterested. Growth is one of those funny words that scares most employers. You need to realize that most companies will try to promote people up through the ranks, at least within the field of office administration, for two reasons: first, it's wonderful for employee morale because everyone sees that the organization recognizes individual accomplishments; second, it's much cheaper than hiring people from the outside! (Cost-per-hire for a promotion is zero. A new position will then be open at a lower level in the organization, that will be less expensive to fill.) No room for growth, consequently, needs to be replaced with a more convincing answer.

When constructing a reason for leaving, follow these two rules:

1. Make it a positive statement.
2. Focus it on the future rather than on the past.

Using these rules, "no room for growth" should be changed to "room for growth" because it's positive and geared toward the future. Still, it uses the no-no word *growth*, which means a lot of different things to different people. Growth may be vertical growth up the corporate ladder and out of administration. It may mean horizontal growth where you're allowed to assume greater responsibilities on your present job. It may mean increased base compensation and benefit perks. Ask yourself, therefore, what growth means to you. Rephrase your reason for leaving accordingly:

- Desire for increased responsibilities and a heavier workload
- Want to work in a more corporate, less entrepreneurial environment
- Prefer a one-on-one reporting relationship with a key executive officer
- Desire a larger company with a full benefits package

By stating a reason for leaving in a positive, future tense, the employer reading the application isn't forced to listen to sour grapes about your past job. "No room for growth," "personality conflict with manager," "not enough money," and "not enough work to keep me busy" are weak reasons that force you to place blame on a past employer. The interviewer cannot do anything with regard to your past problems.

On the other hand, if you're looking for a position with greater responsibilities, a heavier workload, or a larger company with a full benefits package, the employer can think to herself, "We can offer this candidate increased responsibilities and a more varied workload than he's been getting at his present job. If we hire him, his goals will be met by our company's programs." When you phrase your reason for leaving as a future goal, therefore, it has much greater application to the interview process. (Interviews, remember, are meant to determine what type of future impact you'll make on the company.)

The Most Important Questions to Ask—and Not to Ask— Human Resources Practitioners During an Interview

One of the most overlooked areas in interview preparation is determining which questions to ask employers during the meeting. Some candidates mistakenly ask selfish, what's-in-it-for-me questions about salary, benefits, vacation policies, or promotability out of the job that they haven't even landed yet. Others use filler questions about when the company was founded or how many employees there are. (These queries show no insight or depth. A brief trip to the library could have answered those questions!) Worst of all, some applicants ask no questions at all, which tips the employer off that the candidate is either not interested in the job or not very sharp. (The employer's logic is, "You mean you want to work here for the next ten years, and you can't even think of one question to ask regarding the company or the nature of the position?") The purpose of asking questions is not only to gather information, but to reveal your analytical abilities and business knowledge. It's an opportunity for you to shine!

Here's a brief look at poor questions that can disqualify you early in the interview process as well as the five most important questions that will demonstrate your analytical skills and foresight.

Don'ts

A dangerous question is, *"Where does the job go from here?"* Candidates hoping to grow out of a position for which they're applying usually worry employers. Therefore, you should focus on the job at hand, not the illusory career path that this particular position might create. Note that it's possible to raise this question with line management later in the interviewing process, but it should be avoided with HR interviewers because they have no say over promoting you. Only your supervisor can do that.

A disastrous question bound to lessen your chances of landing the job is, *"How much is the position paying?"* There are a lot of internal company factors and external market factors that determine any new employee's beginning salary. (See Figure 6-4.) Let the line manager or department supervisor raise the issue of salary, probably on the second or third round of interviews. Don't raise questions before enough information has been uncovered to allow both parties to come to an informed decision.

An obvious exception occurs when you're interviewing for an ad-generated position. You needn't go through an entire interview with blinders on, hoping the salary is in your range. Most human resources practitioners will share with you right up front what the range is if it's less than what you were making on your last job. If you have reason to believe that a company may not be paying at least what you were making on your last position, it's acceptable to ask human resources, "I was making $46,500 on my last position. Is this position in that salary range?" Or, for example, "I was making $46,500 on my last position, and I'm considering positions in the $43,000 to $50,000 range. Is this job paying in that area?"

Do's

Employers will give as thorough and detailed a job description as possible during the interview. These descriptions will focus on the primary duties of the job. An insightful and analytical question could be, *"Thank you for explaining the primary duties of the job. Could you share with me some of the secondary responsibilities involved—things that may happen only once a quarter*

Figure 6-4. Factors that determine a new employee's starting salary.

I. Internal company policies

A. Compensation structures

Some companies pay "at market," meaning they aim to pay the same as their local competitors. Other companies pay above or below market depending on their name-brand recognition, their industry's appeal, or their market presence and reputation. (More "glamorous" industries like entertainment, public relations, and advertising often pay less than other industries because so many people want to get into those businesses regardless of pay.)

B. Company value of particular skills and/or backgrounds

Companies differ in how much they value certain technical skills, foreign language abilities, years of experience, or degrees. Remember that people tend to hire in their own image. For example, employers with a "pedigree" from a Top Ten MBA school or with *Fortune* 500 experience will often look for those same credentials in the staff they hire.

C. Candidate's current earnings

Your present salary (or ending salary on your last position), **more than anything else,** determines how much the company will offer you. Your current salary represents your market value—how much past employers value your worth, output, or productivity.

II. External market demands

A. Market demand for your position or title

The recession has whittled away many office managerial jobs because middle management was one of the first victims in the layoff squeeze.

B. Market demand for your particular skills

For example, in some cities, Mac secretaries are paid more than IBM PC secretaries because there are fewer Mac people around. That scarcity translates into higher wages. In other cities, however, employers reason that there are fewer companies that use Mac, so the market value of Mac experts goes down. It's a simple supply-and-demand issue.

---

or twice a year?" The question makes the employer surface the incidental tasks that create a more well-rounded picture of your job's overall scope. (Notice that this question comes directly off the T account prep sheet shown earlier in Figure 6-1.)

A trip to the library is invaluable in identifying technical facts about a company. Your goal during the interview, however, is to identify the *emotional* aspects of the company. For example, *"How would you, Ms. Employer, describe the corporate culture of your organization?"* or *"What would you say is the personality of the department where I would be working?"* Corporate personality questions provide insights into the organization's pace (moderate and predictable versus hectic and volatile, proactive planning versus management by crisis), its work style (employees may be expected to work through their breaks and lunch hours and perform unlimited, unpaid overtime), and its communication philosophy (authoritarian decision making from above versus participative input and consensus decision making).

Under certain circumstances you might ask, *"If you don't mind my asking, how long have you been with the firm, Mr. Employer, and what initially attracted you to the company?"* This question can serve as a wonderful bonding opportunity. First of all, it allows you to interview the interviewer and gauge that individual's interest level in the company. Second, it permits employers to share insights about themselves. (Most people enjoy talking about themselves to a point.)

Beware, however, that certain employers believe that interviews are unilateral, fact-finding missions where the goal is to uncover as much as possible about the interviewee while revealing little about themselves. These types of interviewers would probably respond to this personal question with a curt "I'm sorry, but I really don't feel that my particular history with this company has any bearing on this meeting." That response would certainly cool down what might otherwise be a hot relationship, so ask this personal question only of interviewers who you're sure would welcome it.

Another question that will allow you to remind human resources interviewers about the research you've done prior to the meeting is, *"Ms. Employer, I've been to the library to research your company, and I'm aware of your excellent reputation. But, in your opinion, what two or three things make your company unique? What factors account for your company's success?"* It's always best to hear that answer from an insider. (Research does have its limitations!) Again, you're putting the employer in a position where she has to sell her company, and employers may not be used to that, so you may sense some discomfort. However, it's an exemplary question, and you're by no means overstepping your bounds by asking the question because it challenges in a positive manner.

Salary Issues and Company Pay Structures

Remember, salary negotiations don't belong in the HR screening interview. However, salary discussions will almost always surface because the human resources interviewer needs to ensure that you would accept an offer in a particular salary range. For instance, the interviewer might say, "The salary range for this job is $32,000–$36,000. Does that meet your specifications?"

Therefore, the strategy for addressing salary issues is to ensure that the salary range is appropriate. Sell human resources, instead, on your commitment to making a long-term contribution to the organization. *Always put the opportunity above the salary.* For example,

> Ms. Employer, I'd obviously like to make as much money as possible, but the most important thing to me by far is to find a challenging opportunity in a strong company where I can make a long-term contribution.

This type of response is a very logical and safe first line of defense.

Human resources knows how much you're earning because it's clearly stated on the application, and it's easily verified on a reference check. (*Never* fudge about your present salary: That's a rookie mistake that could ruin your reputation. Lying about your base salary will make them think you're capable of embezzling money from the vault!) If what you were making on your last job is lateral to or 10 to 20 percent less than what the present position is paying, then you're officially within the salary range. If, for example, you're earning $30,000 on your present job and are interviewing for a position paying $32,000 to $36,000, then you fall safely into the 10 percent interval. Ten percent more than $30,000 is $33,000, which lies in the $32,000 to $36,000 range. (See Figure 6-5 on page 142.)

Company pay structures or pay grades are usually plotted with a minimum, midpoint, and maximum dollar amount. Companies typically prefer to bring new people aboard at the midpoint of the range so that there is room for salary increases as the employee becomes more effective on the job.

If you tell human resources in the first interview that you'll accept a $30,000 lateral salary, you may be harming your chances of landing the job at $32,000 (the low point on the actual salary curve). If, on the other hand, you specify that you need $36,000 to accept the job (thereby awarding yourself a 20 percent increase over your present salary), you'll lose ground to equally experienced and skilled competitors with lower salary demands.

You'll often not know the salary range for a given position. There's nothing wrong with asking human resources for the position's salary

Figure 6-5. The 10 percent increase rule of thumb.

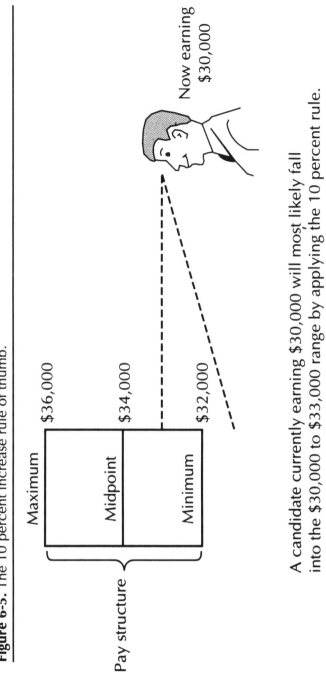

Maximum $36,000

Midpoint $34,000

Minimum $32,000

Pay structure

Now earning $30,000

A candidate currently earning $30,000 will most likely fall into the $30,000 to $33,000 range by applying the 10 percent rule.

curve. It's usually best to explain that you're flexible for the right opportunity, and at this point, do not wish to tackle salary issues until the entire position and compensation package can be explored further.

Remember from Figure 6-4 that more than anything else, your current salary determines the offer to be made. That's the nature of a free market economy. Candidates earning $30,000 currently may feel that they're technically or experientially qualified for a $50,000 job, but no employer would need to give a $30,000 administrator a $20,000 raise because the product can be bought for less. There are exceptions: for example, if a candidate relocates from Tontitown, Arkansas, to Manhattan. Different regional markets vary their pay scales according to their respective costs of living.

The moral of the story is: Don't say anything to human resources during the first interview regarding salary that can knock you out of the running. If you commit to a low dollar figure with human resources, it becomes etched in stone. If you name a dollar figure that is too high, you won't be referred to the department because you're too expensive and your expectations are unrealistic. If you state, "I'm currently making $30,000, and the most important thing for my career right now is to get in with a solid company where I can make a home for myself, and I'll let the salary issue take care of itself once we've had the opportunity to explore each other's merits more thoroughly," you're bound to safely get past the HR screener.

If human resources pushes beyond that, however, and insists on a specific dollar commitment from you, then name one. It's no use to win the battle and lose the war by refusing to play the game.

> "Again, Mr. Employer, I hate to limit myself to a specific dollar figure this early in the interview process, but because it's important for you to gauge my salary expectations, I'll share with you that I'm interviewing in the $32,000 to $33,000 range right now."

The search industry has a name for a candidate's interest level in a particular position. The **interest-demand barometer** says that the more interested a person is in the job, the lower the salary requirements will be. The less interested someone is in a particular position, the higher the salary requirements will be. You'll have to gauge your own barometer on the spot if human resources insists on extracting a dollar commitment from you during the screening interview.

Remember to Ask for the Job!

Most candidates end an interview by thanking employers for their time and bidding them good day. That can't hurt, but it does nothing to further your candidacy. If you're interested in the job, ask for it! Let the interviewer know exactly how you feel. If an interviewer has trouble reading you, the interviewer will interpret that uncertainty against you.

I cannot overemphasize how important this has become since the recession of 1990 hit. The sheer number of job applicants responding to ads has changed the rules of the job-hunting game. As a recruiter, I always felt it was a shame when a qualified candidate who had had an otherwise great interview let the ball drop in the final moments of the meeting. You'd be surprised how often I heard feedback from employers who said, "I couldn't get a feel for her level of interest, so I assume she wasn't really motivated by what we had to offer." Following are examples of various styles that can be applied to close an interview. Remember that job scarcity translates into tougher competition and that your key interview strategy must be to *find ways to stand out from your peers.* If you're not interested in a job, tell your interviewer to have a nice day, then leave. If you really want it, though, try a variation on one of the following themes:

> Ms. Employer, before I leave, I just wanted to share with you that I'm really impressed with your organization. Judging from the people I've met and what you value in employees, I think I'd fit in very well. I hope you'll consider me because I'm very interested in the job.

> Ms. Employer, thank you for your time. I just want to let you know that I feel that I'm geared for progression in my career and think I can make the same contribution to your organization that I'm successfully making to my present employer. I really feel that I could make an immediate impact, and I'd love the opportunity to continue in the interview process.

> Mr. Employer, I've worked in the telecommunications industry for three years now. I would have a minimum learning curve if I were hired, and by lunchtime of my first day, I'm confident I'd be an up-and-running member of the team. I really would like to work here. I hope you'll consider me as a finalist for the position.

> Ms. Employer, I've researched your company, I'm aware of your excellent reputation, and I'd love to work for you not only because of the people I've met and the fact that the company is eight minutes from my front door, but because I'd love the name-brand recognition of being associated with such a prestigious law firm.

If you've closed correctly—sincerely and from the heart—the walls of the room should be reverberating with your parting words. Don't underestimate the desire factor. Selling what you want and how the position ties in to the rest of your life is a key indicator of your potential to contribute to the growth of the organization. Human resources needs to hear it. So does the line manager once you're invited to the second interview.

Chapter 7

On the Grill:
Meeting Smart in
Smart Meetings With Line
Management Decision Makers

Second interviews with line management share many of the same strategies you'll use while interviewing with human resources: Beware of trick questions, ask the employer high-gain questions to reveal your analytical abilities, and, by all means, close the meeting by asking for the job. However, I've found that a general rule of thumb in corporate America is that the higher up the ladder you go, the weaker the employer's formal interviewing skills. I make that point because HR people are trained to interview; line managers, on the other hand, do it only out of necessity, have probably had relatively little formal training in interviewing, and are sometimes more nervous than candidates because they're responsible for filling in the uncomfortable gaps of silence that can come up when unilaterally questioning someone. Therefore, you should prepare yourself for different types of questioning techniques from line management. Second interviews (second interviews, for our purposes, cover third, fourth, and fifth meetings with companies) are make-it-or-break-it meetings. Getting to this stage with the ultimate decision maker is the goal of the whole process.

Variations on interview questioning themes are plentiful. Some employers, however, will take a much more aggressive approach by literally challenging you to answer pressure questions. Pressure-cooker questions are meant to test your poise under fire. Remember that all employers have an inclination to hire in their own image. What may be perceived as a high-pressure query to some interviewers may appear as a perfectly natural question to others. Let's look at some of the more challenging interview questions in an effort to understand what employers hope to find out by asking them.

147

Interviewers' Three Basic Styles

Organizational and behavioral psychologists typically recognize three general business styles. First, there is the **CEO** style: type A personalities with marketing/sales, bottom-line approaches to the day-to-day vagaries of business life. Second, you'll find **analytical,** independent types (we often think of accountants and engineers) who prefer to work solo and who totally involve themselves in their work projects. Finally, **affiliative** types value people and interpersonal relationships over any task at hand. They focus on how others feel and are personally affected by business situations. Understanding which type of business personality you're dealing with will provide insights regarding the questioning style to expect and the types of answers to provide. Of course, these are broad categories, and many interviewers may not fit exclusively into any of them.

CEO Types Focus on the Bottom Line

As a generality, CEO types look for answers that show you have reduced costs for a past employer, saved time, or come up with an idea that increased revenues. CEOs look for concrete proof that you have a track record of improving the bottom line.

Analytical Types Value Independence

Analytical people, in comparison, often look for independence in the staff members they hire. The key to pressing their hot buttons lies in proving that you will respect their independence by assuming work for yourself. Revealing your penchant for functioning as an independent member of the team will fare best for you.

Affiliative Types Care About People

Finally, affiliators will always focus on the people factor involved in any situation. They ask questions regarding your perceptions of others, disappointments and surprises you've experienced that are linked to your relationships with fellow workers, and the like. Affiliators will give off a sincere, personal touch and try to break the ice as quickly as possible by making you feel relaxed in your interview.

Now let's look at some specific questions.

"Tell me about the last time you were angry on the job. Who caused your anger, and what did you do about it?"

Notice how this question focuses on your personal feelings and perceptions. It's a typical pressure-cooker question from an affiliative interviewer. In responding, remember that now is not the time for subjective evaluations. Any time that a personalized question presents itself, diffuse it with an objective response. For example,

> I almost never find myself in a situation where I'm very angry at others on the job. I do get angry with myself at times because I'm my own worst critic. I would say, however, that I can sometimes feel disappointed in others. I guess I expect everyone to have the same commitment to project completion and time management as I do, but that's not always the case.

"Tell me about your last performance appraisal. In which area were you most disappointed?"

Again, this is not an opportunity to justify past decisions and actions. Your past supervisor isn't present to give her side of the story, so anything you subjectively defend will be taken with a grain of salt (at best) and perceived as biased. Objectively evaluate your past performance in light of your strengths and weaknesses. For example,

> My only disappointment—"surprise" may be a better word— was that I received a "meets expectations" grade under the category "coordinated multiple tasks in an efficient and timely manner." I know that my boss realizes that I never let anything slip through the cracks. Our deadline schedules could get very hairy at times, and multiple task coordination was essential to complete the projects on time. I asked my boss why I didn't receive an "exceeds expectations" grade in that category, and she felt that we simply didn't have enough deadlines to necessitate giving a higher grade. Since all my other evaluations were top grade, I didn't question her call any further.

"If you were reporting to two or three bosses and they all wanted their work done immediately, how would you decide whose work needed to be done first?"

It's a very logical question from an analytical boss who wants her time guarded and who looks for logical precision in everything she does. The answer you give will reveal your time and stress management skills, priority-setting abilities, and the delicacy with which you handle interpersonal relationships. More importantly, this analytical interviewer will gain an important insight into how you'll involve her in the boss-sharing process. A strong approach to keep you in good stead with such an interviewer could be:

> Ms. Employer, I see my administrative assistant role as that of a buffer—someone who absorbs some of the shock that's part of every business day in an office. I never want to get my boss involved in areas of my own responsibility. I like running with the ball, and my references will vouch for my ability to get things done independently.
>
> If I had to make a decision on the spot to prioritize my workload, I'd first determine which tasks warranted top priority. I'd order the tasks according to urgency, set time estimates for completion of those tasks, and print out a brief agenda with my plan. I'd deliver the schedule to the three bosses that showed exactly when their particular tasks would be completed. Usually, I find that as long as people know when to expect their work completed, they're fine. If there was a problem at that point, that supervisor could make me aware of her problem, and I'd adjust it accordingly.

"What have you done on your present/past position to decrease costs or raise revenues for your department?"

This is an example of a CEO-style pressure-cooker question. Whether you're asked it or not, it's imperative that you formulate an answer to this question before meeting with any line manager, and somehow bring it up during your discussion.

Any employee in any company at any given time is paid to do one of three things:

1. Decrease costs and/or save time (for staff jobs like human resources, accounting, and administrative support functions).
2. Increase revenue (for line jobs like sales).
3. Make effective leadership decisions for that organization on a day-to-day basis in terms of providing direction to subordinates, delegating work, and achieving project completion goals.

CEOs love this question because it exposes your ability to improve the bottom line. Remember, proper self-marketing means selling yourself as a solution to a company's problems, and every company struggles with increasing top-line revenues and decreasing expenses. Acceptable answers consequently target examples where you've:

- Assisted in converting a manual accounts payable system to a computerized spreadsheet environment
- Created internal desktop publishing newsletters and flyers that formerly had to be expensed to outside vendors
- Revised a manual filing system so that files could be cross-referenced alphabetically and numerically and then purged after a certain period of time where no action was taken
- Added a response section to a marketing letter so that contributions could be made immediately

This type of insight, ingenuity, and know-how represents concrete evidence of your ability to positively impact an organization. It helps you reach your goal of making a company better by your having worked there.

"In retrospect, what have you done on a past job that you now consider somewhat irresponsible?"

Danger! Open mouth, insert foot. You can opt to pass on the question, but then you'd be perceived as less than honest. If you're truly an objective evaluator of your own strengths and weaknesses, you should be able to own up to mistakes you've made. On the other hand, no action should be so egregious as to knock you out of contention. It's best to cite situations where the foul-up can be considered a human oversight. You want the employer to walk away thinking, "Yes, I've done that myself a couple of times." Your strategy is simply to reveal that you're human. Don't damn yourself by surfacing a situation where you really made a seriously poor call that hurt your company (unless you believe that this information will immediately surface on a reference check; if this poor call was the reason you lost your last position, own up to it and explain it).

In addition, by no means should you blame someone else or put yourself above the problem. Here's an illustration:

> Mr. Employer, like everyone else, I'm sure I've had my moments. I wouldn't use the word *irresponsible* to describe my action because I take my work too seriously to grossly overlook anything. But there was one occasion when I forgot to follow up on a case that had been calendar-diaried for that day. We almost blew the statute of limitations because of my error. It was an honest oversight on my part. I owned up to it and apologized to my boss, and it never happened again.

An answer like this reveals your business maturity and ability to accept criticism. You've revealed your shortcomings but also displayed what you learned from the situation.

"With no undue flattery, if you will, grade me on how well I'm conducting this interview. Can you tell something about my management style on the basis of our meeting so far?"

Wow! Could you come up with a better question to gauge an individual's intuition and perception on the spot? What won't work here are flowery adjectives to describe the interviewer's nobler traits. That can seem insincere. Interviewees typically respond to this challenge in one of two ways, and body language tells it all. Some people jump back in their chairs, fold their hands, turn beet-red, and reply with a meek, "Well, how do you mean that?" (gulp!) Others lean forward in their chairs, their eyes open wide, and they smile and say,

> Well, your office is immaculate, so you're obviously a neat and organized person. Just asking a question like this indicates to me that you know exactly what you're looking for. You're very self-confident because you're not afraid to hear a rejection or some kind of critique. That leads me to believe that you're an open, honest communicator who respects other people's opinions without taking things too personally. How's that? Am I close?

Bravo! Guess who just got the job? It's a shocking question indeed, but those challenges are often the best opportunities to clinch an offer.

Holistic Interview Questions: Assessing How the Whole Person Fits Into the Organization

Exceptionally strong, well-trained interviewers ask **holistic questions** to gain an understanding of how you'll fit into the overall corporate plan. Holistic questions attempt to measure the whole person—an individual's work patterns, goals, and ability to see the whole picture and how they as individuals fit in. Holistic questions are usually very broad, open-ended queries that interviewees find difficult to define on the spot. However, they successfully measure people's broad perceptions of their self-worth, self-esteem, and potential abilities to contribute to the firm. (See Figure 7-1.)

Following are some of the more popular applications of holistic interviewing techniques. See how well you fare.

"What are the broad responsibilities of an executive administrative assistant?"

Figure 7-1. Line management's typical questioning barriers.

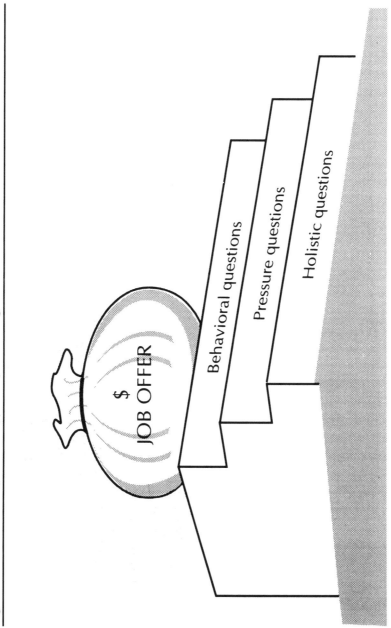

"Tell me how your function contributes to the overall picture."

In answering questions like this, recall that your interviewing goal is to present yourself on a problem-to-solution level. I've seen many a candidate begin to list generic duties like typing, answering phones, and filing—believe me, they gained no points with those answers! Merely recapping secretarial tasks reveals little about your ability to add value to an organization. Frame answers within a perspective of how successful administrative assistants keep the work flowing smoothly by keeping two steps ahead of projects, anticipating their boss's needs, and representing the corporation in the boss's absence. Prove your answer by citing examples of specific accomplishments that demonstrate how you've performed in the past. For example,

> The broad duties of an administrative assistant include lowering company costs by saving time, representing the firm in the boss's absence, and making decisions that further the company's interests. I've achieved these goals, Mr. Employer, by putting together correspondence with grammatical and contextual accuracy, by screening phone calls with a true customer service attitude, and doing anything else necessary in a basic office environment to keep my boss one step ahead of the game. I see the administrative assistant role as quasi-secretarial, quasi-administrative, and quasi-personal. All three areas have to be balanced daily to earn a boss's respect and confidence.

or:

> The broad responsibilities of an administrative executive secretary center around being a contributing member to the team. Whether your function in a company is sales and marketing, human resources, management information systems, or accounting, a key administrator keeps that department running smoothly and properly functioning as an independent part of the whole organization. I always tend to look beyond functional boundaries and envision the whole organizational picture. My goal is to keep my end operating smoothly so that the whole machine remains in sync. The administrative assistant function is the right hand to the executive who oversees either one functional area or multiple areas.

or:

Because my current job (as executive secretary to the vice-president of investor relations) entails such heavy word processing, its broad duties focus on heavy production work that saves my company money. My present boss doesn't rely on me for screening calls. I have an assistant who handles all the office filing. And my boss handles her own personal affairs. That leaves only one thing: production word processing. From the day I was hired, we agreed that I would be responsible for putting together mutual fund prospectuses, annual reports, and 10K filings. I work on a project-by-project basis and get a lot of satisfaction from developing a library of my work. It appears that the job I'm interviewing for now is similar in terms of day-to-day output. So even though I'm not describing the typical broad responsibilities of a generic administrative assistant, these are the realities and expectations of my particular kind of support work.

"Describe how your job relates to the overall goals of your department or company."

My last two jobs have been one-on-one reporting relationships to vice-presidents of sales. In a sales and marketing environment, every member of the department is responsible for generating revenue. The account executives develop business by telemarketing and door-to-door solicitation. My boss's neck is on the line to ensure that the AEs are meeting their numbers. And my role is to ensure that anyone who needs to speak with my boss—our customers are the brokers and agents who market our products—gets timely follow-up and courteous customer service. No matter how much advertising and goodwill a company develops, the customer bond is only as strong as the individual relationships we foster. I've defused many an upset customer and helped to retain accounts that might otherwise have been lost.

or:

After six years working in treasury and accounting, I've been trained to spot areas in which costs could be cut. My boss had the responsibility to keep our company's balance sheet healthy. On a micro level, I accepted that same challenge for our department. For example, I suggested that our department replace fax cover sheets with one-inch Post-it brand notes that could be attached directly to the document's first page. That saved one page of fax paper for every document that we telecopied. Also, when a file needed to be transferred to our in-house counsel, we traditionally used two separate half-page forms for transfer. I combined the forms onto one page, and I saved our organization an estimated $800 on paper costs per year. Learning how to reduce costs is something my bosses really appreciated in a finance environment.

or:

My job related to the overall goals of the company in that my boss, as head of a record label, *was* the company. Everything I did for her affected the deals we were working on, the business relationships we were fostering, and the bottom line. For example, I had to know everyone in the music industry to do my job well. My boss was known for long telephone conversations, and rather than keeping people on hold, I was expected to keep them talking by asking about family members, business trips, and the like. I also had to know when to interrupt my boss for an important call and when to get a caller off the line diplomatically. I was responsible as well for contacting all our department heads to collect report information and schedule board conferences. In short, I kept my boss organized and aided her in maximizing her time management.

"What aspects of your job do you consider most crucial?"

Any employee in any organization is responsible for saving money or increasing revenue. My job was to support the senior vice-president of finance, so as an executive secretary, I focused on decreasing department costs. One way I cut costs was to virtually eliminate rework. Nothing ever crossed my desk twice because of mistakes, and I read each piece of paper only once before taking action. I never kept an in-basket where paperwork piled up. That kind of inefficiency goes against my grain. I also saved time by guarding the gate—I screened stockbrokers', insurance agents', and executive recruiters' calls very heavily. Not that I overscreened potential business relationships, but my boss expected me to save him time by taking accurate messages and giving him the option of returning those calls. Therefore, I would say that the most crucial aspect of my job was enhancing my boss's efficiency by keeping the work flowing smoothly and properly screening unsolicited calls.

or:

Executives and board members are very busy people. Providing individual support to the CEO and president of a $500 million company with six subsidiaries and 2,200 employees had its unique challenges. What really made the job interesting was that the CEO was heavily involved in community and political affairs. She also asked me to coordinate her personal affairs for six properties that she owned and rented on the side. I'm proud to say that I was almost as busy as my boss was! And I've really mastered the art of juggling multiple tasks and setting priorities. Those are the two most crucial aspects of an executive administrator's job.

"In hindsight, how could you have improved your performance?"

In my opinion, secretaries today are vital members of every management team, so they should be responsible for speaking the language of business. I could have improved my past performance if I had had a greater understanding of financial statement analysis and the basics of balance sheets and income statements. That would have allowed me to interpret my past companies' financial signs better and have a greater understanding of how my department contributed to the overall picture. I'm planning on enrolling in a fundamentals of finance course as soon as possible.

or:

Well, I hate to say it, but I've never been particularly fond of filing. There were always so many more important things to do that the idea of filing conjured up images of my mother telling me to clean up my room. It's probably not a major professional shortcoming, but it is something that obviously could have improved my general performance. [Naturally, don't use this kind of answer if filing constitutes a large proportion of the job for which you're interviewing!]

"How many hours a week do you find it necessary to work to get your job done?"

This is obviously a critical question revolving around the hidden agenda of the organization's corporate culture. If these folks work 8:00 A.M. to 8:00 P.M., and you happen to pride yourself on completing your daily tasks by 4:59 P.M., you can bet this won't be a match made in heaven. If you're at a stage in your life where you're not willing to work sixteen-hour days, explain your intentions to leave daily at 5:00 P.M. sharp unless you're needed for a specific project or deadline. In that case, you wouldn't want a job with excessive hours, so you would have nothing to lose if your answer disqualified you.

On the other hand, if the company is known for its Saturday office hours and you want to get into the company at all costs, share your understanding of that practice and sell the fact that you'll do whatever it takes to get the job done. What if you don't know the schedule that this executive or department works? Then you should open it up for discussion:

> Ms. Employer, I've worked jobs that required unlimited time commitments on an ongoing basis, and I've worked for companies that looked down on anyone working beyond normal business hours. I'm capable of excelling in either type of environment. Which style are you envisioning for this job?

You've bought yourself some time with that response. You can now take an offensive position to a question that was meant to throw you into a defensive mode. Answer the question as you see fit for your own needs and expectations.

"What area of your skills do you want to improve upon in the next year?"

Short-term, tactical goals keep people balanced and focused on their present needs. Long-term, strategic goals, in contrast, make up a vision of achievement and a framework of purpose in one's life. A very acceptable answer to a short-term query can easily focus on technical skills, since all employees can bone up on some aspect of their technical abilities. For example:

> My people skills and communication skills are very strong. If I had to choose one area in which I could improve my skills, it would be in my mastery of database management systems. I'm an excellent word processor on WordPerfect and Microsoft Word for Windows. My spreadsheet expertise includes Excel for Windows, Lotus, and Quattro Pro. I've even mastered Ventura Publisher and Pagemaker desktop publishing softwares. But I've rarely had to use relational databases in my work. I'd like to focus, therefore, on mastering Q&A or Paradox or dBase IV. It's the only exposed area in my PC arsenal.

or:

> I would guess that my Gregg shorthand has gotten a little rusty. I tested at 90 words per minute at an employment agency recently, but I was at 120 words per minute when I left the Katharine Gibbs secretarial school. It probably wouldn't take too long to get back up there. I would just need to make the time to practice.

Hypothetical Interview Questions:
Weak Indicators of a Candidate's Potential

Interviewers sometimes ask **hypothetical questions,** or "what would you do if" questions. These are limiting because they only test candidates' abilities to theorize about their potential future performance. There's no guarantee that the performance would really come out that way. Besides, most interviewees naturally put themselves in the best light possible to impress the employer. So hypothetical questions often lead to exaggeration.

Behavioral Interview Questions:
Projecting Potential From Past Performance

To counteract this tendency toward hyperbole, behavioral psychologists and interview theorists developed **behavioral interview questions,** which attempt to relate your answers to specific past experiences. The past experiences reveal how you indeed acted in a specific past situation, and are therefore much more reliable indicators of how you'll act in the future. Behavioral interview questions do not deny that people can learn from their mistakes and alter their behaviors, but they assume that your future behavior will be closely reflected by your past actions.

Behavioral interview questions probe both past and present situations and call for on-the-spot self-analysis. There are two main types of behavioral questions: self-appraisal and situational questions. **Self-appraisal queries** ask, "What is it about you that makes you feel a certain way or makes you want to do something?" For example, "What is it about you that makes you get totally involved in your work to the point where you lose track of the time?" Similarly, the self-appraisal format may ask for a third-party validation of your actions: "What would your supervisor say about that?"

Other examples of self-appraisal queries include:

"On a scale of 1 to 10, how do you see yourself as a supervisor? Why?"

"If you had the choice of working in a marketing environment or a finance environment, which would you choose and why?"

"In the future, how do you think you would handle an employee termination in those same circumstances?"

Situational queries, like self-appraisal queries, look for concrete experiences as an indicator of future behavior. The typical behavioral interview questioning format begins with the paradigm, *"Give me an example of a time when you acted in your boss's absence,"* or *"Tell me about a circumstance in which you assumed responsibility for a task that was clearly outside of your job description."* Notice the specific linkage to past concrete experiences and situations.

The beauty of this questioning methodology as far as interviewers are concerned is that its applications are limitless. It can be applied to anything: your greatest strengths and weaknesses, your supervisory style, your communication skills, or the last time you fired someone.

Behavioral queries ensure spontaneity since you, the job candidate, can't prepare for them in advance. Rehearsed answers to traditional interview questions go by the wayside in this ad hoc environment. Even though every question within this format cannot possibly be anticipated and formulated, it's worth your time to explore some of the more common applications. Watch where behavioral interview questions lead this conversation.

Employer: Tell me about your greatest weakness.

Candidate: My greatest weakness probably lies in delegating work to others. Sure, I trust other people to do excellent work on their own. It's just that with especially important projects, I feel that I'd better do them myself to make sure they get done the way I like.

Employer: I see. *Give me an example of a time when* your not wanting to delegate work to someone else left you in a bind because you had to do other people's work to meet a deadline.

Candidate: Well, there was a time when I had to stay in the office till 7:00 P.M. one night to get out a proposal for a consulting bid due the next morning. It was a rather frustrating experience because I had another obligation that night, but it was just too important to leave to someone else.

Employer: How did you handle that type of situation the next time it happened? Could you have done anything differently in retrospect to have delegated that work to someone else? What is it about you that drives you to work so hard?

Figure 7-2. The unpredictable course of behavioral interview questioning.

" **Tell me about a time when you** . . . felt it important to take it upon yourself to bring bad news to your boss."

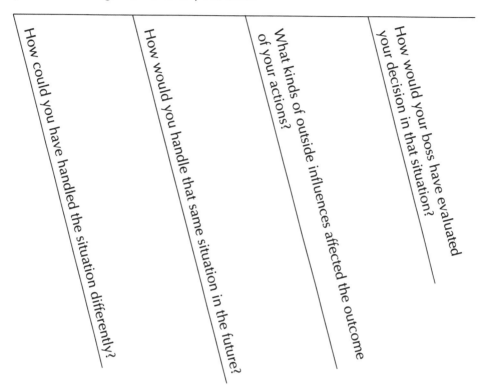

Following are other optional questions the interviewer might choose in this particular questioning scenario:

> *"Tell me about an experience you had in which* this inability to delegate work to others possibly left one of your subordinates feeling frustrated that he or she wasn't allowed to get deeper into a project or assume more responsibilities working for you."
>
> *"Tell me about the last time you* reached the boiling point in terms of handling everything yourself."
>
> "What type of mentoring style do you have? Do you see yourself as a delegator if you believe it could lead to a subordinate's growth?"

You can see that, depending on your responses to the initial behavioral question, an interviewer has a lot of directions to pursue. If you diagramed the behavioral interview question and its potential outcomes, it would look something like Figure 7-2.

The exercise isn't meant to overwhelm you. It is meant, however, to illustrate where the most sophisticated interviewers can lead you. Universities across the nation and independent management training seminars are teaching employers to measure individuals by their responses to behavioral questioning techniques. The questioning formats are both sequential and logical. They test your ability to account for the ramifications of your actions. They can also reveal discrepancies in your answers.

Again, the point isn't so much that you can prepare to answer the myriad variations that develop from behavioral questions. It is instead important to realize what the interviewer is evaluating when taking you through these exercises. Behavioral questions can be lots of fun because they make the meeting a challenge. If you've really got a sharp employer weaving you in and out of your past actions to gain insights into your future performance, rise to the occasion! You've got an excellent boss on the line who may be a valuable mentor in your career.

Those Awful Generic Interview Questions

I don't know what else to call them. These are the ones that register more in your stomach than in your head. Actually, they can be fun too. No interview preparation for a final meeting is complete without them. These questions are challenging because they're hard to put your hands around. Think about how you would answer them before reading the example responses.

> *"Why do you want to work here?"*

> Well, I really need a job so that my mortgage doesn't go into foreclosure, and you're the closest I've gotten to being hired in the last thirty-seven interviews!

Perhaps that has a little bit of truth in it, but it's not likely to catapult your career to new heights! By the time you've gotten to the final stage of the interview (whether this is a second, third, or fourth meeting), you're expected to know why you want to become part of the organization's assets. If an untrained interviewer blurts out a generic question like this one, your best strategy is to link your desire to become part of the organization to one of three things:

1. *The company:* its reputation as a quality employer, its high-profile brand-name recognition, or the fact that it's expanding rapidly and offers a ground-floor opportunity to help the company grow.

2. *The position:* its variety, challenge, pace, reporting relationship, or scope of authority.
3. *The people:* everyone you've met is so likeable; you feel you fit in, could be a member of the team, and would feel appreciated and recognized for your contributions.

Compliment any of these three things, and you're complimenting the company and its people. It's always best to focus on what you could do for the company, and not what the company could do for you. (Forgive me for paraphrasing John F. Kennedy's words.) Don't state that you want to work somewhere because the benefits are superior, the pay is above market, or the opportunities for growth are excellent in the company. Benefit packages change. If you're solely motivated by money, the employer may view you as recruiter's bait, staying only until a higher-paying job surfaces. And again, if you make the mistake of appearing eager for growth potential before you're even hired for the job at hand, shame on you! You know better than that, having read this far in this book!

"What do you know about our company? Tell me about your understanding of the job you're applying for."

(*Gulp!*) Trying to answer this one in thirty seconds or less can be harrowing. Instead of attempting to regurgitate everything you've learned through library research and the six people you've interviewed with before getting to this last meeting, smile, relax, and say, "I'd love to answer that question. Would you mind if I looked at my notes?" (T account prep to the rescue! Refer back to Figure 6-1 on page 125.) The T account is all laid out on one neat page with company information on the left and job information on the right. Account for the highlights in both categories enough to give the employer the sense that you have total mastery of the company's function and the job's primary and secondary duties. Watch how smoothly this answer rolls:

Well, Ms. Employer, I know that your *company* is one of the largest property and casualty reinsurance companies in North America. You're based here in Chicago with about 7,000 employees worldwide, and your annual revenues are about $800 million. You enjoy a reputation for reinsuring or spreading the financial risk of six of the ten largest U.S. insurance companies, and from an article I located in the *Wall Street Journal,* you project your market share to grow by 2 percent per year over the next three years.

The job is *titled* executive secretary *reporting to* you, the president and chief operating officer. I realize that this is an IBM

WordPerfect and Lotus environment in which I'm totally fluent. The *primary duties* of the job include taking shorthand minutes at board meetings, keeping your schedule balanced, and double-booking your travel arrangements on the corporate jet with a commercial airlines back-up. Is that a fairly accurate overview?

The italicized responses come straight off the T account outline. It allows you to manage this somewhat cumbersome question easily.

"What can you do for us if we hire you?"

Remember that you're probably talking to the CEO type now. Line managers wield this question to gain positive, concrete reasons why hiring you will make the company a better place. We've already covered this answer in an earlier chapter in terms of linking your achievements to decreased costs, saved time, increased revenues, or your effective decision-making abilities. Realize again, however, that even if this question per se isn't asked, you've got to have an answer to it that you somehow bring up in the meeting.

Responses to Illegal Interview Questions

Most interviewers who ask illegal questions don't deliberately set out to break the law. To understand this, it helps to see how businesses often develop from sole proprietorships into large companies.

The typical life cycle of a business begins with an individual or small group of founders with a product or service that is aggressively marketed and that produces adequate sales revenues to sustain growth. Expenses are kept to a minimum because they typically come out of the owners' personal checking accounts. Each employee is a factotum, doing everything from answering the phone to licking envelopes to closing big deals. The environment is entrepreneurial and fluid in terms of an employee's responsibilities; there are no departmental boxes or definitive specifications that limit an individual's role to that of a specialist.

As the business matures and employees are added to staff, company founders typically layer on a bureaucracy to protect themselves from legal exposure and to bridge the gap between executive-level management and the operational employees. Human resources departments, for example, set up formal equal opportunity guidelines, develop equitable compensation practices, and train internal management in the do's and don'ts of pre-employment interview inquiries.

You'll rarely encounter an HR interviewer who asks questions that blatantly transgress the guidelines established by the Equal Employment

Opportunity Commission or the Department of Fair Employment and Housing. The founders and line managers, on the other hand, may have assumptions more like, "It's my company, and I'll say who's to be hired and for what reasons." Unfortunately, this mentality can sometimes circumvent laws meant to bar various forms of discrimination. Again, the higher up you go in the interviewing process, the more all bets are off in terms of what can be asked or suggested during an interview.

Let's briefly take a look at some of the more common unacceptable pre-employment inquiries that are floating around out there, and then strategize how to field them.

1. It is not acceptable for a company or interviewer to ask you for your maiden name. That can discriminate against marital status. It is okay, on the other hand, for an interviewer to question whether there is additional information concerning a name change in the past (not necessarily due to marriage) that will allow the company to verify your past work experience and education.

2. Companies may not ask your age, birthdate, or dates of elementary or high school attendance. The Age Discrimination in Employment Act of 1967 protects workers from forty to seventy years old. It promotes the employment of older persons based upon their abilities rather than their age. There's no problem listing the year of college graduation because people can graduate from college at any time in their lives, so there's no way to figure out the person's age. But nearly all high schoolers graduate at age 17 or 18, so an individual's date of birth can readily be determined by subtracting 18 from the year of graduation.

A special note of interest: Many employment applications ask for the month and day of birth. Many candidates erroneously list their year of birth out of habit. Don't make that mistake! It works against you in two ways: first, it reveals that you show little attention to following written directions, and second, it puts the company representative in an embarrassing position because that person is not supposed to know your age before you get hired. Out comes the white-out to remove the information as the employer attempts to protect himself from a possible age discrimination claim later down the road.

3. Birthplace and citizenship inquiries may not be asked. For example:

"Are you a U.S. citizen?"
"What is your mother tongue?"
"How did you acquire your ability to speak a certain language?"

These questions transgress the guidelines regarding national origin and birthplace/citizenship. Company representatives should instead ask,

"Can you, after employment, submit verification of your legal right to work in the United States?"

   4. Companies may not ask about marital status or family issues.

"Can you make adequate provisions for child care?"
"Do you live with your parents?"
"Is pregnancy a part of your personal plans for the near future?"

Whoops! A big no-no on the company's part. It's a legitimate concern to wonder whether a potential employee can meet overtime demands or report to work on time. As much as CEO and line types want to cut to the chase and get straight to the point, they are limited by law to stating such facts as the hours, any overtime demands, and company travel expectations and simply asking whether you would have any reason why you couldn't meet those requirements.

   5. Photographs may not be attached to applications. Questions regarding a candidate's height and weight are unacceptable except where those factors are proven to be bona fide occupational qualifications. A photograph may be required after employment for a company badge, but not before an offer is extended.

   6. Questions about your religion are illegal. It's okay if the employer states that weekend and holiday work is required. The employer may then ask whether this is acceptable to you as a condition of employment. Asking whether your religion prevents you from working on weekends obviously discriminates on the basis of religious affiliation.

   7. Companies may not ask whether you are disabled. The Americans with Disabilities Act (ADA) of 1992 requires businesses to make their facilities accessible to the mentally and physically disabled and prohibits job discrimination on the basis of disability. The ADA says that a company can't exclude a qualified person from a job if that individual can perform the job's "essential functions," either unaided or with a "reasonable accommodation." The terms in quotation marks are, of course, subject to legal interpretation. You should know, though, that a company may not ask:

"Do you have any disabilities?"
"Are you currently receiving workers compensation payments?"
"Do you have any previous major medical problems?"

Company representatives should instead ask whether you are capable of performing the position's essential job functions, which should be typically mapped out in a written job description.

   8. Asking whether you have ever been arrested is unacceptable. Employers may ask if you have ever been convicted of a felony, but this question must typically be accompanied by a statement that a conviction will not necessarily disqualify you from consideration for a job. If you're wondering what the difference is between being arrested and being convicted of a felony, it's that a felony record may legitimately disqualify you for certain types of jobs. Merely having been arrested, however, tends to discriminate against inner-city, poorer residents who may be arrested because of association—being at the wrong place at the wrong time. Besides, people may be arrested for misdemeanors (like smoking marijuana at a Saturday night party) that may have little bearing on the workplace. They may also be arrested and later found innocent.

9. *Military service questions must be limited to relevant skills acquired during service.* It is unacceptable for an employer to ask you the dates of service or type of discharge.

10. *Questions about your credit rating, economic status, bankruptcy, or garnishment history are not allowable during the interview.* There are no acceptable alternative questions that allow employers to address these issues before the hire.

Employers are perfectly within their rights, however, to make employment offers contingent upon credit checks. After an offer is extended, you may be asked to sign a clearance that allows the prospective employer to gain information regarding your:

- Mortgage payment history
- Bankruptcy history
- Credit limits
- Pending lawsuits
- Personal loans
- Foreclosures and repossessions

By signing, you agree that the credit information constitutes a condition of employment.

Historically, companies performed credit history checks only on employees directly involved in cash handling. Nowadays the use of a credit check as an employment screening tool has been expanded to cover many professional hires and yes, even administrative support hires. Apparently, the belief is that your spending and saving patterns as well as your ability to manage your own personal affairs are indicators of your character. Agree or not, a poor credit report can function as a negative swing factor in the final decision. As of this writing, we're seeing more and more credit verifications and urinalysis drug screenings in the post-offer screening stage. The tendency throughout the 1990s will be an increase in the various screening tools in the employer's recruitment and selection arsenal.

11. A prospective employer may ask you to list someone to be notified in an emergency, but not the nearest relative to be contacted. Obviously, that could border on discrimination by national origin, race, or marital status.

Well, this is interesting information, but what do you do with it? As the saying goes, somewhere between the theory and the practice falls the shadow. You can count on this shadow rising up at some point in a meeting with first-line management. How you handle the query will obviously depend on the vibes you're getting: Is the employer asking out of ignorance of the law or is she a bigot? Do you want to correct the employer by explaining the rules of interviewing? Or do you want to simply answer the question by promising yourself to forget it was ever asked? (If you make believe that the question was never asked, however, you may be establishing a precedent that will be difficult to change in the future.)

Each instance will have to be judged on its own merit. One polite response to such a question might be, "With all due respect, I'd like to pass on that question because I feel it would compromise my candidacy and past achievements." If the interviewer still looks perplexed, you might continue, "With all due respect, Ms. Employer, although I'm no expert in labor law, I feel that question may be delving too deeply into an issue that isn't really a factor in the pre-employment screening process."

As with most things in life, it's not what you say, but how you say it. You'll fare best by assuming that the interviewer is simply unaware that the question is out of line. Embarrassing employers by instructing them on the fine points of interviewing will most likely make them feel uncomfortable enough to not want to pursue you any further. Let your intuition be your guide.

Questions to Ask Employers on a Final Interview

The beauty of the questions we asked human resources earlier is that they were all subjective, opinion-type questions. Therefore, they can all be used again:

> "What two or three criteria make someone successful in your organization or department?"
>
> "How do you describe the corporate culture or personality of ABC Company?"
>
> "What would you add to the background or skills of the last person who held the job that could have made that person more effective?"

> "If you could choose three adjectives to describe the personality of the ideal candidate, what would they be?"

Employers don't compare notes and ask each other what questions particular candidates asked. Even if they did, these opinion questions would yield different answers under different circumstances, so they may be asked over and over again.

Other questions that reveal your depth of intellect and business savvy include:

> "What short-term plans has the organization developed to compensate for the more challenging business environment?"
>
> "What other industries or outside influences have a direct impact on your company's operations?"
>
> "Do you feel that, as a whole, employees are encouraged to assume responsibilities beyond their written job descriptions or to adhere strictly to defined duties?"

Although it's typically not advisable to bring up growth opportunities beyond the job you're applying for, if the company intimated in its recruitment process (whether in an ad or through a contingency recruiter) that the position has definite growth potential, ask,

> Because your ad clearly emphasized that you want this position to lead to greater responsibilities, I'd like to know in what time frame you'd like the candidate to master the job at hand. Also, what criteria will you use to measure that achievement? Finally, what will an employee need to accomplish to move on to the next stage of responsibility?

How to Find a Really Good Boss

Before we leave the topic of questions to ask the potential employer during the final rounds of interview, let's discuss questions that you could ask to get a realistic look at what it would be like to work with this supervisor on a day-to-day basis. Be careful, though; you don't want to insult anyone. But if you phrase the question tactfully and ask it with an inquisitive smile, you'll be surprised what you can learn about the other person.

Lead into your conversation like this: "Mary Jo, no one you've hired in the past may have asked you these questions, but I feel very comfortable with you and I'm obviously looking to make a long-term commitment to you as my boss. Let me ask you:

- What is it like working for you? What should I expect on a day-to-day basis?
- What kind of mentoring and training style do you have? Do you naturally delegate responsibilities or is that difficult for you?
- In what area do you have the least amount of patience?
- How do you approach your work and balance your career with your personal life?"

You'll certainly stand out among other applicants. In addition, you will have armed yourself with critical information that will help you determine the outcome of this job search venture should you ultimately be offered the position.

Don't Forget to Ask for the Job!

The meeting is ending, and it's time to make that powerful close again. You're right: We've seen this before in Chapter 6 when we were discussing interviewing with the folks in human resources. However, this close is a lot more important! You know that your first close worked with HR—that's how you got passed on to this final interview round.

But remember how we said that once you've met the basic qualifications of the job, 70 percent of the hire is based on a personality match, a meeting of the minds, so to speak? The opportunity now to ask enthusiastically for the job and share with the employer that you want to become a contributing member of the team helps lock in that feeling of camaraderie.

I once received a phone call from an employer after final rounds of what had been an intensely competitive search. The interviewer was 99 percent sure she was going to hire candidate 3 and almost cancelled the meeting with candidate 4. The client ended up keeping the meeting with candidate 4, but only because it was too late to change it. Here's the twist: The follow-up phone call I got from the client sounded like this:

> Paul, you're not going to believe what I'm going to tell you. I know I was dead-set on hiring Julie, but I really think that Shannon has her beat. I was expecting to give Shannon a courtesy interview, but she absolutely wowed me! The more I listened to her, the more I related to everything she had to say. And did she convince me to hire her! She researched our company, she complimented us on our reputation, and she said she'd mesh perfectly into our corporate culture. She was so sincerely excited about the whole thing that I got motivated by the meeting! I can't remember the last time that happened.

Once you've reached this stage of the interview process the hire is primarily based upon *personality match* at the office administrator level. Let your personality come shining through in those final moments of the meeting.

With these powerful interviewing tools in hand, you can move on to Chapter 8, where we'll look at postinterview follow-up techniques. These are more important than you may think.

Chapter 8

Creatively Staying in Touch: Post-Interview Follow-Up Techniques

Before we jump into the final stages of evaluating company benefit plans and weighing the strengths versus the weaknesses of the job opportunity, it's time to examine one more critical aspect of the employment process: creatively staying in touch with the company after your interview. You've got two strategies in this case:

1. *Thank-you notes,* the best way to remind your interviewers who you are and what you could do for them.
2. *Creative follow-up agendas,* useful after you've interviewed with a company on an exploratory basis where no real opening existed at the time of your interview.

Make Your Thank-You Notes Work for You, Not Against You!

Should you send a thank-you note? To whom, and when? And most importantly, what should you say? Well, I'm a big believer in thank-you notes. I would go as far as saying that they're mandatory in today's job market. But be careful with this tool because it's a two-edged sword: As easily as an excellent thank-you note could be just the right touch to secure an attractive offer, a poor one could ruin your candidacy and kill a job prospect.

No exaggeration here, folks! I've seen too many people send thank-you notes with typos, name misspellings, and sloppy penmanship that totally put the employer off. As a matter of fact, many recruiters in the search business require that their candidates fax their thank-you notes to the recruiters before mailing them to the company! Why? Because recruiters are protecting their investment. They've gotten you all the way to the finish line and want to ensure that no amateur mistakes knock you out of the running at this point. And that's great for you, because no matter what the recruiter's motive, she's promoting your best interests.

Thank-you notes may either be typed or handwritten. The handwritten format dictates a much more casual style, but it's a much more personal approach. In today's world of word-processed form letters, a handwritten note is more appreciated and more appropriate in most cases. Still, if you think that the receiver could perceive that as too personal or too informal, then typing the note may be more appropriate. Finally, the suitable stationery for handwritten notes is typically a standard, blank, fold-over thank-you note. Typewritten letters, in comparison, should be on bond paper of heavyweight stock just like your resumé paper. Just be sure *not to use your current employer's letterhead* (if you're currently employed) because you'd be using company product for personal affairs, and that's not going to win you many points with your prospective employer!

The Three Components of a Winning Note

Thank-you notes typically contain three sections:

1. The "thank you/it was a pleasure meeting you" opener.
2. Either the "I feel I'm particularly well suited for the job because" reinforcement or the "although I'm lacking in one particular area, my other skills will allow me to compensate" recovery.
3. The "I feel I could make an immediate contribution to your company" and "I really want the job" close.

Here's how they work best: Thank-you notes need to begin with a very cordial and friendly opener. How friendly or how formal a conversational style you lend your writing is up to you. Obviously, you want the tone of your letter to match the flavor of your interview. If the meeting was witty or humorous, your writing style should reflect that. If your interviewer took more of a formal posture, then a "proper" business letter would be more suitable. The only style I would caution against is the legalese approach that could leave even a lawyer feeling cold and clammy. "Pursuant to our meeting dated July 7th in which we discussed the mutual benefits that an offer of employment would proffer, . . ." Yuk! There's no humanity in that. Even if you're interviewing with an attorney, make your offer letter come alive with your personality. Save the legal argot for the contracts. Thank-you notes are person-to-person communications.

The second issue in a thank-you note can go one of two ways: If you're a near-exact fit for the job (meaning you come from a competitor, you have the exact same reporting relationship with your current employer that you would have with this prospective employer, or your technical skills and softwares are head-on), then use the body of the thank-you note to hammer home why you're the perfect person for the position. For example:

> Mark, I just wanted to share with you that I really feel that this position suits me exceptionally well. I'm currently reporting to a principal/partner at another Big Six CPA firm. My WordPerfect and Lotus skills are exceptionally strong, and I would love the opportunity to work for you because of your excellent reputation in the field.

or:

> The fact that your CEO has so many ties to the entertainment industry really motivates me. There are very few real estate development executives with a strong entertainment network. With my eleven years of experience in entertainment and my knowledge of the key players in the business, I feel I could represent the CEO's office particularly well and possibly introduce her to some of the people in my own network.

The point is to reinforce what makes you uniquely qualified for the job and what makes you stand apart from the competition.

On the other hand, this middle section could be used to overcome any objections the employer might have about you. If you saw the interviewer wince when you mentioned that you don't have formal Gregg or Pitman shorthand, you might add a few sentences about your experience using fast notes to take corporate minutes at board of directors' meetings. Similarly, if you feel that your lack of Windows experience puts you at a disadvantage, write something like this:

> Evelyn, we discussed the fact that you're in a Microsoft Word for Windows and Excel environment. Even though the majority of my computer experience has been in a DOS environment using WordPerfect and Lotus, I have a Windows book at home that could get me up and running in no time. The employment agency that referred me offered me a three-hour training session on Microsoft Word and Excel, and I would be happy to enroll in a class immediately to enhance my skills even further. Therefore, I could have a solid fundamental grounding by the time I come aboard.

Another example of overcoming objections in a thank-you letter might focus on the fact that you were earning $49,000 in your last job and are now interviewing for a $38,000 job:

Jim, I was making $49,000 in my last position, but the realities of today's marketplace have made those kinds of high-paying positions quite rare. Like many other executive secretaries, I have had to adjust my financial expectations to the new realities of the 1990s, and I want to assure you that I'm interviewing in the $38,000 range with other companies now. Please consider my performance track record and my career achievements more than my salary at my last position.

One of the keys to overcoming objections is to surface them yourself (as opposed to letting the other party raise them) and thereby *stay in control* of the situation. If you recognize the objections by holding them up under the light, then logically overcome them by presenting solutions like the ones we detailed above, you'll also reveal excellent problem-solving skills. That business maturity reveals a key personal characteristic that has a direct bearing on your business decision-making approach.

The final thought within a thank-you note focuses on closing the employer by reconfirming how much you want the job. Try something like this:

Candi, I've always felt that one of the biggest factors in the selection process lies in how much the candidate wants the job. I am truly eager for this position and believe I could make an immediate contribution to your organization. Because of my industry knowledge, technical skills, and understanding of the pressures involved working one-on-one for a key corporate officer, I would need minimal training or downtime to become an up-and-running member of your company. I would consider myself very fortunate to become a member of your business team.

Sample Thank-You Notes

Let's take a look at some sample thank-you notes and pull these ideas together:

Example 1:

Dear Brigette,

I wanted to take a moment to thank you for meeting with me today regarding the executive assistant position to Ms. Jones. You made our meeting very comfortable and amiable, and I really feel that I understand your organization and its corporate culture that much more because of your efforts.

I've been preparing myself for a position like this throughout my career. You're aware that my scope of responsibility has risen over the years as I increased my reporting relationships from senior to executive level management. This position would be my ideal next move because I want to represent the office of the president. I've researched your company, I understand the pressures and protocol common to the telecommunications/high-tech industry, and I feel that I'm ready for the increase in responsibilities that would go along with this opportunity. Thank you again for your time and consideration.

Sincerely,

Example 2:

Dear Mr. Johnson:

I would like to thank you for the opportunity to meet with you yesterday regarding the sales secretarial position at your branch office. As I shared with you, I am very interested in becoming a part of your company because of the exciting growth plans ahead of you. Also, I have long been aware of your company's excellent reputation, and I would be proud to become a contributing member to your business team.

Mr. Johnson, during our meeting you shared with me that your keys to hire include bilingual Spanish abilities, Genesis loan processing software experience, and the ability to provide world-class customer service. I used both my language and technical skills very heavily in my last position, and my references will speak for my customer service abilities. I know that I could become an asset to your company, especially with your focus on developing the Hispanic market. I hope you will permit me to continue in the interview process. Thank you very much.

Sincerely,

Example 3:

Dear Doris,

I want to thank you for a thoroughly insightful and open interview. You obviously love what you do, and I'm sure XYZ Company appreciates the motivational interviews you provide to your prospective employees. Interviewing isn't much fun, and many employers show very little empathy for what it's like being on the other side of the desk. Thank you so much for your understanding and humor. I really feel that I understand the company better because I now know one of its key employees.

I hope I'm a finalist for this job because I believe I would be able to make a unique and immediate contribution based on my previous industry background and similar technical orientation. But even if it doesn't work out for whatever reason, I want you to know that I appreciated your honesty, openness, and your goodwill. Continued success in your career, and I hope to hear from you soon.

Regards,

As you can see, the tone and style of these notes vary widely. The key to writing thank-you notes lies in allowing that letter to *be you*. The thank-you note is a written reminder that arrives two or three days after your interview to refresh that interviewer's memory of who you are. (I recommend mailing thank-you notes to everyone who formally interviewed you on the same day as your meeting.) Since you can't go back to pop into the office in person, then your short note has to conjure up a picture and rekindle the emotional aspects of your personality. So let your personality come out! Sell the future benefits you'll provide on the basis of your past achievements, overcome any weaknesses in the backs of their minds, and close them on how much you want that job! You'll find that a thank-you note, placed at the finish line after all rounds of interviews have been completed, can be an extremely effective tool for clinching an offer.

Creative Ongoing Follow-Up Techniques

What do you do if you're interviewing with a company on a proactive basis and no opening currently exists that fits you? Or what happens if you're not chosen for the job, but you still want to become part of that company in the future when another position surfaces? Well, the thank-you note remains step 1 in the follow-up process, but let's face it, any thank-you note has only a short-term effect. Most employers won't remember you two months after your interview on the basis of a thirty-minute meeting or a brief thank-you note. So, understanding the very limited shelf life of the thank-you note, you need to develop a longer-term, creative follow-up agenda for staying in touch with a company. *It is a mistake to assume that just because you weren't chosen for a particular job that you're no longer in the running for future openings!* Very often human resources professionals check their databases once new openings surface before enlisting the aid of classified newspaper ads or recruiting firms. You've just got to put together a methodology for consistently contacting companies so as to establish an ongoing positive relationship without becoming a pest.

First things first. There's one way in which you're guaranteed to become a pest: by calling on the phone (or leaving a voicemail message) that says, "Hi, Ms. Employer, this is Jane Doe. We interviewed about three weeks ago, and I was wondering if you have any openings for me. Please call me back to let me know." Yeah, right! I'll get to it somewhere between the two hundred resumés I'm evaluating for my fourteen openings and the six interviews I've got scheduled to come into my office today! Employers aren't going to return those calls because they're time-wasters. If the employer had something for you, it would be in her best interest to get you back into the office immediately! So your unsophisticated phone call isn't going to usher in any golden opportunities that happen to be waiting in the wings for you.

Also, because you're now more in tune with the time management pressures facing human resources professionals, your creative follow-up agenda will have to keep their needs in mind. The way to do that is by employing written or faxed communications rather than spoken messages. In other words, now that you're aware of the sheer volume of phone calls that the HR practitioner faces from all different fronts, then you'll realize that the best means of communication will be in a form that employers can get to at their leisure. I call this the **silent contact follow-up agenda,** and it has one key benefit to employers: A letter or a fax allows employers the flexibility to focus on your communication at their leisure rather than having to measure and prioritize it against the twenty-two other voicemail messages on their answering machines.

So what are you going to write or fax to them? Come on now, you know. *Your research!* This is exactly how I found my present job. I developed a solid working relationship with one of my clients by sending waves of research over to her. I didn't make a lot of fluff phone calls, and I contacted her only when I had information of specific interest to her. When an opening surfaced for a recruiter/trainer not too long after our initial contact, I was invited to join the company! Let me tell you, it feels great to be recruited and invited to go inside with a client. And I owe most of that opportunity to my library research, which opened the door!

One of the most sophisticated approaches to following up with companies consequently lies in providing information that benefits them. After all, you've got all this wonderful material that you've developed from your active and passive research activities. Now's the time to feed that back to the employer so that she'll appreciate your unique willingness to serve as an informational resource.

Sample Research Reminders

It's simple. Make a photocopy of the article you found in the *Seattle Times* and mail it to the human resources contact with a short, handwritten letter (mailed or faxed) like this:

Example 1:

Dear Ms. Employer:

I found this article today in the *Seattle Times,* and I thought I'd fax it to you right away. I'm doing everything I can to learn about your company and what makes it unique so that when an opening becomes available for a sales assistant, I'll be the first person you think of. Congratulations and continued success!

Regards,

Example 2:

Dear Marlene,

I hope all is well. It's been about three weeks since we met for an interview, and I thought I'd share some of the research I originally did on your company that prompted my call to you in the first place. I know that when people are busy with their jobs, they sometimes don't have the time to develop a P.R. portfolio of what's being written about their company. So I thought you'd appreciate this printout from the newest issue of *A.M. Best's Insurance Ratings.* Congratulations on your renewed A++ status!

Please keep me in mind once a staff accountant position becomes available. Again, I'm very excited about the prospect of joining your company. Thank you.

Sincerely,

Example 3:

Dear Henry,

I interviewed with you last month for a receptionist position in your loan services department. Although I didn't land that position, I'm still very interested in becoming a receptionist in another department. I didn't want to call you to see whether there were any openings for fear of disrupting your work. So I decided to mail you this one-page write-up from the *Value Line Investment Survey.* It's the newest edition, and it ranks your company's projected stock performance over the next year as rock-solid.

Congratulations and continued success. And again, when an opportunity surfaces for which I'm qualified, I hope you'll give me the chance to interview with you again. Thank you very much.

Sincerely,

Can this really work for you? Of course it can work! You'll gain an awful lot of points by doing this. Also remember that you don't have to unload all your research in one fell swoop. You can make three or four contacts over a period of two to three months and spread out those follow-ups. This is one of the ways that recruiters develop human resources clients. (Present company included!) As a matter of fact, this is a key sales strategy for account executives in all fields of sales who want to penetrate new accounts. With recruiters, though, it can take a year or two to crack a really tight account. You don't have that much time, so some of these follow-ups will merely fall by the wayside.

On the other hand, put on your human resources hat for a moment. When 90 percent of the candidates fall off the planet after your interview, and the 9 percent who do follow up make ho-hum phone calls hoping against hope that you've got the ideal job for them and you just forgot to call them about it, consider how you'd feel if someone pursued you intelligently and thoughtfully. Even if you didn't originally like the person, you'd have to admire and respect her smarts. After all, isn't this what networking is all about? A candidate who goes out of her way to share information that has a direct and immediate benefit for you will stand out like a diamond in a sea of onyx! Besides, the way I figure it, you've already done all the research. Why let it collect dust when you could put it to such positive use?

What happens if the company doesn't want you, though? Will you be perpetuating the law of diminishing returns by pursuing a company that won't hire you no matter what you do? Sure, the HR person will appreciate this follow-up information, but will it get you another interview?! Unfortunately, no one can answer that. But I can tell you that if your gut and intuition tell you that the company has a real interest in you, and you're incredibly excited about becoming a member of that organization, then this creative follow-up strategy could be just the thing to get you upstairs into the accounting department for an interview. What's the worst that could happen? Unrequited love—you never hear from them again. So what? You're still showing that you're smarter than the rest of the population, and that's got to make you feel good!

Of course, this exercise will be limited by the number of companies you originally researched. If you've got only ten firms in hand, then this creative follow-up strategy won't take up much of your time. If you've got a hundred companies, this could take longer, so prioritize the ones you want to pursue.

By the way, this same technique can be used to land an initial interview. Once you've sent a resumé and haven't heard back, don't make a call asking whether they received your resumé. The answer is yes; they just can't find it right now from among the two hundred or so others in the office. Instead, send a follow-up letter with another copy of your resumé explaining that your resumé was sent two weeks ago, and that you hadn't heard back from them. Share the research that helped you identify the company in the first place, and then explain that you'd be interested in meeting with them on a proactive basis even if no current openings fit your background.

I would then recommend that, about a week after mailing that follow-up letter, you make a phone call (yes, sometimes it's okay to make a phone call!) presenting yourself to that company. That's when you could ask the human resources manager whether he prefers that you register with a particular employment agency or whether he might consider meeting with you on an exploratory basis. But that's material we've already covered in Chapter 2, so you can jump back there for more tips on making initial presentations to companies.

Finally, when should you give up on these creative follow-up strategies with a particular company? You've sent information about the company that you found in *Fortune* magazine (which you located via the *Reader's Guide to Periodical Literature*), you mailed an article about the changes in the industry, and it's been about two or three months since you first mailed in your resumé. Well, wipe the dust from your sandals. You've probably reached a dead end, *but you're still the smartest and most considerate job candidate that employer has ever seen.* So even if she doesn't return your calls, know that you impressed her.

Okay, your tools are laid out neatly, you understand the practical rules as well as the philosophy behind job search, and you're about to get that offer. Now what? Well, don't panic. Let's again remove the *mystery* and focus on the *method* that will help you come through this final test with flying colors. See you in Chapter 9!

Part III

The Finish Line: Winning That Perfect Job

Chapter 9

Anticipating the Offer:
Don't Stumble Now!

Welcome to the finish line! You've come a long way in understanding how to tap into the hidden job market, write impressive resumés and cover letters, tackle the most difficult interview questions, and creatively follow up with companies to maintain a high profile after the interview. You've suddenly arrived at the final, and most significant, stage in the entire process: accepting the offer.

Not to be too negative, but this is the part where many a fine candidate has bungled what up to then had been a beautifully executed plan. Every recruiter in the search business knows that most deals are lost at the resignation interview when the candidate's "buyer's remorse" typically sets in. Perhaps the candidate didn't accept or reject the offer in the same time frame that the employer made it. Maybe he was thrown for an unexpected loop by his existing employer, who played on his sympathies and proposed a tempting counteroffer. Perhaps his salary demands showed him to be more interested in lining his own pockets than focusing on furthering the company's interests. Whatever the case, there are some tricky pitfalls awaiting you in this liminal zone where you're between jobs. Grace under pressure at this stage dictates total success. One flinch at the wrong moment and *zap!* The deal is off.

Accepting an Offer

Saying yes or no to an employer's offer at the time the offer is made is the most critical step in the whole process. Peter Leffkowitz, search industry trainer extraordinaire (of The Morgan Consulting Group, Kansas City, Missouri) once shared with me that *the first decision a company watches you make is acceptance or rejection of the offer.* The people who made the offer focus on your ability to collect the appropriate information in the necessary time frame to reach a definitive conclusion about what's best for your career. Flinch under pressure, hold out for more money, or show yourself to be indecisive regarding your career plans, and you could be out.

The time to contemplate the pros and cons of offer acceptance is *not* at the time of the offer. Those stages of decision making needed to happen while you were making the rounds from interviewer to interviewer over the past two weeks. Employers don't want to sell candidates on why accepting the job offer will benefit everyone. "If I've got to sell them to accept the position in the first place," the employer reasons, "then I'll be establishing a pattern of weakness and employee dependence that is very unhealthy. I'll end up creating an environment of high-need employees, and that could throw morale into a tailspin."

For some strange reason, many employees, both at the administrative and executive management levels, have come under the impression that holding off on accepting an employment offer for twenty-four hours enhances their candidacies. "I don't want them to think I'm too desperate by jumping at their first offer" goes this warped line of logic. "Maybe if I hold out for twenty-four hours, I may even enhance my chances of getting more money because they sure won't want to lose me at this late stage." Wrong! If you can't gather adequate information to accept or reject their offer within the same time frame that they've made that offer, then your decision-making skills are weak and your motives will be questioned. You might just find out that in twenty-four hours the offer will no longer be on the table. Beware: Whether your interests were selfish or simply poorly thought out, the end result will be a note in your file that says, "Pass. Indecisive about offer. Probably had some other offer on the line for which she was holding out."

Salary Negotiation

Up to now we've kind of danced around the dollar issue. In your first round of meetings with human resources, you did your best to keep the lines of communication open by not limiting yourself to a specific dollar commitment. Naming a dollar figure with HR has a double danger: If you name a figure that is too low right from the start, you severely restrict your chances of increasing that dollar amount because the company knows that you find that figure acceptable. On the other hand, if you name a figure that is too high from the outset of the employment process, you may be pricing yourself out of the market because the company feels that it can't afford you.

To keep the doors open, therefore, your strategy has been to tell HR what you were making on your last job and to state that (a) the long-term opportunity with the company is more important to you than the initial salary, and (b) you're considering the base salary in conjunction with the whole benefits package so that you have a whole compensation picture (of which base salary is only one element). You closed that statement with the open-ended question, "What's the salary range for the position, Ms. Employer?" Hopefully, whether with the human resources interviewer in round one of the interview process or later on during your meeting with line management, you discovered the range for the position.

Note that your communications with human resources will probably reopen at this final-offer stage. Here, however, your dialogue with human resources will be in a negotiation context, as opposed to the simple discussion format assumed in the first interview. In many companies, human resources assumes the role of ultimate salary negotiator and makes all final offers. In other organizations, the line managers themselves initiate starting salary issues while you're sitting in their offices.

Timing plays a role as well regarding which company official assumes the negotiating posture: If you're being made an offer on the spot, your prospective supervisor may consummate the deal. If you're being called two weeks later with an offer, human resources will most likely finalize your salary with you over the phone. Just keep in mind that the salary negotiation scenarios that follow will apply no matter who negotiates your final offer.

Thank goodness, you also know how employers make salary offers according to the 10 percent rule. (Refer back to Figure 6-5 on page 142.) And we've discussed that lateral moves and even cuts in salary can sometimes be appropriate if you were an exceptionally highly compensated employee in your last position, and your local marketplace isn't producing many jobs in those salary ranges any more. See Chapter 6 for more information on salary discussions with human resources representatives.

But now's the time to face that critical issue head-to-head. Let's see how you should handle it. Whether you know the salary range for the position or not, *your first step is to determine how much you want the job*. This, once again, will be a function of your interest demand barometer. Remember, that's the rule that says the more interested you are in the position, the fewer demands you'll have. Conversely, the less interested you are, the more demands you'll have. Your gut will play a role in this process as much as your head, so let the two run wild in determining your interest level.

The second step is to determine at what dollar figure you'll accept an offer, and at what point you'll reject one. This is a critical exercise for you because once you're set on a number, you have a target or goal from which to leverage your negotiating posture. If you're not sure what you want, you'll be more likely to accept an offer that is less than ideal.

Now, let's assume that you're making $30,000 on your present or last job, and you know that this position will pay $30,000 to the low thirties. If you're unemployed right now, you could bet that the offer will come in right where you left off on your last position, at $30,000. That's a good call on the company's part, because it's certainly not lowballing you, and it's offering you a chance to get off the unemployment line and become a contributing member of the team again. You'll not have lots of negotiation leverage in this case, because when you're in career transition, your marketability goes down somewhat.

On the other hand, if you're happily employed where you are right now, but a recruiter presented you with this stronger opportunity even though you weren't actively looking at the time of the recruiter's call, the company may need to up the ante to pull you away from your present company. In that case, you might share with the employer something like,

> You know, Mr. Employer, I'm flattered to be at the offer stage with your company because I admire and respect your corporate reputation, and I really feel that I could make a unique contribution to your firm based on my background working for a competitor. Still, I wasn't actively interested in making a career move at the time of the recruiter's phone call, and, with all due respect, I'd like to see myself come in with a meaningful increase to justify making the transition. I was told that the position was paying in the low thirties, and I'd really like a 10 percent increase in my base pay. That would put my salary needs at $33,000. What are your thoughts about that?

The employer may acquiesce right away or hesitate a little and share with you that what he meant by "low thirties" was $31,500. If you're a soft negotiator, you'll avoid any type of confrontation and accept that dollar figure. If you're a hard negotiator, you'll welcome the opportunity to haggle and convince that employer by sheer force of your own will that you deserve every penny of that $33,000 offer. On the other hand, if you're a principled negotiator who believes in positional bargaining, you'll be open to hashing out the pros and cons of the offer according to the merits of your case and the employer's arguments.

In that case, you might surface issues like:

- You've researched the company in the library to learn more about the company's key players, short-term marketing strategies, and long-term corporate philosophy so that you could make an immediate contribution to the company and ensure a smooth transition into the new workplace.
- You've worked for a direct competitor and are familiar with the pressures, protocol, and parlance of the industry.
- You've held the exact reporting relationship, which means that you understand how to represent the office well.
- You've got the same technical systems (such as softwares and

shorthand), which will ensure a minimal downtime and learning curve.

Those tangible benefits carry with them a definite dollar value. And you've objectively presented your case well to justify the higher end of the salary range.

Of course, the employer may then bring you to a dead end with a take-it-or-leave-it proposition.

Employer: Sarah, we really can't go above $31,500 for internal equity reasons. If we bring you in at $33,000, you'll be compensated more highly than another executive assistant who holds the same level of responsibility and who has comparable experience. Unfortunately, we can't offer you a penny higher than $31,500, so you'll have to accept the offer or reject it at that starting salary.

Darn, this isn't easy! (Nothing worthwhile ever is.) Now you have to pull out your secret weapon: the **out-of-cycle review.** It works like this: If, for internal equity reasons, the employer can't initially offer you more than $31,500, that doesn't mean that in ninety days or six months the company will be barred from increasing your base pay. Let's do some quick math: The difference between $33,000 and $31,500 is $1,500 per year, or roughly $125 per month. So your question goes as follows:

You: Well, Mr. Employer, what are your thoughts about allowing me to earn the difference of $125 per month via an out-of-cycle review, say in ninety days?

Employer: Unfortunately, Sarah, that's not an option either. We really can't formally pay you more than the other person while you're still in your first year. It just wouldn't be appropriate pay policy on our part.

Let's keep this rolling:

You: Mr. Employer, do you have any thoughts as to how we could address that $125 difference? [Notice that you should always use the smaller number ($125/month) as opposed to the larger number ($1,500/year) because it's a much less threatening and much more doable amount.] Will there be an annual bonus plan at year's end? And if so, will it be based on individual performance or the whole company's profitability? What would the outer limits of the bonus range be?

Now you're rolling! You're certainly giving the employer options to salvage the hire. These ventures into raising your salary may give you a green light (for example, if the bonus potential is $5,000, then the $1,500 offset will pale in comparison). Or, alas, they may end with no fruitful results: no out-of-cycle review and no year-end bonus. Yet you still have two arrows left in your quiver:

You: Are there opportunities to work overtime, Mr. Employer? I understand that overtime is typically paid at time-and-a-half, and I'm amenable to working heavy overtime.

And if overtime isn't an option:

You: I think I'm seeing the picture a little more clearly. Please don't mistake my assertiveness for lack of appreciation; just being considered as a finalist candidate is an honor. It's just that the ten minutes we spend discussing compensation dictates my take-home pay for the next twelve months. I know companies at times offer sign-on bonuses for key personnel.* Has your company ever offered a sign-on bonus to someone at the administrative support level? If so, I'd hope that you would consider me a candidate for that special exception.

Bully for you! You're fighting for yourself, and you're doing it very nicely. (This is a very powerful negotiation wrapped in a soft and humble presentation.) Your persistence may force them to rethink their compensation strategies in your special case. If all of your suggestions don't work, so be it. Accept or reject the offer at $31,500 based on the merits of the job and the perceived opportunity for increased responsibilities. Remember, though, that even if you didn't make that $1,500 up in one way or another right now, you'll have planted a seed in their memories that will remind them that you're very serious about receiving additional compensation at some point in the future. Maybe it'll take a year until your next review, but you might see a higher-than-average jump after you've proven yourself. Whatever the case, don't underestimate the significance of your efforts in creating a set of expectations that the company will need to fulfill to keep you happy.

Request a Written Offer Letter

I recommend that you request a *written* offer letter whenever possible. Many companies confirm all verbal hires with a written follow-up letter stipulating monthly salary and start date. That's an excellent corporate

---

*Sign-on bonuses of, say, $1,000 were not uncommon in the late 1980s as a tool to attract high-caliber administrative people to companies. They are a lot less common in the 1990s but might still be found in certain parts of the country for specific jobs. However, you should use this request only as a last resort. Remember that it never hurts to ask!

policy because it protects the company right from the start from any miscommunications or unresolved demands from new employees. Besides, if it's written down, the company reasons, it has greater legal enforceability.

Those same reasons are why you want a written offer letter as soon as possible after the verbal hire is made. Being a recruiter, or employment broker, so to speak, where I helped companies find the right people to fill their needs, allowed me to see lots of deals happen from a third-party, objective standpoint. There have been occasions, rare though they may be, where candidates have tried to wrangle some added benefits from the employer, claiming that those benefits were orally promised during the interview process. There have even been cases where companies, after having made an offer that the candidate accepted, later balked at their decision and ended up not bringing the person aboard. (That's terrible in and of itself, but the bad news is compounded by the fact that the employee quit her past job to accept this new one!) The employer committed a legal violation called wrongful failure to hire, and if that ever happens to you, having a written confirmation letter will help you collect in court.

It's a simple request, and even if a company doesn't have a formal policy for mailing out official offer letters, most organizations will oblige your special request. Even if the company representative tells you that it's simply not company policy to mail out offer letters to new hires, there's no reason why you can't write your own offer letter specifying the terms of the hire, and then mail it to the company. The typical offer letter contains information regarding your:

- ☛ Official job title
- ☛ Starting salary (typically quoted on an hourly or monthly basis) along with commission or override specifics and percentages
- ☛ Start date, time, and location for reporting on the first day
- ☛ Any arrangements regarding a pre-employment physical or drug screen

Here's a sample offer letter to help you visualize what a typical one looks like.

Dear Ms. White:

We are pleased to confirm our offer for the position of departmental secretary in our payroll area. The position's starting salary is $1,950 per month. As discussed, you will begin work on Monday, July 24, at 8:30 A.M. Please report directly to the human resources department on the second floor, where you will be asked to complete our new employee hire materials.

We look forward to having you join our organization. If any questions surface that we can answer for you in the meantime, please call.

Sincerely,

Benefits Evaluation: Understanding the Total Compensation Package

Your final task in accepting or rejecting an employment offer must briefly delve into the value of benefits. It's your obligation to become an educated consumer of health care and financial products. One company's offer at $31,500 may be vastly better than another organization's offer at $33,000 if the first company has a dollar-for-dollar match on the 401(k) plan and the second company offers no tax-deferred retirement plan. Dollars need not be totally liquid to be counted: Deferred savings and noncash incentives can go a long way in sheltering your income, reducing your taxes, and letting you sleep at night knowing that your retirement nest egg is compounding tax-deferred in a solid, growth-stock mutual fund.

Just so you're aware, expenses related to employee benefits programs amount to a large percentage of a company's payroll costs—anywhere from 10 percent of the total expenditure for wages for a bare-bones program to as much as 40 percent or 50 percent of payroll for more elaborate plans. Do companies legally have to provide benefits? With the exception of social security, worker's compensation, and in most states, unemployment insurance, the answer is no. Companies don't even have to provide workers with vacation, although common practice has made vacation a universal benefit.

What is a **benefit?** Anything you receive from a company besides cash wages typically qualifies as a benefit. And those "anythings" could really add up in terms of reduced taxes, lessened out-of-pocket expenses, and special services. Let's focus first on the out-of-pocket expenses typically associated with major medical plans, then move on to special services and retirement planning options. For your needs, those three areas will have the greatest impact on the overall value of the employment offer. Although dental coverage, life insurance, and long- and short-term disability plans are certainly important, they have less bearing on your aggregate annual payout, so we'll bypass those lower-profile benefits in this book.

Major Medical Expenses: Premiums, Deductibles, and
Coinsurance Payments

Health maintenance organizations (HMOs) have become increasingly popular with American workers since their initial development more than twenty years ago. HMOs focus on preventive care by encouraging members to pursue help early on, before an illness has a chance to become more serious. HMOs cover members **prospectively,** meaning they receive a set monthly fee or premium for the number of participants enrolled regardless of patient usage. What that proactive payment approach means to you is lessened headaches in terms of payments and paperwork: When you visit an HMO doctor, you typically make a small copayment (around $5), get care, and then leave. There are no deductibles to calculate, no reimbursement forms to fill out—a wonderfully simple solution to a potentially complex process. On the other hand, you must choose a doctor and health care facility within a network that may not be extensive.

Under a **preferred provider organization** (PPO) arrangement, by comparison, you can go to any doctor or hospital you wish, but you'll be reimbursed at a higher rate if you choose one enrolled in the plan. Typically, 80 or 90 percent of your costs are covered when you go to plan doctors, while 50 to 70 percent are covered when you opt for doctors outside the PPO system. Yet with this luxury comes an increased price: PPOs and indemnity plans cost significantly more in terms of monthly premiums (the cost of belonging to the plan), deductibles (the up-front amount that must be paid before insurance kicks in, typically somewhere between $250 and $1,000 per person), and coinsurance payments (the amount per visit you must pay once the annual deductible has been met, typically 20 percent of the cost of the visit in an 80/20 plan).

Finally, a newer choice available to you is the **point of service** (POS) plan, where, usually for an increased premium and/or higher coinsurance payment, you can choose to go beyond the HMO network's doctors and facilities while still enjoying the overall cost savings associated with HMO plans. POS plans are hybrids between HMOs and PPOs. Under certain circumstances, point-of-service plans may allow you to leave the HMO system without any financial penalty. As of this writing, they aren't nearly as widespread as HMO and PPO programs, but joining choice plus cost savings seems to have a bright future on the medical scene.

It's crucial that you find out these after-tax, out-of-pocket costs before accepting or rejecting an employment offer. However, I don't recommend surfacing benefits questions on a first round of interviews. Instead, save those questions for the final round, when you're anticipating the offer. Compare what you're paying for premiums, deductibles, and coinsurance costs at your present employer (for yourself or your family) with the plan offered by the prospective company. You may learn that you could save $200 a month in insurance premiums, adding that amount to your total income package.

Special Services and Other Tax-Favored Benefits

As part of the major medical package you're considering, you may find that your prospective employer offers orthodontic or chiropractic care.

Some plans include **employee assistance programs** (EAPs) that provide you with professional counseling assistance to help you and your family with substance abuse and even legal and financial planning. EAPs are meant to help employees work through personal problems that could affect their job performance. Furthermore, there is a strict confidentiality agreement between the EAP provider and the company that mandates that any employees seeking treatment will not run the risk of having their identities exposed. The only reporting requirement is that the EAP organization provides your company with the number of employees participating in the program in a given time period.

Similarly, some companies offer **wellness programs** that provide counseling and workshops on fitness, weight control, stress management, cardiopulmonary resuscitation, and quitting smoking. The philosophy behind wellness programs is simply to keep members well so that they have less of a chance of getting sick. The long-term costs associated with stress, smoking, and obesity could be vastly minimized by early treatment. An ounce of prevention is certainly worth a pound of cure. Obviously, these plans can have a significant cash value to you if any of these areas concern you.

Educational reimbursement programs reimburse you for coursework taken toward furthering your professional credentials or even working toward an MBA. The philosophy behind educational assistance plans rests on the premise that an educated worker will be more productive in the long run and will also feel an enhanced sense of loyalty to the firm. Companies handle this benefit differently: Some reimburse expenses only for work-related courses; some base tuition reimbursement on a fixed percentage of costs ("We pay 80 percent of all your coursework taken toward your bachelor's degree"); while others link payback to your grades ("If you get an A, we reimburse 100 percent, a B equals 80 percent, . . ."). Not a bad perk at all if education is your lifelong pursuit!

Section 125 plans, also known as flexible benefits or cafeteria plans, allow you to pay certain expenses related to child care, elder care, legal fees, and unreimbursed medical costs (such as deductibles and copayments) with pretax dollars. The money is taken out of your monthly paycheck via payroll deduction and actually reduces your gross income dollar for dollar. In other words, if you earn $18,000 a year, and you pay $2,000 a year in child care expenses via a company's flexible spending plan, the IRS will tax you as if you earned $16,000 that year, not $18,000. This plan could be a valuable benefit, but you need to plan very carefully: It is a use-it-or-lose-it plan because you forfeit anything left over in the account at the end of the year.

You may learn in the interview process that a company typically provides outplacement services for its employees should an unforeseen layoff or performance problem occur. Although no one likes thinking about layoffs, they've become a probable occurrence in the 1990s. Companies that provide outplacement services demonstrate exceptional concern for their workers' well-being.

Here's how it works: Outplacement firms are paid by companies that are downsizing to assist displaced workers in finding jobs. When companies demonstrate concern for hastened reemployment, they foster a sense that people are well taken care of, and that automatically minimizes the traumatic impact on remaining employees. As far as the company is concerned, the cost of outplacement is far outweighed by the altruistic and practical benefits which allow it to continue its business operations without undue interruption.

As far as you're concerned, outplacement programs are typically worth 10%–15% of your base salary. Working with an outplacement counselor includes individualized resumé writing assistance, interview training (often with video playback), aptitude testing, and national online job databank access. Most importantly, outplacement firms are staffed by employment executives with vast networks of contacts who will help you land your next position much more quickly. By no means should you underestimate the significant value of this option if it's part of a prospective employer's benefits package.

Finally, look for other special services that can significantly cut your out-of-pocket costs. Subsidized food services on company premises can significantly cut down on your daily lunch tab, and product discounts, credit unions, and employee gymnasiums may provide added perks that significantly enhance the job's desirability.

Company Retirement Plans

Let's take a brief look at pension plans and contribution plans. This is where the tax-deferred benefits could really add up over the years to provide you with a substantial retirement income. There are two types of retirement vehicles available in many organizations: defined benefit plans (pension plans) and defined contribution plans (contribution plans).

Defined benefit plans are the traditional pension plans you think of if you picture a senior citizen rocking on his porch swing waiting for the pension check to come in. They're called defined benefit plans because the benefit, or the amount the employee is to receive, is specifically set forth by the company. (That benefit is typically calculated using a formula that includes the employee's years of service and average earnings preceding retirement.) In this type of plan, the employer has been making annual payments to a trust fund over twenty or more years so that its fiduciary obligations to its retiring workforce could be met. The company assumes all the investment risk and annually invests what it must to reach its investment goals.

These traditional pension plans typically reward a workforce that has dedicated many years to the company. **Cliff vesting,** the most common vesting methodology, states that no pension credit is vested until the employee has been covered by the plan for five years. After that, the employee is fully vested. (*Vesting* simply means that you're guaranteed the right to receive that benefit even if you leave the company.)

As you might guess, the only problem with this scenario is that most people these days don't work for the same company all their lives, so reaching that five-year vesting threshold can be relatively difficult. Also, companies with formal pension plans face heavy vesting, funding, eligibility, tax, and reporting requirements. For these reasons and others, many companies have favored defined contribution plans over traditional pension plans.

In a **defined contribution plan,** the amount that the company contributes is determined every year and may be fairly arbitrary. The company invests what it can afford, not what it must contribute to reach certain preplanned goals. From that point on, employees assume the responsibilities and risks of managing their own portfolios. There's no guarantee how much money will be in the account at the time of an individual's retirement.

One kind of contribution plan is called profit sharing. With **profit-sharing plans,** companies distribute a percentage of their net profits (usually about 10 to 15 percent) to employees as a bonus. The value of the plan lies in providing additional compensation while giving employees a sense of ownership in the company. Profits may be paid to you either in cash (taxable), as a contribution to your retirement fund (tax-deferred), or both. Under a profit-sharing arrangement, only the employer puts in money. With a 401(k) plan, in comparison, the employer generally only matches (usually by 50 percent or less) the contributions that you make.

Employee stock ownership plans (ESOPs) allow companies to obtain tax incentives by permitting a portion of the organization's earnings to be excluded from taxation if those earnings are assigned to employees in the form of stock shares. Similar to the profit-sharing concept, ESOPs encourage employees—"shareholders," I should say—to have a greater stake in the success of the company. Keep in mind, however, that stock prices are unpredictable, which means that the value of your retirement portfolio could fluctuate considerably. Another danger with ESOPs is that you can fall prey to putting all your eggs in one basket: If the company goes down, so does its stock. Therefore, both your job and your retirement nest egg could be jeopardized.

Finally, the most common type of contribution plan is the **401(k) plan,** so called because it's Section 401(k) of the tax code. In a typical 401(k) arrangement, the employee contributes money on a pretax basis into the plan. For this reason, 401(k)s are often called salary reduction plans because they make it appear as if you're earning less income by sheltering that income from the IRS. For example, if you invest $3,000 a year into a 401(k) plan and you earn $26,000, the IRS will tax you as if you earned $23,000. Features of these plans vary from company to company.

The other feature often available with 401(k)s is the company matching feature, although not all companies provide matching options. Companies may match your investment dollar for dollar, or they may match $0.25 for every $1 you invest. On the other hand, some companies match your contributions using a one-time, fixed dollar amount. For example, the company may match the first $500 you invest and no more. Whatever the case, 401(k)s are extremely popular because of the multiple benefits of reducing salary, enjoying a company matching feature (when available), and investing for your retirement on a tax-deferred basis. (You don't pay taxes on your interest or earnings until you withdraw the money at retirement. At that point, you'll probably be in a lower tax bracket, so you won't feel the tax bite as much.) Finally, unlike a true pension plan, some plans allow you to borrow against your 401(k) money if necessary.

Just to avoid a common confusion, the incorrect term bandied about by many employers is "401(k) profit-sharing plan." That's a misnomer because, practically speaking, employers do not offer both a profit-sharing plan and a 401(k) plan (which is simply a type of profit-sharing program). What sets 401(k)s apart from other profit-sharing plans is the tax-deferred status of employee and employer contributions to the accounts.

Retirement investing is clearly a complicated matter, and any questions you have should be directed to the company's HR department or your personal financial planner. Still, realizing that these options exist can open up new ways of evaluating company offers. And that ties in rather nicely with your statement to the HR interviewer in the first round of interviews that the base salary was only one component of the total compensation plan you were considering.

When Is It Time to Leave Your Present Company?

I could have decided to ask this question on the first page of Chapter 1. It is, after all, the fundamental reason why you purchased this book in the first place. I assumed that you wouldn't be reading this if you didn't have an active and serious interest in advancing your career. Instead I chose to discuss this topic here because examining your feelings about your present job is crucial to how you accept a new employment offer. So let's formally tackle this self-interest question by honestly examining your fears and motivations about job change.

Resigning is a painful rite of passage. It's a confrontational task that can play on your emotions of guilt, remorse, fear of change, and loyalty.

But since you know that one of the first things prospective employers observe about you is your acceptance or rejection of their offer, you've got to come to terms with leaving your current employer.

A job change will happen only when the pain of staying with your present company outweighs the pain of change. And a large pain it is! Job change ranks right up there with fear of moving, fear of public speaking, and fear of death in terms of causing anxiety in us humans. And rightfully so—severing the ties with your corporate family, the familiar restaurants where you have lunch, and the comfortable chair that you've broken in to fit your back conjures up intense fear in lots of people.

> What if the grass *isn't* greener on the other side? What if the new company has an unforeseen layoff? At least here I've got tenure and I'd probably survive the first cut. I've heard of a lot of people getting axed because of the LIFO method. "Last in, first out" means that I'd be the first out on the street. Is my present job really so bad? I mean, at least I like the people. Help, I'm having buyer's remorse!

Okay, let's take a look at this objectively. When you're working with a strong recruiter, she'll do everything she can to help you come to terms with your feelings in advance. The way I stated it to my candidates was, "Anna, you're about to go in for your final meeting. The offer could be made directly to you on the spot, and I don't want your emotions at the time of the offer to cloud your better business judgment. Let's talk now about how you'd feel if I told you 'We want you to become a member of our company.' How would you feel? What would your gut be telling you?" I've also pushed candidates further by asking, "On a scale of 1 to 10 (10 being you can't believe how much you want it, 1 being you're not interested), where do you fall? If you're anything less than a 10, what would have to be added to or subtracted from the offer to make you a 10?" And so goes the drill.

Recruiters typically have no problem with candidates accepting offers. That's how they make a living. They also, believe it or not, have no problem with candidates rejecting offers. That's because the search business is a numbers game and statistically, only about one in eight candidates who interview with a client company will even generate an offer. However, most recruiters have serious problems with candidates who can't make up their minds. That doesn't make the recruiter look good in front of her client. It's not a clean way of doing business. And too many wishy-washy candidates mean the recruiter will most likely lose the account.

So let's run through an exercise that will help you finalize your thoughts in terms of accepting another position. I hope it will help crystallize the objective and emotional criteria that you're using to weigh the opportunities associated with change. (It will also help strengthen your relationship with your recruiter!) Remember while you go through this exercise that salary is not a primary motivator for the majority of the population. As a matter of fact, salary issues usually rank fourth in job offer considerations behind the more important issues of personal involvement in your job, recognition of your accomplishments, and the potential impact you have to effect change in your area.

The checklist shown in Figure 9-1 will help you measure your sense of self-worth and your perceived contributions to your existing employer. It will also cover issues of safety from layoffs and the overall health of your company and industry.

This exercise uses a weighted ranking scale, which means there really aren't absolute yes/no types of answers. Instead you'll weigh each feature on a scale of 1 to 5, 1 being weak/bad/negative, and 5 being strong/good/positive. For example, if you feel that you're in the hottest industry in America, rank *industry* with a 5. If, on the other hand, you believe that your company is a target for a corporate takeover, rank *company* with a 1 or 2. At the end, you'll add up your points and divide them by the number of categories to come up with an objective numerical ranking. (There are lots of variations on this ranking method theme. You can customize them more specifically to your needs.)

Now let's assign a grade in order to score your results. There are no absolutes here, but it's fair to say that if your present company isn't meeting two-thirds (or 20 points) of your needs either because external factors are jeopardizing your job safety or internal issues are stifling your personal growth, it may be time to move on. If you totalled 25 or more, stay put! You're on the high end of the fulfillment scale. If you totalled fifteen to nineteen points, you're ready to make a healthy career move and reinvigorate yourself with new challenges. If you scored less than fifteen points, you're subjecting yourself to a harsh work environment. A move is necessary. Remember that there are two types of employees who quit jobs: (1) those who quit and leave, and (2) those who quit and stay. You're not doing yourself or your present company a favor if you fall into the latter category.

On the other hand, remember to balance your equation fairly. Jumping too soon could be a premature decision. If you're in a company going through a merger and acquisition, your particular job may get wiped out along with everyone else's in your department. Still, mergers typically impact senior managers much more than the operational departmental employees. The radical staffing changes inherent to the merger process may actually create new opportunities for you. And that boss who seems to be blocking your career may support your decision to fill out a request-for-transfer form and move you into a new area within the same company.

Figure 9-1. The time-to-leave checklist.

1. Take stock of the external, objective factors beyond your immediate control that affect your industry, company, and department.

- *Industry:*

  Is your industry healthy overall? Is there a lot of job growth in it? Or is it more cyclical in nature and about to move into a falling phase? (Aerospace and military-related companies that manufacture magnetic-tape disk drives and aircraft or weapons parts will remain on the decline. In comparison, high-tech multimedia communications, international long-distance telephone carriers, and alternate-fuel transportation manufacturers, as of this writing, are creating jobs at a fairly rapid pace.)

1	2	3	4	5
Weak industry				Strong industry

- *Company:*

  Is your company being outflanked by its competition even if the industry is in an overall growth pattern? Is there excessive turnover in the senior management ranks? Has the company posted consecutive quarterly losses in revenue? Is the stock's performance getting whipsawed or battered on Wall Street? If so, the next corporate strategic move may be to slash payroll in an effort to reduce variable expenses and streamline operations, and that means layoffs!

1	2	3	4	5
Weak company				Strong company

- *Department:*

  What's the mood in your department? Are people getting along, or can you cut the atmosphere with a knife? Is there excessive turnover? How is your department performing as a cost center relative to other departments? (In other words, is your department overstaffed and underperforming?) How is your department performing in terms of meeting its own goals and compared to its performance last year at this time?

1	2	3	4	5
Weak department				Strong department

  Total score for external factors: _____ /15 points

Figure 9-1. *(continued)*

2. Evaluate your personal, subjective feelings about your ability to make a positive difference to your organization.

- Grade your ability to effect change in your company:

1	2	3	4	5
It doesn't matter what I do				My job adds value and I have input

- Evaluate your personal rapport with your immediate manager:

Do you have honest and open communications? Is your opinion valued? Do you feel as if someone closed the door on you in terms of keeping you in tune with the information grapevine? Do you find yourself having to justify your actions that were previously accepted? Are the semisocial encounters that brought you and your boss together for an occasional lunch gone? Are you the victim of benign neglect and indifference? Do you find yourself with diminished responsibilities? Does your boss keep changing the definition of what's acceptable so that you don't know what's consistently expected of you? If so, your fall from grace may have landed your career at a point where the inertia makes life in the corporation intolerably mediocre.

1	2	3	4	5
Poor rapport				Very good rapport

- Examine your perception of your worth to the company and your chances for upward mobility via increased responsibilities:

Do you get the "psychological income" that goes along with a job well done? Are you at the top of the salary range in your department and consequently barred from receiving a significant salary increase? Do you believe that you're miserably underpaid relative to the general marketplace? Do you find yourself going through the motions of your job because no matter what you do or how hard you try, you get no recognition or financial incentive?

1	2	3	4	5
Little upward mobility				Great upward mobility

Total score for internal factors: _____ /15

Grand total: _____ /30

Remember that longevity is the number 1 factor that can help or hurt you in the job change process. Sticking it out through changes in management and even waves of layoffs will portray you as an individual with excellent staying power in the face of diversity. Giving up the ship without speaking with your supervisor and exploring internal opportunities first could very well shortchange a successful career path for you. Again, I don't advocate staying with a company where there's a corporate culture mismatch, benign neglect, or a lack of respect for the individual. Yet, as a recruiter, I can't advise a prospective candidate to pursue other opportunities until every option within the present company has been exhausted. If I were to forget to first send a prospective candidate back to her supervisor at her present company before inviting her into my office, I might very well become a victim of something known as **candidate counteroffer acceptance.**

Counteroffer Acceptance: Courting Career Ruin

Counteroffers are simply enticements by your present employer to keep you after you've given notice. Employers have been known to appeal to an employee's sense of loyalty, guilt, and fear to keep that person aboard once the person announces her resignation. I've heard of candidates being offered promotions, salary increases, and other such lures to prevent them from jumping ship.

The problem with counteroffer acceptance is that the offer isn't always made with the employee's best interests in mind. Solid companies with well-developed human resources management practices don't subject themselves to counteroffer coercion. Their policies allow their employees the freedom to accept other offers if those offers appear to be stronger opportunities. Employees leave those organizations as smoothly as possible with a minimum of friction and histrionics.

Candidates who accept counteroffers may be deceiving themselves if they think that the majority of the problems that led them to the conclusion to leave will change. Throwing money or promotions at people in a last-ditch effort to salvage them may make things seem better in the short run. More often, however, the same problem that originally motivated the person to change jobs is still there. Problems very rarely disappear, and unless some very concrete steps are taken to correct past actions, those problems usually get a lot worse quickly. Now that the situation has been brought to a head, so to speak, it manifests itself more dominantly than it may have before.

Accepting counteroffers won't always hurt your career, of course. There are times when staying put actually opens doors for you. However, I can honestly say that I have seen very few occasions where the counteroffer helped the incumbent employee. There's a logical reason. Employees who subject their employers to counteroffer coercion put themselves in a tenuous position: They have shown themselves to be disloyal, and the mental break they made to look elsewhere will generally land them outside of the inner circle at work.

Furthermore, because those employees have shown themselves capable of making the break, so to speak, the company typically will put out antennae to locate a replacement or at least have one waiting in the wings. That's simply a good business decision on the company's part since it can't afford to keep the position open for any significant period of time.

Many recruiters actually take their candidates through resignation drills that role-play how the candidate will handle the resignation interview with her boss. Again, that's to avoid surprises at the finish line that wipe out the whole deal and all the work that's gone into the search to get that candidate to this stage in the offer process. So it's practical business sense that leads the recruiter down this path. It needs to be practical business sense for you too.

If there's any doubt whatsoever about leaving your present company, overcome it before you begin the job-hunting process! Don't go through all the emotional swings of job search and job change to be convinced by your present employer to stick it out. It's poor career management, it's poor decision making, and the resentment that will grow inside your employer's mind will seriously damage your chances for advancement or increased responsibilities. I would hazard a guess that 50 percent of all employees who accept counteroffers are gone within six months. When the problems don't go away and you've raised the specter of disloyalty, you shouldn't all of a sudden expect to be back on the fast track. Make your decision to move, stick with it, and don't respond to the false temptation of a counteroffer unless you truly feel that your boss has your best interests at heart.

For further reading in the area of leaving your present company or contemplating a counteroffer, see Jacqueline Hornor Plumez's *Divorcing a Corporation: How to Know When—and If—a Job Change Is Right for You* (New York, Villard Books, 1986) and Madelaine and Robert Swain's *Out the Organization: How Fast Could You Find a New Job?* (New York, MasterMedia LTD, 1988).

The Resignation Interview

First issue: corporate etiquette. The first person you should notify about your decision to leave your present company is your immediate supervisor. Not human resources, not your boss's boss, not your best friend in the department. No matter how tempting it may be to let others know and share in your excitement, if your boss hears it from anyone else in the company before you get to her, it's an insult. It's one thing to lose an employee; it's another thing if the whole company seems to know about it before your immediate supervisor learns about it. That's the ultimate form of disrespect, and it will make your resignation interview a lot harder if, on top of everything else, you've got to apologize for having had "loose lips."

When you inform your supervisor about your decision, explain that you received an offer that, from a business and career standpoint, you simply couldn't refuse. Thank your boss for the investment she made in you via training, trust, delegated responsibilities, and goodwill. And by all means, give two weeks' notice to allow her ample time to find a replacement! It's a poor career decision to leave a company in a hurry. Although you're not legally bound to offer two weeks' notice, it's an unwritten law of goodwill that shouldn't be broken under any circumstances.

Why not? First of all, you'd end up leaving your company in a bind and preventing a smooth transition of the work flow. Second, and more significant, you could end up ruining everything you've worked for by damaging your reference! Take the case of Dana, a sales assistant at a major Wall Street brokerage house. She had a track record of outstanding accomplishments, longevity, and promotability through the ranks with her last employer. Sure that her boss would give her rave reference reviews, she couldn't wait for me to make the reference-check call. As you probably guessed, although most of her references' feedback was solid, one of the first things her former boss shared with me was that she only gave one week's notice. That apparently left the boss in an awkward enough spot to remember Dana's lack of consideration. Why leave your last boss with hard feelings about you?

Second issue: No matter how tempting it may be to give your boss the old Johnny Paycheck line about "Take this job and shove it," you have to resist the urge to get things off your chest. The resignation interview is a time for objective sharing of a business and career decision, not subjective griping. Very little good comes out of a meeting where the resigning employee complains about goings-on within the company. Once you're gone (and that will be in about a half hour), you're gone, so very little heed is given to your recommendations to fix problems that were obviously egregious enough to make you quit.

More importantly, complaining on your way out could raise bitter feelings in your boss. Don't risk retaliation at some later date. After all, *this employer will be providing reference-check material about you for the next ten years.* Thinking that you're walking away a free person, never to have any dealings with that company again, is a naive misunderstanding of the job search process. Don't ever allow a past employer to rewrite your employment history, so to speak, because you'll need him again sooner than you think.

Finally, after your meeting with your manager, you may be asked to write out your formal letter of resignation and deliver it to the human resources department. HR will most likely conduct an exit interview where you'll be invited to share your story again. Yet the same rule applies: Keep it objective, explain that your decision is based on a business and career opportunity that will provide you with increased responsibilities, and make a clean break. If the HR professional begins fishing for emotional or subjective reasons why you're leaving, remember that the individual is asking only to see whether there are any patterns of problems with your supervisor (especially if there's been heavy turnover in your department), not to provide you with an audience to air your frustrations. Once the exit interview is complete, pat yourself on the back. You've just come through one of the most angst-ridden events in your life, and you passed with flying colors!

Now that you've properly evaluated and accepted your new offer and made a clean, professional break with your current employer, there's only one thing to look forward to: your new future. Here are some final tips regarding successful transitions into the new job.

The Two Biggest Challenges in the First Six Months of a New Job

Adjusting to a new company is hard. No matter how self-confident you are or how much self-esteem is bursting out of your shirt collar, it's lonely, intimidating, and disorientating to be the new kid on the block. Starting from scratch in terms of proving yourself and earning others' respect can be a daunting task. But take a deep breath and walk into the office with a smile.

Remember that 70 percent of corporate America steps down (or gets fired) from a job not because of technical incompetency but because of personality conflict. The goal, therefore, is to *establish yourself as someone with a wonderful personality*. To do so, there are two things you need to do in addition to keeping that smile shining like a laser beam. First, remember all managers are looking for value in the people they hire nowadays, and the way you show value as an employee is by assuming responsibilities beyond your basic, written job description. Volunteer to help out in areas that aren't really your immediate responsibility. Show yourself as a team player willing to assist wherever you can. Nothing goes further in raising your personality quotient than establishing yourself as someone who constantly looks for things to do. You'll quickly develop a reputation as a doer, and increased responsibilities will soon follow. You'll be establishing a pattern that will quickly lead to co-worker confidence and promotability.

Next, *ask for meetings with your boss on a proactive basis*. Ninety-nine percent of corporate America fears confrontation, and many fine employees have lost their breakfasts at the thought of having to attend a performance review with the boss. The problem is that they avoid meetings because of a fear of the unknown. However, soliciting feedback can be done in a comfortable, informal way. Establish a pattern of keeping the lines of communication open.

For example, by asking your boss for quarterly or even monthly performance updates, you'll show yourself as someone looking for ways to improve yourself, an individual open to constructive criticism, and a person with outstanding communication skills. Most significantly, you'll get a steady stream of feedback that will help you improve your performance. That way, when it comes time for the annual performance appraisal, you'll have had a headstart on gathering the information necessary to have fixed most of the weaker issues in advance! This is a winning strategy for a well-informed, career-conscious, information-hungry employee geared for career progression.

This book's final investment in enhancing your career will focus on answering your questions. Up to now, we've removed much of the mystery of the job search process and replaced it with a method to enhance your candidacy consistently. Chapter 10 covers all the main areas of this book, but from the standpoint of a personal, one-on-one question-and-answer session. It will tie together all the big-picture ideas we've covered so far and apply them to more specific experiences.

Chapter 10

Concise Questions and Answers to Offbeat but Real-Life Job Puzzles and Quagmires: Fielding Your Questions

Now's the time for us to sit together and address your specific needs. Changes in interviewing strategies and questioning techniques occur fairly rapidly. Our venture together wouldn't be complete without covering the nuances, trick questions, and exceptions to the rule that I've come across in my years as a human resources manager and contingency recruiter. Working both sides of the employment desk does have its advantages in terms of seeing the bigger picture, and I hope you could benefit from my dual experiences. We'll address these issues in functional clusters so that you can more easily locate groups of related topics.

Reasons for Leaving Revisited

"I left my last two positions to follow my boss to new companies. Is that an asset or a liability in terms of how a prospective employer will view my motivation for change? How do I address it most effectively?"

Reasons for leaving past positions (RFLs) are significant indicators of your work values, your individual career path strategy, and your loyalty. RFLs are one of the most critical areas in "silent employee evaluation"— what the employer is thinking about you even if she isn't saying anything.

I believe that following your boss is a very acceptable and favorable reason for leaving one company and moving on to another. Sure, a prospective employer might view you as someone more loyal to your specific boss than to the companies that have employed you, but the decisions you've made to follow your immediate supervisor are certainly understandable. After all, your relationship to your boss and the people in your work group represents your bond to the company. Therefore, most employers will view that loyalty as a plus.

One caveat here, though: You can be sure that the interviewer will focus in on your current relationship with that same boss. If the interviewer learns that this boss whom you've been following has now retired from business, you'll be considered a safe hire. If, on the other hand, your old boss is now working for a competitor across town, you'll be considered a risk who's capable of leaving the new firm to repeat a past pattern of behavior.

"I pride myself on never having been laid off. I've always left a company on my own before the layoff happened. How would a prospective employer view that?"

Red light! Proceed with caution. This one can really trip you up. Contrary to what many people believe, a layoff is a very acceptable reason for leaving because it's totally out of your control. Downsizing has become the corporate religion of the 1990s in light of megamergers, leveraged buyouts, hostile takeovers, and lean and mean corporate operational strategies. As a result, great people have been caught up in massive divisional layoffs that in no way reflect those individuals' work habits or achievements. It's simply an accepted reality and mentality in the current employment marketplace.

People who leave companies on their own—especially those who leave one company without having another firm position in hand—run the risk of being viewed as people with little staying power, the ones who jump ship once the going gets tough.

So, when it's your decision to leave a company and you appear to change companies too often, you run the risk of being viewed as a job-hopper, a worker with a low potential return on investment for a prospective employer's training and orientation, payroll, insurance, and benefit costs.

"What do I do if I fit the profile of the person you just mentioned in the preceding answer—namely, a person who left some past companies before the corporate layoff happened?"

Well, the crux of the answer lies in your wording "before the corporate layoff happened." If there truly was a bona fide layoff coming your way, describe and substantiate it. Make it as factual as possible, and make sure your references can back you up. For example:

Ms. Employer, I left XYZ Company because word came down
that a layoff was in the works. I found a new job before I got

caught in the downsizing. As a matter of fact, two months after I left, the marketing department was reduced from a staff of eight to a staff of three. My former boss was laid off, and since the other administrative assistant had more tenure than I did, I would have been displaced as well.

On the other hand, if you left the company for other reasons (besides potential layoff) or the layoff you expected to happen never materialized (which means your whole department is still intact and no one there can vouch for your decision to leave when giving you a reference), then find another reason that was, preferably, beyond your control:

> There was excessive turnover in the ranks of senior management, and I felt it might be better to explore opportunities with a more stable organization.

> My responsibilities were downgraded because of an internal reorganization, and I felt I could increase my level of responsibilities and make a stronger impact at another firm.

> My boss was replaced, and there was no suitable opening for me elsewhere.

"I've been through a series of layoffs in the past four years. I've held five different jobs, and now I've been laid off again. Will an employer think that I don't know how to pick a company, and can that jeopardize my candidacy?"

Multiple layoffs are not uncommon, and even though that's out of your control, if it's happened too many times recently, some employers may have doubts about hiring you. Although bad luck hits all of us at certain points in our lives, if it seems to hit the same person too often, doubts are raised about the individual's patterns of successfully overcoming adversity. Besides, the prospective employer reasons, "Why haven't you been able to guard yourself against the same problems that plagued you in the recent past?"

Too many candidates hide behind a layoff to avoid saying *fired*. The employer's unspoken rationale: "Was this person individually laid off, in other words, fired, or was she part of a larger company downsizing each time?" Be aware that companies often lay off individuals who don't fit in or pull their weight.

There is a strategy to allay an employer's fears in this instance. The key lies in *qualifying the layoff*. First, let's look at industry. If you've been in the aerospace or defense-related sectors, then the multiple layoff factor won't play as great a role in your individual evaluation. Everyone knows that the erosion of the military-industrial complex has wreaked havoc on employment in those industries. If you're now interviewing in the private/commercial sector, you can simply state that your goal is to move out of military/aerospace and transfer your skills and abilities to the private/commercial sector.

On the other hand, if you've been through multiple layoffs in an industry that's relatively healthy, then you have to focus on the particular companies where you've worked. The litmus test is, "Should you have known that this particular company might end up laying you off?"

Here's how to build a case for yourself. First, qualify each layoff when filling in the reason-for-leaving box on the employment application. Instead of simply writing *layoff*, write:

> "Layoff: Company underwent a Chapter 7 total liquidation."
> "Layoff: Company underwent a Chapter 11 reorganization and reduced staff by 60 percent at corporate headquarters."
> "Layoff: Owner retired and business was disbanded."
> "Layoff: East Coast pharmaceuticals division was relocated to corporate offices in Chicago."

In these circumstances, you couldn't have known that these company relocations, bankruptcies, or owner retirement were going to happen. If you're specific about the circumstances, you'll do a much better job of removing potential doubts from an employer's mind.

By the way, when sending a cover letter and resumé to a company, dedicate a paragraph to these reason-for-leaving issues. You'll immediately wipe away an employer's doubts as to your ability to make a long-term commitment to your next company. Try something like this:

> Mr. Employer:
>
> Please accept my resumé for the **office administrator** position listed in this Sunday's *New York Times* classified ad section. I believe that I am uniquely qualified for this position because. . . .
>
> Please also note, however, that I have held four positions between 1990 and 1994. Although I planned to make long-term commitments to all four organizations, each company had a unique reason for downsizing or closing. The owner at ABC Company suddenly retired and the company closed. DEF Company defaulted on a bond payment to its creditors and was placed into Chapter 11 bankruptcy. (Corporate staff was reduced by 60 percent.) Also, GHI Company relocated its pharmaceutical division back to Chicago.

I am truly eager to make a long-term commitment to my next employer. Please note that I held a ten-year position before joining ABC Company in 1988. That kind of stability is what I'm looking for again.

"I've heard that 'better opportunity' is a good reason for leaving when filling out an employment application. How would a prospective employer view that motivation?"

Actually, an employer would look at that excuse as a poor reason for leaving a past company. We discussed in Chapter 6 why writing down "no room for growth" on an employment application is a poor strategy: Employers translate that into "bored, tired, and unmotivated." All employees have an obligation to motivate themselves! The company's responsibility is to pay those employees for their hard work and contributions to the corporate mission.

Similarly, "better opportunity" as a written reason for leaving on your employment application throws up a big red flag in the interviewer's mind. What kind of better opportunity did this worker leave for? More money? Increased responsibilities? Or was this person simply tired of the same old grind and needing a change of scenery?

"Better opportunity" needs to be qualified. It indicates that you orchestrated your own move to the next company. (In other words, you weren't laid off and didn't have the situation forced on you.) And since you coordinated the move, then your reasoning behind that decision will obviously reveal a lot about your values as a worker. So qualify your response by being more specific when filling out that application. For example, write "Opportunity at XYZ Company to gain exposure to the marketing side of the business," or "Opportunity at ABC Company to report to a senior executive on a one-on-one basis." In other words, that better opportunity should be as concrete as possible! Desire to join a particular company or to get into a certain industry are very acceptable reasons as well.

What if you left for more money? Fine. No one can fault you for that unless you've made too many recent moves for more money. Then you run the risk of being viewed as **recruiter's bait,** ready to move the next time someone dangles a higher base salary in front of you. However, you obviously don't want to jot down "Opportunity to earn more money at DEF Company." It will be very clear from your filled-out application that you were given a raise to move from one company to the other. So what should you write? Well, there's always more than one reason why someone leaves a job. Money may have been a key motivator, but it probably wasn't the only one. Therefore, focus on another critical reason (like desire to assume greater responsibilities or to increase your workload) and phrase your answer as we've outlined above.

A special note: I wouldn't recommend listing "better opportunity" as a reason for leaving if you made a job change that didn't include an increase in salary. The employer would reason in that case that you made a move that wasn't necessarily a better opportunity at all—it was just a change. And change for change's sake scares employers. Remember that patterns of longevity in past employment boil down to return on investment for the company: If you typically stay with organizations for five years at a clip, then it's reasonable for the interviewer to believe that you'll stay with his company for five years. So all the training, orientation, and knowledge imparted to you will benefit the company for that long. And if the company pays a fee to a contingency recruiter for you, then that cost may be amortized over the five years you remain on board. Hiring you for your patterns of staying put is a wise investment because it's based on concrete evidence. And that's one less thing an employer has to worry about in the tricky business of employee selection.

More Resumé-Writing Pointers

"I'm a recent high school (or college) graduate. My resumé doesn't show much longevity, but most of the jobs I've held were part-time while working my way through school. How do I reflect that?"

Oh, that's an easy one! I've seen many recent grads create chronological resumés without making reference to the fact that their jobs were part-time or school-related. Rather than getting credit for having helped finance their educations, they set themselves up to be viewed as job-hoppers. The simple solution is to write down under your job title "Part-time position while in high school" or "Seasonal work to help finance my education." That little disclaimer quickly turns what otherwise might be construed as a deficit (spotty, short-term jobs) into an asset. Most employers agree that students who help finance their own education show business maturity, preplanning skills, commitment, and appreciation for hard work. Your resumé will make a lot more sense at first glance if it provides that kind of critical detail.

"Can I leave off my resumé a job that I held for, say, three months? More importantly, can a future employer check on my whereabouts if I don't provide any employment information?"

Well, here's a gray and murky area, indeed. As an author and employer, I strongly recommend against misstating anything in your employment history. Murphy's law seems to find its way into these situations at the most inopportune times! Misrepresentation is grounds for dismissal. You don't want to start a new job with a liability hanging over your head and the feeling that you misrepresented yourself to get the job.

Still, truth be known, prospective employers don't have access to your W-2s or tax returns to determine your various sources of income. The breach of ethics involved, however, should be enough to make you steer clear of any temptation.

"What are the most misrepresented factors on a resumé?"

There's a fine line between resumé misrepresentation and resumé fraud. I don't want to paint a picture of life behind bars because of an exaggerated issue on a resumé, but bear in mind that the resumé and employment application are the two paper documents upon which the decision to hire you is made. Any misleading or exaggerated statements found out after you've begun working for a company could bar you from keeping your job. Worse, if you falsified your resumé to land a position and are later wrongfully terminated by that organization (for something that could be totally unrelated to your resumé misrepresentation), federal courts have held that you may be barred from receiving damages against the employer. So this is serious stuff!

The biggest area of concern lies in the education section of the re-sumé. Either you have a degree or you don't. There's no middle ground here. Even being one class or one unit away from a degree counts as non-degreed. There's nothing wrong with explaining in a cover letter or employment application that you're three units shy of your bachelor's, and that you plan on completing the degree within three months. But never, and I do mean never, misrepresent your academic history. That one mistake has unnecessarily unseated many good employees from their jobs.

Notice that I didn't say *candidate* in that last sentence. Education checks can sometimes take several weeks to complete depending on the university's policies on releasing student information. So it's one thing to lose out on a great job offer because of misstated facts on a resumé. It's a whole other ball of wax to be dismissed after only a few weeks on a new job! Try explaining that one on your next round of interviews or even ten years down the road. The reason for leaving your past company was to join the ranks of this new company. Yet the new job only lasted two weeks. Wow! A foolish mistake that could cast a long-term shadow on an otherwise brilliant career.

Speaking of misrepresentations, the second kind of falsification that is much less serious in nature can be found in the technical skills section of your resumé. As a contingency recruiter specializing in administrative support placement, I'd seen many candidates exaggerate their typing and shorthand skills. The resumé says "Type 65 WPM," but in the office they actually type 54 words per minute with seven errors, which nets 47 words per minute. The difference there is not only of a technical nature. Employers frown upon people who exaggerate their skills. "If they're embellishing in that area, who knows where else we're seeing some untruths?" goes the logic. My advice: List your raw skills more accurately on your resumé, or get your skills up to speed with your claims. Just don't get caught in the middle!

"I've attended several colleges, but I'm not degreed. What's the best method of documenting my schooling?"

Strangely enough, there always seems to be an inverse relationship between scholastic achievements and the amount of time candidates spend talking about their schooling on their resumés. I've seen Harvard MBAs list their education in two lines:

MBA, Harvard University, Boston, Mass. 1995

BA, Political Science, DePaul University, Chicago, Ill. 1989

And I've seen people without degrees list four to seven colleges where they've attended courses, taking up half a page on a resumé.

What's the catch? Well, it appears to me that people who don't complete degrees have a need to prove that they're college material by documenting as much of their coursework at various institutions of higher learning as possible. The Harvard MBA, on the other hand, lets the degrees speak for themselves.

My advice is to follow the Harvard grad's example. If you list too many colleges and can't show a degree as a result of your efforts, it might tell an employer that you don't have the tenacity to complete projects you start. And if that's the way an employer reads that resumé, then you've damaged your credibility. Instead, list the one college where you've completed the most coursework or the best-known institution. Add to your description following the college name something like this:

College of the Canyons, Valencia, Calif. 1993–present. Completed one year toward AA degree.

Even if all of your coursework wasn't completed at that school, it's still acceptable to name only one college on your resumé since the majority of your work has been completed there. At some later point in the hiring process, the prospective employer may want more details about your academic history for reference-checking purposes. At that time, you could provide the details of particular coursework taken at other schools.

Additional Interviewing Tips: Don't Leave Home Without Them!

"I seem to be getting more and more telephone interviews recently. Why the sudden increase? Is this the new thing in employment circles, and how should I handle them?"

Telephone interviews are an employer's defense to the sheer numbers of people applying for jobs these days. You remember that HR has historically been responsible for *screening interviews*—brief meetings to ensure that a candidate meets the minimum requirements of the job and fits the organization's corporate culture. Telephone interviews take screening interviews one step further: They attempt to determine candidate suitability in a shorter time (roughly ten to twenty minutes) with less commitment (no courteous small talk and no paying for candidate parking).

The strategy for handling a telephone interview is twofold: First, prepare your notes in advance so that you can deliver a clear and convincing presentation; second, close the meeting by asking for a personal interview. Let's handle each issue separately.

When you lay out your notes before the telephone call, use bullets to capture your main points. Don't write out a presentation: It will be too hard to follow and customize on the spot. A verbatim written presentation will only make you nervous and remove all spontaneity from the conversation. The bullet form, in contrast, briefly covers the most significant highlights and gives you more confidence in clarifying your main points (see Figure 10-1). The advantage of using this form is that you can preplan your strategy, feel confident that you'll cover your key points in a short amount of time, and most importantly, be able to check off the areas as you cover them so that nothing will be repeated.

"I was fired two years ago for insubordination. (I had a personality conflict with my manager, and one day we both said things we shouldn't have. Well, at least I shouldn't have: I was fired shortly thereafter.) How do I explain that without jeopardizing my chances of landing a new job?"

This is the trickiest of all. My first piece of advice is this: Don't try to justify your actions by blaming the other party. There's a twofold danger with that approach: First, your past boss isn't present to explain his side of the story, which means that your interpretation of the events leading up to your dismissal will be taken with a grain of salt at best. Second, and more importantly, employers tend to take sides with other employers in these matters. Practically speaking, most employers have been on the wrong end of a past employee's complaints and exaggerations, so it becomes a psychological defense mechanism for employers to distance

Figure 10-1. Telephone interview format.

Interviewer's name/phone number: ———————————————

Company address: ————————————————————— ———

————————————————————————————————

Date and time of personal interview: —————————————

Directions to company: —————————————————————

————————————————————————————————

1. Why I want to work for your company:
   o
   o
   o

2. Why I feel I'm particularly well qualified for the job:
   o
   o
   o

3. My greatest achievement/accomplishment that this company would be interested in (in terms of winning departmental awards, decreasing departmental costs, saving time, and/or increasing revenues)
   o
   o
   o

4. Close the conversation by asking for an in-person interview! (For example, "Thank you for your time over the phone. I'd just like you to know that I'd very much like the opportunity to meet with you in person.")

themselves from any employee complaining about a past boss. Whichever the case, you'll either be seen as biased in your explanations or have your version dismissed outright. (Of course, you won't be told that. You'll just get a rejection letter in the mail a few days later.)

Instead, the best thing is to show yourself as an objective, third-party evaluator of the situation. Accept responsibility for your actions (which in itself shows tremendous business maturity), and get off the topic as quickly as possible. For example,

> Ms. Employer, I was "dismissed" [not *fired* or *terminated*] from XYZ Company. Unfortunately, I had some difficulties communicating with my supervisor, and the relationship just didn't work out. But that's long behind me now. I'm sorry for the outcome, but I learned a lot from the situation, and I don't anticipate anything like that happening again.

> *"Would it be too strong a close (on a telephone or in-person interview) to say at the end of the meeting, 'Mr. Employer, if you don't hire me, your company will really be missing out on a very special person'?"*

This is more a question of personal taste and matching your style to the employer's. Personally, I really dislike that kind of hard close. I feel it's arrogant and cocky. As a recruiter and employer, I've always preferred a more humble and self-effacing approach. The tone of this book, I believe, assumes that people need to simply talk with each other during an interview. No showmanship, no games, and no sales pitches. Your personal style may be able to apply this selling technique better than I ever could, and it might enable you to stand out in an employer's memory. A good number of employers, however, might view this as pure grandstanding and look elsewhere for a somewhat more sophisticated prospective employee.

Instead, I would recommend a more humble approach complimenting the company's achievements or emphasizing your personal interest in joining the company. For example:

> Thank you for your time, Mr. Interviewer. I'd just like to share with you that, on the basis of our meeting this morning and the research I was able to collect on your organization before the meeting, I would really like to become part of your company. I hope you'll consider me as a finalist for this position because of my prior industry experience and similar technical orientation. I would be proud to work for your company. Thank you for meeting with me.

"What about asking the employer, 'What can this company do for me'?"

I strongly advise against it. It waxes insincere. The employer has no obligation to sell you on why you should join the firm. If you can't articulate why you want to become a member of the organization, then you're ill prepared for the meeting. Many candidates use this as a standard question because they view interviews as a give-and-take process: The employer is interviewing them, but they're also interviewing the company.

Well, although I agree that the interview is a give-and-take communication exchange, it's not give-and-take in the sense that the employer has to provide you with reasons to accept her job offer. It is give-and-take in the sense that you're gauging the corporate culture, the salary and benefits package, the nature and scope of your responsibilities, and the personalities of the folks with whom you'll be working most closely. That's your end of the give-and-take process. Don't make the mistake of expecting the employer to entice you. That would be a very dangerous assumption for your job search campaign.

Is it okay to ask an interviewer at the end of a meeting, "Do you think I'm the right person for the job?"

This question backs an employer against a wall. If he believes you're the right person for the job, he really shouldn't tell you that because a reference check or a drug test could still eliminate you. Furthermore, no employer wants you to figure out that you've been eliminated because of a reference check since that information could get the employer named in a lawsuit, along with your past employer who provided the negative reference information. These issues can obviously open a Pandora's box of terrible alternatives. Instead, when a candidate gets knocked out on a reference check, the employer typically sends a generic rejection letter stating that the individual's background doesn't fit the company's needs. It's quick, easy, and safe for the company.

On the other hand, if the employer believes you're not the right person for the job, then he'll feel obliged to tell you why you're not. That can lead to embarrassment (yours or his) or confrontation. No one wants that to happen during an interview. Therefore, I'd suggest not asking that question.

"Is it favorable to walk into a company cold for an interview? Do I stand a better chance of landing an interview if I go in person than if I send a resumé?"

My gut response is no. Although different approaches work better for some people than others, in today's business environment, a cold-call knock on the door probably won't fare well. The employer may consider an unscheduled meeting as an infringement upon her time. Although literally knocking on doors worked in the past (specifically from 1984 to 1989 when nationwide unemployment was close to 4 percent and qualified people were very difficult to find), it will probably meet with very limited success in today's more competitive market because of the increased demands of the search process and the time constraints of hiring officials.

If you plan on making point-to-point canvassing or cold calling part of your job search strategy nonetheless, go to the building first in order to identify its tenants. Then head out to the library to learn about those companies before you simply barge in unannounced. You'll stand a much better chance if you walk into a company and explain that even though you don't have an appointment, you are aware of the company's reputation and you've taken the time to research the organization before arriving.

"Do I have to tell an employer how much I'm currently earning? I don't feel that my present salary really should dictate how much I'm worth in terms of potential performance. Also, I've heard that if I'm earning too much money now and want to take a pay cut to get a particular job, then I may get knocked out because the employer will be afraid that I'll leave in the near future to make more money. Shouldn't I be the one to decide whether I'm willing to take a pay cut or not?"

You absolutely have to tell an employer how much you're currently earning! Sorry, but that's the primary rule of the game, and remember, it's the employer's game even in the tightest of labor markets. First of all, verifying your current salary on a reference check is very easy to do, so the employer will find out how much you're making. Second, and more importantly, your current salary is a reference point or anchor of your market value. It is what your current or last employer felt you were worth in terms of your years of experience, technical and communication skills, and ability to influence the organization. No one gets measured strictly in terms of potential performance. Past performance is a much more reliable indicator of your ability to affect your working environment. And, like it or not, salary is a solid link to performance potential.

Finally, in terms of taking a pay cut to land another position, understand why many employers are hesitant about hiring people at salaries significantly lower than what they were earning before. Like most things, it boils down to experience: Many employers have been burned in the past by hiring someone who claimed not to mind a large pay cut, only to see that individual leave within six months to locate a position paying what she was making in the past. Although you may be sincere beyond any doubt that you're willing to accept a pay cut, you're swimming upstream on this issue because employers' experiences and instincts say that bringing people on board lower than where they were on the last job encourages turnover. It's a tough sell, so map out your reasons for wanting the job and account for your ability to be able to afford the cut. For example,

> Ms. Employer, I know this position is paying 25 percent lower than the base pay on my last job. Please understand, though, that the long-term opportunity to excel at your firm is much stronger than what I had before. I've always wanted to pursue work in the advertising field, and I know that because you're a glamour industry, the pay typically isn't as strong as in some other industries. But your benefits package is outstanding and much stronger than what I had before, and I would be proud to say that I work for your company. Quite frankly, I can afford the cut. My spouse's income is primary, and my earnings are secondary. Therefore, I'm at a time in my life where I can afford to pull back on the salary somewhat in order to get into the field that I've always wanted.

"I absolutely hate taking tests! I know I type faster than those five-minute tests measure. Help me! What can I do?"

There are a few issues here. First, know that most secretaries, junior-level accountants and financial analysts, receptionists, claims adjusters, customer service reps, and bank tellers get their typing tested. Now that we're all in the same boat, let's take a look at the reasoning behind the test.

Typing speed used to be a critical issue in the old days when secretaries sat together in pools and banged out documents on typewriters. (Please understand that I'm answering this question strictly from a technical standpoint, not from an overall opinion of how much the role of office administrator has developed to cover many more responsibilities than before.) If one person typed forty words per minute and the other typed eighty words per minute, then, other things being equal, an employer would feel that the second person had twice the production potential of the first. Back before the arrival of the personal computer in 1980, secretarial pools were very clerical and mechanical in nature.

Today, it's a fallacy to equate typing speed with an individual's potential output. Personally, I'd rather have a 40 WPM typist who can dance in and out of various software applications and put together camera-ready artwork than an 80 WPM typist who's PC illiterate. The key to production nowadays lies in software capabilities, not speed.

However, speed does have a role in the concrete evaluation of a prospective employee's productivity—not so much because it dictates the new hire's potential (you're hired for a lot more than your typing capabilities, heaven knows!) but because it's so easy to measure uniformly and compare. Interviewing results can depend on a person's mood, reference-check feedback can be inconsistent or one-sided, but typing tests are concrete, scientific evidence. And like it or not, many employers still do equate typing speed with output. (Don't hold that against them, though. They just haven't sat down to think about what they hire administrative support staff to do. Old habits and ways of thinking are hard to break.)

Also, remember that it's common for candidates to exaggerate their typing skills on a resumé or job application. It says sixty words per minute on paper, but the test showed forty words per minute. That kind of discrepancy, barring any outstanding circumstances like a sprained finger, is pure misrepresentation. So employers and agencies give the test.

What we're seeing more of is the proliferation of testing softwares that measure a candidate's abilities to manipulate basic and advanced features of PC and Mac word processors, spreadsheets, databases, and graphics applications. Software tests along with typing tests are the keys to determining technical competence.

My advice when taking a typing test is to always go for accuracy more than speed. It's better to score sixty words per minute clean than seventy words per minute gross with ten errors. Seventy words per minute with ten errors usually nets sixty words per minute, but with some companies' magic math formulas, seventy minus ten equals fifty words per minute because—you guessed it—they take off two points per error.

Let me put this in the proper perspective (and I'm not exaggerating here): Imagine you're an administrative support recruiter responsible for interviewing ten candidates a week. Of the ten, nine will tell you that they hate testing and never do well. It almost wants to make you hire the one person who doesn't complain, even if she performs poorly on the test! So don't psych yourself out, and don't sound like all the other whiners out there! Go slowly, remember accuracy more than speed, and keep this hurdle in perspective: After all, it's only one evaluation factor.

Career Strategies: Advice to Keep You on Top

"I want to explore other opportunities for various reasons, but I'm relatively happy where I am, and I feel a little noncommittal toward the time and energy needed to conduct a job search while still employed. What's the first thing I should do?"

Do some soul-searching and become relatively clear about what you want and where you feel you'll be wanted most. Obviously, as a recruiter, I believe it's good policy to keep yourself abreast of potentially stronger opportunities if the occasion arises. Where you can damage your own credibility, though, is if you haven't given much thought to where you want to be and why: In that case, in a meeting with a prospective employer, you'll probably come across as indecisive and noncommital. That boils down to a waste of time for the employer because you're not taken seriously. The employer may be left with the feeling that you're just window-shopping to get a feel for what's out there, or worse, that you're fishing for a job offer so that you can go back to your present boss and negotiate a raise for yourself (with the threat of leaving if you don't receive it).

Refer back to pages 117–118 for a checklist of issues to consider when thinking about a job search. You'll need to address them when meeting with a prospective employer on an exploratory interview. Pay particular attention to your reasons for wanting to leave your present position. This is really a key issue, since a prospective employer will need to gauge whether she can provide you with what you're missing on your present job. If it's a simple matter of benefits or of company name-brand recognition, that's easy. If your primary reason for leaving your present job is that you don't feel that your creative abilities are being used to their fullest right now, that may be a little tougher for the prospective employer to satisfy, but at least the employer knows where you're coming from. Just don't let indecisiveness damage your reputation.

"I hate my present job. Should I leave my current position to dedicate my efforts to a full-time job search campaign?"

I strongly advise against it! Let me explain why. First and foremost, your marketability drops once you become unemployed. So many people have become the victims of corporate downsizings, relocations south of the border, and bankruptcies, that if you're fortunate enough to be holding a job currently, you'll have an advantage in the employment process. I don't want to exaggerate this point, but many employers look at the fact that you're currently employed as a plus in your column. In many cases, employers have been so overwhelmed by the number of unemployed people applying for positions that employed candidates are somehow thought of as people who have made the cut. (It's for this very same reason that most retained executive search firms typically only place candidates who are currently working.)

A second reason why leaving one job without having another firmly in hand may damage your candidacy lies in the perception of what I call your business maturity. In today's tough economy, an employer may reason that your inability to stick it out when the going gets tough directly reflects your intolerance threshold. You may throw up a red flag showing either that you're not a long-term player or that you had no idea how difficult landing a full-time job could be—hence, the three or six months that you've been looking for work. If the latter is the case, the employer may fault you for not having had enough insight to learn about the marketplace before deciding to leave your last job.

However, don't get an ulcer over it! Keeping things in perspective will dictate at times that you should leave your job to find work elsewhere. Period. And that's a universally human experience because many employers have gone through it themselves (or at least seriously thought about it).

So if you left your last position without having another one waiting for you, present it as a virtue rather than an ill-thought-out action. Reveal your commitment to doing the best work possible while employed, and share that the environment or circumstances at your last position didn't allow you to make the type of contribution to the company that you were used to making, so you left to find other work. You might also mention that you didn't want to compromise your work performance at your last position by taking time off to look for a new position, so to be fair to yourself and your employer, you decided to dedicate yourself to a full-time job search.

"I have an MBA, and I'm afraid that certain employers will hold that against me for fear that I would be overqualified for administrative positions within their organizations. Should I leave my MBA off my resumé?"

This again is an opinion call. I believe that having an MBA is an outstanding achievement and that the business acumen derived from that kind of educational training is priceless. If you applied with my company as an administrative assistant, I would find it hard to not hire you with those qualifications. You'd really have to do something bad on the interview to miss out on at least being a finalist because, as an employer, I value education tremendously.

In the real world, that's not always the case. I've seen companies that demand bachelor's degrees in their job specifications for nonexempt, administrative support workers. I've seen other organizations where it's mandatory that candidates not be degreed for fear that a degreed employee would be less than challenged in an administrative support role, even if that person had been working as a secretary for the past ten years! It really boils down to the particular employer's personal experience: If the employer is intimidated by support staff members with more education than she has, or if that employer has a lousy track record of keeping degreed individuals happy, that employer will simply shy away from degrees.

But you can't know that! It's not even the issue that certain companies prefer or don't prefer bachelor's and master's degrees; most often particular bosses call the shots. So my opinion in this matter is simple: *List it! Be proud of your achievement!* You don't want to work for a company that's going to be intimidated by your educational track record. Besides, just look at the courses that organizations like the American Management Association offer for secretaries and administrative assistants:

- ☛ Fundamentals of Finance and Accounting for Executive Secretaries and Administrative Assistants
- ☛ Management Skills for Executive Secretaries and Administrative Assistants
- ☛ Business Writing for Secretaries and Administrative Assistants

These tell you how important advanced business skills are for everyone in this segment of the corporate pyramid.

"Which softwares are in most demand today?"

Your software capabilities can open lots of opportunities for you. As a matter of fact, the technical skills section of your resumé is one of the first areas where employers look when screening resumés. The really hot softwares as of this writing are the Windows-driven operating systems that allow multiple windows for performing multiple tasks. The demand for Microsoft Word for Windows and Excel is steadily increasing in corporate America. Of course, organizations that demand lots of graphics traditionally rely on the Macintosh, and Macs are still predominantly seen in the advertising, public relations, design, and entertainment areas. (Bear in mind, however, that Macs lie outside of the mainstream of business computing. Roughly 90 percent of desktops used in business are IBM-compatible.) So depending on the type of work you do and the industry you're pursuing, choose to strengthen your Windows and/or Mac skills.

Unfortunately for you DOS lovers, the DOS-based softwares are going the way of the dinosaur. Windows is quicker and easier to manipulate for most people, so that workforce productivity goes up. (*DOS* stands for disk operating system, which relies on a text-based user interface—in other words, you type in all your commands. By contrast, Windows uses a graphics-based user interface, in which you point and click at pictures and icons on your computer screen.)

I would recommend rounding out your software capabilities by mastering softwares in the following areas:

1. Word processing
2. Spreadsheet
3. Database
4. Graphics

If you've got hands-on experience in each of these categories, then your marketability will go way up.

Of course, the computer industry is probably the fastest-changing market the world has ever seen. Therefore, if you want to find out what are the hottest softwares out there at any given time, either check out the classified ads or call your local employment agency. Either resource will steer you in the right direction regarding the current softwares in demand.

"Have the 1990s changed the ways companies look at people? Are there any big trends out there regarding how to present yourself to a company on a problem-to-solution level?"

In the 1980s it was more accepted that people would change jobs often in pursuit of higher salaries and personal development. In the 1990s that trend has given way to keeping your job. Revenues and profits have been drastically trimmed, budgets have been pared down, and the number of employees necessary to run the company has gone down as corporations have "trimmed the fat of middle management." Consequently, we know that productivity per employee has had to increase to compensate for the decrease in labor.

One of the trends, therefore, that has surfaced is in an individual's ability to reevaluate and reinvent her job in light of her company's new needs. Most jobs are no longer confined to a neat little job description that puts the employee in a finite box with definitive parameters. Most people have had to take on more responsibilities and redefine their jobs. (This is sometimes referred to as job reengineering.) That may have meant doing relief receptionist duties, taking over specific functions for a job that has been eliminated (for example, the company year-end party now becomes your responsibility), or returning to the classroom for advanced training and certifications. It may also have meant assuming advanced responsibilities without adequate training and being left on your own to reinvent the wheel, so to speak.

On the company side, employers have been busy training their staffs to adopt what's known as an economic advocate approach. The goal of **economic advocacy** is to train employees to become cost-sensitive. Teaching staff members how the business operates from a profit-and-loss point of view allows workers to understand how they fit in to the larger business picture and empowers employees to gain a greater sense of ownership in the company's success. It removes the veil of secrecy that historically surrounded many companies' operations in the assembly-line days when workers were expected to master only one particular set of skills and make one specific part of the finished product.

The significance of all this is that if you've been responsible for reinventing your job in light of the new demands of your company, then you should provide an in-depth explanation to your interviewer. That employer will walk away with a greater sense of your potential if you show yourself to be a person who can objectively, creatively redefine your role within a company.

If you're interviewing prospective candidates on behalf of your company, on the other hand, ask questions that bring out these economic advocate tendencies in those being interviewed. Helping a candidate highlight her achievements in the cost-cutting area by redefining work will ensure that you're hiring someone who's flexible, creative, and committed to the bottom line.

"I've been out of the workforce for eight years. I was making $28,000 as an executive assistant at a Big Six CPA firm. If I were still working, I'd be making around $38,000 today. So I'm hoping to split the difference, and I want a base salary of $33,000. Will the employer agree with my logic?"

Nope! You get an A for effort in your logical formulation, but most employers won't give you a premium for the time you were out of the market. They're more likely to see your time on the sidelines as detrimental to your skills because software demands have changed drastically in a very short time. Your next starting salary will depend on the type of job you're applying for, the industry, and the technical skills involved. My guess would be to position yourself to get back into the workforce at $28,000—exactly where you left off. But don't be surprised if you get offers below that amount. Again, like everything else in business, when it's a buyer's market (the buyer is the employer), wares can be had at a discount. Labor costs are no exception to the rule, and most people are faced with taking a cut in pay when a transition is forced upon them through layoffs, relocations, and reentry into the workforce.

"I'm planning on reentering the workforce after ten years of raising a family. What strategy should I employ when interviewing? Will employers want to know about my domestic responsibilities, or will they strictly focus on my potential ability to contribute to their companies?"

Don't underestimate the significance of your stay-at-home activities. People run day-care centers out of their homes or contract themselves out for word processing assignments to bring in some extra money. Others pour blood, sweat, and tears into the full-time job of raising their children. All these areas should be explained in an interview.

Running a day-care center involves licensing, billing, collectibles, and outstanding supervisory skills. (I'm not kidding—supervising children is a challenge that relatively few can master!) Similarly, The National Association of Secretarial Services can attest to the challenges associated with running a business from the home, and it is a wonderful support organization dedicated to enhancing that line of business. (More on this in Appendix C.)

Bear in mind, however, that although dedicating yourself to the kids for ten years is exceptionally admirable, you'll still be facing a hurdle because you'll have been out of the labor market for so long. Even if you can link some of your duties and responsibilities directly to the day-to-day operations of a business, your involvement in clubs, committees, PTAs, choirs, and other volunteer or family-oriented organizations won't exactly match the needs of most employers.

Understand that you're facing a unique challenge, and be very open about why it's so important for you to make the transition back into the workforce at this point in your life. If those skills you've developed match any of the employer's needs and there's a nice rapport between you and the interviewer, there will be a good chance that your commitment and performance potential will suffice to qualify you for the job.

I would also strongly recommend that you register with a temporary help agency to sharpen your work skills. You might be able to take advantage of one of the newest hiring trends in business today: **temp-to-full-time hire.** Also known as *temp-to-perm* and *temp-to-hire*, this arrangement allows companies to pay you temp wages and observe your performance for sixty or ninety days before putting you on the corporate payroll. Companies typically prefer to hire people on a temp-to-hire basis because they don't have to base a hiring decision on a one-hour interview. Instead, by actually observing you in the workplace, that company has much more information upon which to base its hiring decision.

Temp-to-hire can open wonderful opportunities for someone reentering the workforce because it sets you up to prove your skills and abilities rather than get judged on an outdated resumé. It also significantly narrows your competition: Full-time workers won't typically pursue temp-to-hire arrangements because they are restricted job offers with no guarantees. (Of course, no job is guaranteed, but once you're on a company's payroll, that organization becomes much more committed to making it work, since there is then corporate liability for your unemployment insurance, worker's compensation, wrongful termination, and the like.) Therefore, your competition in a temp-to-hire arrangement limits itself to the unemployed workforce, and that's more than ten times smaller than the employed workforce.

"Is there one final career tip that you feel supersedes all others?"

Yes. One of the best pieces of advice I ever received was to figure out what you want your resumé to say in the future, and then go from there. I firmly believe that the secretarial and administrative support role has become a respectable career path that offers variety, responsibility, and independent decision-making. If your goal is to become a key executive administrative assistant in a Fortune 500 company or to ultimately move up to a management position, you've got to prepare your career moves right now.

A receptionist looking to become a staff secretary needs to refine technical skills and establish a pattern of assuming responsibilities beyond the call of duty. A staff secretary looking to report directly to a vice president of finance should acquire an understanding of business accounting that enables her to grasp the larger fiscal issues facing the company and thereby makes her more valuable to her boss. An administrative assistant interested in joining the ranks of management at her company should be prepared to assume profit and loss responsibilities, which may entail giving up a comfortable salary for commissioned earnings.

Whatever your goal may be, it's your responsibility to map out your ultimate plan on paper right now. Then mark your calendar for quarterly and annual follow-ups to measure your own progress. Remember, we're all responsible for motivating ourselves and determining our career destinations.

It's really amazing when you think about it: You don't know where the journey's going to take you, but sometimes one little strategy, if closely adhered to, can be the link for progression in your life.

*   *   *

I hope you enjoyed reading this book as much as I enjoyed writing it. May it give you a better of understanding of the world of employment, and more importantly, of yourself—your wants, your strengths, and your weaknesses—so that you can maximize all the opportunities that are awaiting you out there.

Good luck, and enjoy the journey along the way!

Appendixes

This section contains further details regarding issues that were showcased throughout the book. There are also a few special topics I've saved for you that should provide greater insight into your job search campaign.

Appendix A

Reference-Checking Questions

The questions that employers ask about you when checking your references will allow you to understand how they perceive your value to their companies. They'll also help you put together a menu of your achievements and accomplishments that you can focus on during your future interviews. Following are some of the most advanced and sophisticated questions floating around the employment world right now. My special thanks to Peter Leffkowitz of the Morgan Consulting Group in Kansas City, Missouri, who originally developed many of these questions to help contingency recruiters gather more in-depth and meaningful background information on their candidates.

Here's how to use this information. Put your name in the question blanks below. Then imagine how your past four or five supervisors would grade you in each area. You'll probably notice some consistent trends surfacing as you run through this exercise. Your strengths and weaknesses will begin to cluster around certain types of questions. Your goal, then, will be to sell those strengths to a potential employer. Your mission will also be to assess your weaknesses fairly and objectively and develop an action plan to overcome them.

Remember that this information *will* be gathered before your next job offer is made. It's too late to go back and rewrite history. Still, preparing an action plan for strengthening areas where you need support, and honestly assessing your business capabilities and limitations, will go a long way in revealing your business maturity and objectivity. Most importantly, you'll avoid placing yourself into the "victim" role where you blame others for your failures or inconsistencies. That posturing alienates even the most empathetic interviewers. No one, after all, wants to hire "excuses."

You remember from Chapter 2 how crucial it is that you go back to your past supervisors at the onset of your job search campaign to ask them to vouch for you as a reference. When you take that very important step in contacting past bosses, use the following questions as a basis for your conversation. If you ferret out your strengths and weaknesses in advance, you'll end up having a much more candid and professional conversation with your former supervisors than if you simply asked, "So how was I when I worked for you?" Evaluate yourself first, then ask your boss to confirm your findings. You'll find that the phone call will produce much more tangible results in a shorter time.

> Please comment on _____'s ability to interface with upper-level management, peers, and customers.
>
> How would you grade _____'s ability to predict needs before they arise? In other words, how would you evaluate her intuition, timeliness, and proactive business style?
>
> How effective were _____'s oral and written communication skills?
>
> Did _____ typically show a strict adherence to job duties or did he assume responsibilities beyond the basic, written job description?
>
> Does _____ need close supervision to excel or does she take more of an autonomous, independent approach to her work (by finding work to keep herself busy)?
>
> How structured an environment would you say _____ needs to excel at work and reach his maximum potential?
>
> What can we as a management team do to support _____ and increase her productivity?
>
> Would you comment on _____'s ability to accept constructive criticism?
>
> Would you define _____ more as a task-oriented person or a project-oriented person?
>
> Seeing that _____ came out of an environment working for you that demanded both high volume production and quality, which of these two work styles matches his personality better?
>
> Would _____ excel (a) in a more moderate, even-paced environment, (b) in a faster-paced atmosphere with deadline pressures and time constraints, or (c) in a hypergrowth, chaotic type of culture?
>
> Would you recommend _____ for a position with a one-on-one reporting relationship or a multiple reporting relationship?
>
> Would you consider _____ more of a people person or a technically oriented person?
>
> Tell me about _____'s technical capabilities. What softwares were used in your department? Would you consider her level of competence basic, intermediate, or advanced?
>
> How would you describe _____'s day-to-day attitude?
>
> How would you grade _____'s organizational skills?
>
> Has absenteeism or tardiness ever been a problem for _____?

What would you consider to be _____'s greatest achievement or accomplishment within your company?

What one or two areas of improvement could _____ work on right now? What should we look out for in terms of giving him added support?

Is _____ rehirable? If not, why not?

What was _____'s reason for leaving your company?

What was _____'s ending salary?

What were _____'s dates of employment?

Appendix B

Dressing the Part

Okay, it's time for me to play fashion consultant. Here's a quick overview of the do's and don'ts of interview dress. Of course, the part of the country where you live and the industry you're interviewing in play critical roles in dictating the proper etiquette of dress. Still, there are some hard-and-fast rules that will do you well under almost all circumstances, so they're worth reviewing.

The primary rule when it comes to creating the image you want to portray is to *dress for the interview, not for the job*. Even if you're interviewing at the hippest ad agency on Madison Avenue, you need to make a corporate conservative first impression. Once you get the job, then you can wear the worn-out jeans with holes in the knees or whatever other style the company deems acceptable. But, as the saying goes, "you never get a second chance to make a first impression." And every hiring authority wants the reassurance that the new hire understands appropriate business attire and can make a sophisticated impression when the top brass makes its occasional visit.

My experience as an employment agency recruiter had been in placing administrative support staff into financial service companies in the downtown Los Angeles area. Our clients were law firms, investment bankers, ad agencies, and real estate developers. Currently I'm a manager of human resources in a mortgage banking firm. Please keep that orientation in mind as we go through this topic so that you can filter my recommendations through your own screen of experiences. If you're interviewing with any of these types of companies, then dress as if you were interviewing with IBM. Corporate culture in this case dictates a "blue suit and pearls" approach to interview dress.

If you're meeting with a manufacturing company, public-sector employer like county governments or state universities, or a local business owner in a small, rural town, guess what? Do the "blue suit and pearls" thing anyway! Although it may not be generally expected to dress to that level of sophistication, get as close to it as you can. You won't be penalized for dressing as if you were preparing for a meeting with IBM.

Sophistication is the norm for being hired in today's market. Office staff members represent their companies in their bosses' absence, interface with customers, and create an image of what it's like to deal with that organization. Therefore, interview dress must always be conservatively appropriate.

Now, this proverbial "blue suit and pearls" is a stereotype. After all, you might not own a business suit. Allow me, then, to walk you through your own closet at home and help you create the ideal interview outfit.

Accessories

Rule 1: Your peripherals speak very loudly about your style. Write with a nice pen. You don't need a $300 Mont Blanc, but a Cross, Parker, or Calibri pen would be nice. I strongly disapprove of a Bic with the lid chewed off!

Next, I recommend that you bring a leather-bound note pad (or $10 vinyl look-alike) with your notes and your T account inside (refer back to Figure 6-1 on page 125). The portfolio is advantageous for two reasons: First, it keeps you organized, which in itself will enhance your self-confidence and give you an air of control. Second, it keeps your hands busy so that you're not twiddling your thumbs or rubbing your palms together like a fly in a honey bowl. There's also nothing wrong with jotting down the employer's answers in your notebook or asking questions that you've written down before the meeting. As a matter of fact, most employers I know prefer to see that kind of organization and preplanning. It shows respect for the interviewer's time and a serious approach to your job search campaign.

A leather attaché case or briefcase is preferable to a casual tote bag. I'm not exaggerating when I say that I've interviewed candidates who carried shopping bags, library books, and children into my office. Let's just say that you don't want to distract from yourself by clouding an employer's impression of you with such "accessories." (Nothing against the kids; it's just not the right time or place for them!) Also, a leather attaché case or briefcase should suffice to carry *all* your belongings into an interview. Don't carry a briefcase *and* a large purse because it will be hard to manipulate both when shaking hands or signing documents. Try to squeeze the contents of the purse into the briefcase. If you have to carry a separate purse, make sure it's small so that it won't get in the way.

Rule 2: No perfume or cologne on the interview. Period! The reason: Most people put on their "Sunday best" for a job interview and end up overdoing it. They smell like the fragrance department of the local department store and either give the interviewer a headache or an allergic rash. "So what if I use just a little?" you ask. My response: reread rule 2! Soap and water will make you smell just fine.

Rule 3: Keep your resumé in some kind of manila envelope or protective jacket **unfolded** *and crisp.* Your resumé is the first work product (besides your job application) that you're producing for this company. Don't pull a folded, wrinkled piece of paper out of your breast pocket that curls up when the employer tries to read it. Tacky, tacky, tacky!

Women's Dress

Starting from the ground up, here's what I recommend:

- Polished black or dark shoes with heels no higher than one inch.
- Clear hose (no ankle bracelets, please).
- A business suit with jacket and matching skirt. The best interview colors are navy blue, battleship gray, or glen plaid. Flat black probably isn't the ideal color for an interview, but it will do if it's the only suit that you already own. (Still, I wouldn't buy a black suit if you're running out to the store tomorrow to purchase that first interview outfit.) Pinstripes are fine; chalk stripes are a bit much. Flannel works only when it's cold; cotton works all year long. The skirt should extend below the knee. The jacket's length should be parallel with your knuckles when your arm is hanging down freely at your side.
- A white or pearl blouse. It should definitely be pressed and free of wrinkles. Remember, this isn't a fashion show; you're supposed to blend in with the wallpaper. If you happen to intimidate the interviewer because your plunging neckline is too revealing, you may end up with a courtesy interview.
- A taut string of pearls hanging down roughly four inches below the neckline or a narrow silk scarf tied in a bow would complement this outfit well.
- Earrings that rest against your ears—no hanging baubles, in other words.
- Neatly combed hair. Long hair should be pulled away from your face and ideally formed into some kind of braid or bun.
- Last, but not least, minimal makeup! Perhaps apply light blush and eye shadow with a lightly toned lipstick. No more is necessary. If you overdo the makeup, it will detract from your *natural* good looks. Similarly, fingernails should be well shaped, relatively short, and done in a clear or lightly toned color.

P.S. If you don't own a business suit, a business dress will do. Color schemes, length, and peripherals will be the same as above. Just no prom gowns, party dresses, or formals, if you please!

Men's Dress

Beginning from the ground up, I'd suggest:

- Black leather wing-tip shoes with shoelaces. Tassels and slip-ons are not viewed as favorably as laced shoes, but you don't need to go out and spend $80 on a new pair of laced shoes as long as your black shoes are in near-new condition. If wing-tips are too conservative for you, go with a more stylish black leather tied shoe. Just make sure that both the shoe and the heel are freshly polished.
- Solid socks that match the color of your suit. (If you wear white socks with your blue suit and the employer gives you a tour of the office, it's not because she wants to hire you; it's because she wants to show you off so that everybody can get a look at those "white-walls." No, that's very out of place in corporate America, and there's no excuse since you can buy a pair of navy blue socks for $3.)
- A business suit. Single-breasted is preferable to double-breasted only because it's a lot more common and acceptable. Double-breasted styles may be viewed as too hip, but if your only suit is double-breasted, wear a conservative tie and shirt combination to add a more conservative tone to your outfit.
- A solid white, well-pressed shirt. (It's typically worth $1.50 to have your interview shirt pressed at the cleaners.) Some shirt collars have buttons at the tips to attach the collar to the shirt. Those are fine; shirts without the extra two buttons on the collar tips are equally acceptable.
- An appropriate tie. Ties, ah ties . . . power ties, paisley ties, theme ties, bow ties. We do have choices, men, don't we? Well, the strategy is to blend in with the wallpaper, so anything too loud will stand out too much. I recommend a tightly knotted, silk "power" tie in fire-engine or burgundy red. A dotted tie pattern or striped design at larger intervals is ideal, as long as it's not too "busy." I'd pass on the paisley. I would definitely recommend against wearing ties with pictures of your favorite cartoon characters plastered all over them! And, please, do make that knot tight and small. Those huge knots that covered your whole neck and a substantial part of your upper torso went out in the 1970s.
- No stubble. Clean-shaven is in. If you're one of those people who gets a five-o'clock shadow by lunchtime, bring an electric shaver to work and give yourself a once-over before your 4:00 interview.

P.S. If you don't own a business suit, then a nice pair of slacks, a crisp white shirt, and a power tie will do. You can successfully circumnavigate the Catch-22 of "I can't buy a suit until I get a job, but I can't get a job unless I have a suit" by leaving out the jacket while still adhering to all the other rules for dressing previously mentioned.

For more information on corporate interview dressing etiquette, see John T. Malloy's *Dress for Success* (New York: Warner Books, 1975).

Appendix C

Professional Associations and Accreditations

Secretaries and Other Office Support Staff

Certification in the secretarial profession has become a reality thanks to **Professional Secretaries International,** which offers a one-day, three-part exam covering finance and business law, office systems and administration, and management. The Certified Professional Secretary (CPS) rating ensures an employer that you "possess a mastery of office skills, demonstrate the ability to assume responsibility without direct supervision, exercise initiative and judgment, and make decisions within the scope of assigned authority." Also note that many schools offer college credit toward a degree for achieving the CPS rating.

Even if you're not a secretary, attaining certification is achievable through PSI's Office Proficiency Assessment and Certification Program. This entry-level certification program for office workers is designed to test basic office skills. The three-and-a-half hour exam includes skills analysis in the areas of keyboarding and word processing information, language arts skills, administrative support skills, records management, and financial applications and record keeping.

Joining Professional Secretaries International means becoming a member of a professional association with about 40,000 peers who make up the top ranks of administrative support in corporate America and around the world. Membership entitles you to a subscription to *The Secretary* magazine, membership newsletters, conventions (United States and Canada), and local networking groups.

Annual membership cost in 1994 was $42, plus a one-time $15 processing charge for members at large; those who join specific chapters pay additional dues at the local level. For more information on PSI membership and professional certification, contact:

Professional Secretaries International
10502 NW Ambassador Drive
P.O. Box 20404

Kansas City, MO 64195-0404
(816) 891-6600
(816) 891-9118 Fax

*   *   *

The National Association of Executive Secretaries (NAES) publishes the *Exec-U-Tary,* a monthly newsletter written exclusively for the professional secretary, which includes an annual salary survey. NAES has 5,000 members, and it sponsors seminars and an annual conference. Membership also includes free job referral service and a member network.

Annual membership cost in 1994 was $30. For more information, contact:

National Association of Executive Secretaries
900 South Washington St., No. G-13
Falls Church, VA 22046
(703) 237-8616
(703) 533-1153 Fax

*   *   *

The National Association of Legal Secretaries has 14,000 members. It sponsors legal secretarial training courses for legal support personnel through 500 chapters across the United States. Legal education is the primary focus of the monthly and quarterly chapter meetings. Many chapter and state organizations award scholarships.

NALS is the exclusive provider of national certification for legal secretaries. The Accredited Legal Secretary (ALS) designation is obtained after successfully completing a six-hour examination. The Professional Legal Secretary (PLS) designation is achieved after successfully completing a seven-part, two-day examination.

NALS publishes four specialty newsletters in the areas of litigation, business/corporate law, law office management, and probate/estate planning. NALS has written several textbooks including *The Career Legal Secretary* (1993), *The Manual for the Lawyer's Assistant* (third edition, 1994), *The Probate Handbook for the Lawyer's Assistant* (1993) (all available through West Publishing, St. Paul, Minn.).

In addition to continuing legal education, the association provides national certification programs for leadership training. *The Docket* is the association's bimonthly magazine, which contains articles promoting the professional growth of the membership. Furthermore, NALS has beginning and advanced employment skills tests available for law firms hiring legal support personnel.

Annual membership cost in 1994 was $45, not including local and state dues. For more information, contact:

National Association of Legal Secretaries
2250 East 73rd Street, Suite 550
Tulsa, OK 74136
(918) 493-3540
(918) 493-5784 Fax

* * *

Our final selection of professional membership organizations, **The National Association of Secretarial Services,** has 1,800 members. NASS offers a twist on what we've seen above because it focuses on *independent* secretarial services offering office support services including word processing, telephone answering, copying, desktop publishing, and dictation/transcription. The organization's purpose is to provide sales and marketing ideas as well as consulting assistance for independent contractors in the field of administrative support services. Membership includes the *NASS Newsletter* as well as the *National Membership Directory* and discounted pricing on industry-specific manuals.

Annual membership price in 1994 was $120. A subscription to the *NASS Newsletter* only is available for $48 a year. For more information, contact:

The National Association of Secretarial Services
3637 4th Street N., Suite 330
St. Petersburg, FL 33704-1336
(813) 823-3646
(813) 894-1277 Fax

Human Resources Professionals

Professional designations in human resources management are available at universities throughout the country. Program completion typically necessitates fulfillment of somewhere between six and eight core courses that cover the major areas of HR management, including:

- Recruitment and selection
- Benefits and compensation
- Training and development
- Affirmative actions and EEO (equal employment opportunity) programs

- Financial aspects of human resources management
- Organized labor, arbitration, and mediation
- Behavioral science and organizational psychology
- Organizational development

In addition to such university programs, the **Society for Human Resource Management** (SHRM) offers two professional designations in HR for earlier-career and advanced HR practitioners. The Professional in Human Resources (PHR) designation is awarded after completion of a four-hour exam focusing on the tactical and operational aspects of successful human resources programs. The PHR designation gears itself toward HR practitioners with fewer than five years of experience who hold *functional* positions in the field, such as managers of compensation and benefits, affirmative action officers, and training specialists.

In addition to the PHR certification, the Senior Professional in Human Resources (SPHR) designation avails itself to HR professionals with *strategic* responsibilities in terms of integrating the corporate HR function into the overall company plan and aligning HR's goals with the organization's mission. Candidates for the SPHR designation need a minimum of five years experience to qualify for the exam.

For further information regarding the PHR and SPHR certification exams, contact:

HR Certification Institute
The Society for Human Resource Management
606 North Washington Street
Alexandria, VA 22314
(703) 548-3440
(703) 836-0367 Fax

Contingency Recruiters

Certification for contingency recruiters and temporary specialists is available through the **National Association of Personnel Services** (NAPS). Contingency recruiters can receive their Certified Personnel Consultant (CPC) designation, and temporary recruiters can obtain their Certified Temporary-Staffing Specialist (CTS) designation by passing a four-hour exam that covers the basics of employment law, industry history, and business ethics. 1994 costs of the exams were $279 for NAPS members, $605 for nonmembers. Certification exams are administered twice a year.

Annual membership price in 1994 was $475. (This is either company membership or individual membership, but to qualify as an individual member, you must already have your CPC or CTS designation.) For further information regarding joining NAPS and/or receiving employment industry certification, contact:

The National Association of Personnel Services
3133 Mount Vernon Avenue
Alexandria, VA 22305
(703) 684-0180
(703) 684-0071 Fax

Appendix D

Choosing a Recruiting Firm or Temporary Agency

Whether you're a job candidate or a company interviewer seeking a qualified full-time placement or temporary service, locating an organization can be a challenging task. There are many recruiting firms to choose from with various discipline specialties and geographic locations. Although I truly feel that any agency is only as good as the recruiter (or recruitment team) who represents it, your chances of becoming a happy consumer increase when you're dealing with a firm that comes personally recommended to you.

Candidates

Your first logical step is to ask friends and acquaintances whom they recommend. Specifically ask for the name of the recruiter being recommended, not just the name of the agency. Be sure to qualify not only how nice and friendly that recruiter happens to be, but how effective that individual has been in finding qualified jobs with excellent companies for your friends. Ask about that recruiter's listening skills as well. If you're fortunate enough to locate a "proven performer" recruiter who will listen to you and put your needs first, and who has strong endorsements from your peers, you'll truly be maximizing an exceptionally effective job-hunting resource.

Company Hiring Officials

Word of mouth is the best way to locate qualified search and temporary-staffing specialists in your area or industry as well. Although many full-time and temporary-staffing services will be knocking at your door at any given time to develop a search assignment, check with your competitor companies to see whom they're using. It makes sense for recruiters to develop market specialties even for administrative support placement. If you can locate a recruiter who understands your business and has successfully placed secretaries, accountants, salespeople, and customer service people at competitor firms you respect, then that recruiter will likely have a smaller learning curve in terms of understanding your company's specific needs. And from my experience, most HR professionals would be very willing to share with you whom they feel are the most talented recruiters in town.

Also notice the level of customer service that the agency provides in its client development literature. I know that a lot of firms *say* they believe in customer service, but the proof lies in their commitment to their profession:

- Has the agency researched your company before making its initial presentation?
- Has the placement firm received professional certification through NAPS (or a state association like the California Association of Personnel Consultants)?
- Can the company provide you with tests to measure candidates' software, accounting, data processing, and clerical skills?
- Will the company fax you those tests before an interview takes place with one of its candidates? (Note here that I don't think it's necessary for agencies to fax you ten pages of test scores and references in order for you to judge whether that candidate is worthy of an interview. That would be an administrative nightmare and would put an undue and unfair logistical burden on the recruiting firm. On the other hand, once you've agreed to meet with a candidate, it's certainly within your rights to meet the candidate on paper before that person arrives. Most agencies will gladly oblige that request since they've already locked the candidate into an interview time.)
- Does the agency have the capabilities to cross-train a candidate on your particular company softwares?
- What kinds of value-added services will the agency provide you? Suggestions: hot lines for legal questions, gratis salary surveys, assistance with job description development, and personal company visits.

Remember that ultimate customer service in the employment business will be witnessed by agencies that are willing to outservice their competition. What that means to you is quality candidates within reasonable time frames. "Fee" usually ranks third or fourth in terms of measuring what companies look for in selecting placement firms. I don't mean to down play the cost issue, but remember that a good agency is worth its weight in gold if it can provide you with quality staffing solutions when you need them. Don't let a few percentage points in a contingency sales relationship stand in the way of selecting the agency that will provide the highest-quality and most consistent service.

The National Directory of Personnel Services

There's yet another excellent tool for selecting a recruiting firm or temporary agency that will more than likely stand out from its competitors. The National Association of Personnel Services (NAPS) offers its *National Directory of Personnel Services* for $20.95. The directory profiles 1,200 member firms in the contingency and temporary fields of employment. It's divided by job specialty and geographic location to make the job of selecting a placement firm that much easier. And again, companies that have spent the dollars and energy to pass professional exams in order to become better service providers to their clients stand a much better chance of presenting successful solutions to your staffing needs.

Appendix E

How to Work With a Headhunter

We've already profiled some very specific ways to maximize a relationship with a contingency search firm. I can think of nothing more beneficial to you and your recruiter than what we discussed in Chapter 2 on customizing your own marketing plan—namely, researching companies where you would be proud to work and then handing that list over to your recruiter. It's a blueprint for success: You do the legwork in learning as much about the organization as possible and then rely on the recruiter's sales skills to set up an initial meeting.

Of course, helping a recruiter prepare a customized marketing plan around your background is only one aspect of the entire candidate–recruiter relationship. Let's talk briefly about both parties' expectations. Your expectations as a candidate focus on generating interviews with solid companies. Whether you arrange those interviews through networking and research, classified ad response, or with the help of a headhunter, you want to meet with employers who interest you. Therefore, your needs walking into a relationship with a recruiter center around:

1. *The recruiter's listening abilities to hear what your needs are.* For example, you might want to work only in a given part of town, at a certain minimum salary, or within a certain industry, and anything else would be a waste of your time.
2. *Ample information about a company where a meeting has been set up for you,* including the salary range for the position, the company's primary product lines and its clientele, the number of employees, the year founded, and the location of its corporate headquarters.
3. *"Insider" recommendations about the company where you're interviewing,* namely, the personality of the interviewer, the dress code, and the corporate culture of that organization.
4. *Concrete and timely debriefing information after an interview* to understand what the next step is (or how you could have performed better, if there's no further interest on the company's part).

What does a recruiter expect from a candidate?

1. Two hours to complete the agency's registration process. That time includes thoroughly filling out an employment application (see pages 134–138) and undergoing fairly extensive computer and paper tests.
2. *A commitment on your behalf to a serious job search.* (The biggest nightmare in the recruiting business occurs when a candidate decides not to go to a scheduled interview and doesn't call the recruiter in advance. Too many no-shows and that recruiter will most likely lose an account.)
3. *Your immediate feedback after an interview so that the recruiter is then armed to provide the client with information regarding your interest level.* After all, if you're really interested in the position but fail to call your recruiter right after the interview, then the recruiter has no ammunition to fight for you. The client calls and says, "Gee, we're really interested in pursuing Pam. How's she feeling about us?" And the recruiter clears her throat, flinches, and then sheepishly says, "Well, I'm really sorry, Ms. Employer, but we just haven't heard back from her yet." There went the recruiter's (and your) chance to lock that employer into a second interview!

So now that we've cleared the air in terms of everyone's expectations, where do both your needs converge? Remember that recruiters are salespeople who get paid to fill a client company's openings. They aren't paid to find jobs for people. That fact underscores one of the greatest challenges I found in training new recruiters. You see, recruiters more often bond with their candidates than they do with their clients. That's because the candidates are in and out of the agency's office quite frequently, they spend two hours with the recruiter right up front in the initial interview, and then the recruiter checks all their references and gets to know them very intimately. Clients, on the other hand, are often only seen a few times a year and typically don't share that intimate a relationship with the recruiter.

Capitalize on that intimacy. I'm not saying that every recruiter you meet should become a career confidant. I am suggesting, however, that you keep an ear to the ground to locate one recruiter out there who could become your eyes and ears to potentially stronger job opportunities. That's nothing less than "career insurance" in today's day and age. Besides, a recruiter's influence on your career could be beneficial or it could be benign, but it will rarely be detrimental. The worst-case scenario in working with a headhunter is that you go through the whole application process and never hear from that agency again. So what? You have the right to apply with as many agencies as you like. As long as your relationship with your recruiter is mutually beneficial, then nurture it. Once it becomes less than productive, then pursue opportunity elsewhere.

One of the most-often-asked questions I received from job candidates who had been to other agencies before coming to me was, "Why don't some agencies call you back?" You'll never really know that answer. Some people have more success with agencies than others because their backgrounds lend themselves more to a recruiter's *general* needs. For example, they typically have excellent longevity at companies with high brand-name recognition, their skills are solid, and they dress the part. Remember, fee-paid hires command a premium in talent. On the other hand, some agencies may simply be looking for *specific* pedigrees in candidates' backgrounds at any given point in time to match particular clients' needs.

I guess my biggest recommendation in working with a recruiter would be to keep the lines of communication open. You deserve to know which companies that recruiter wants you to meet with *before* an interview is set up. One caveat here: Sometimes recruiters will describe the company only in terms of its location, line of business, and the nature of the job without revealing the organization's identity. That's because the client doesn't want the word put out on the street that a particular opening is vacant. That information should still be enough for you to make an advanced decision about whether you want to meet with that organization. (Of course, if you agree to the interview and the company sets a meeting, your recruiter will then reveal the company's identity so you can get to the library to research that organization ahead of time.) Similarly, the recruiter deserves to have a candidate who is seriously committed to landing another job and who will provide that recruiter with informational updates that keep the headhunter in the loop. This way, everyone's needs are met and there's a "win-win-win" situation among client company, candidate, and recruiter.

Appendix F

Where the Jobs Are (and Where They'll Be Through 2005!)

Within the field of administrative support, certain jobs will be undergoing significant growth while others will shrink away between 1995 and 2005. Take heed of these important general trends that will help you make the right long-term decisions in your career. By aiming for expanding occupations, you'll be guaranteeing yourself the greatest opportunities for career growth, compensation, and job availability.

Let's put some big numbers into perspective. The Department of Labor's January 1993 *Employment and Earnings Report* shows that the United States has approximately:

> 4.2 million secretaries
> 2.3 million bookkeeping and accounting clerks
> 1.5 million word processors and typists
> 900,000 receptionists
> 271,000 file clerks

Now, in terms of projected job growth through the year 2005, here's how the occupational growth patterns are projected to stack up:

Projections of Occupations with the Largest Growth Potential

Title	Number (in thousands)		Percentage Growth
	Jobs in 1990	Projected Jobs in 2005	
Medical Secretaries	232	390	68
Legal Secretaries	281	413	47
Receptionists	900	1,300	47
General Office Clerks	2,700	3,400	24
Customer Service	109	120	10
Secretaries (non-legal/med)	3,064	3,312	8

Other Projections

Bookkeeping/Acctg. Clerks	2,276	2,143	**−6**
Word processors/Typists	972	869	**−11**
Admin. Support Industry (overall)	2,200	2,500	**12**

Source: Department of Labor, Bureau of Labor Statistics: U.S. Government Printing Office, *Outlook 1990–2005,* 1992.

The numbers tell the story very clearly. *Specialize!* Bookkeeping and typing jobs are on the decline, so secretaries should pursue opportunities in the medical and legal fields for top compensation and job security. Be somewhat wary of positions that might be replaceable through office automation and computerization. And review the prospects for your job type from time to time at the library. The Bureau of Labor Statistics' data are available even at most smaller libraries and can be accessed very quickly with the help of your librarian.

Index